P9-CKP-941

THE COSTS OF HIGHER EDUCATION

*How Much Do Colleges and Universities
Spend per Student and
How Much Should They Spend?*

A REPORT PREPARED WITH THE SUPPORT
OF THE EXXON EDUCATION FOUNDATION
AND THE FORD FOUNDATION
AND ISSUED BY THE CARNEGIE COUNCIL
ON POLICY STUDIES IN HIGHER EDUCATION

Howard R. Bowen

THE COSTS OF HIGHER EDUCATION

How Much Do Colleges and Universities
Spend per Student and
How Much Should They Spend?

 Jossey-Bass Publishers
San Francisco • Washington • London • 1980

THE COSTS OF HIGHER EDUCATION
*How Much Do Colleges and Universities Spend per Student
and How Much Should They Spend?*
   by Howard R. Bowen

Copyright © 1980 by: The Carnegie Foundation
                     for the Advancement of Teaching

                     Jossey-Bass Inc., Publishers
                     433 California Street
                     San Francisco, California 94104

                     Jossey-Bass Limited
                     28 Banner Street
                     London EC1Y 8QE

Copyright under International, Pan American, and
Universal Copyright Conventions. All rights
reserved. No part of this book may be reproduced
in any form—except for brief quotation (not to
exceed 1,000 words) in a review or professional work—
without permission in writing from The Carnegie Foundation
for the Advancement of Teaching and the publishers.

*Copies are available from Jossey-Bass, San Francisco,
for the United States and Possessions, and for Canada,
Australia, New Zealand, and Japan.
Copies for the rest of the world are available
from Jossey-Bass, London.*

Library of Congress Cataloging in Publication Data

Bowen, Howard Rothman
   The costs of higher education.

   Bibliography: p. 267
   Includes index.
   1. College costs—United States.   2. Universities and
colleges—United States—Finance.
I. Title.
LB2342.B63   379.1'18'0973   80-8321
ISBN 0-87589-485-2

Manufactured in the United States of America

JACKET DESIGN BY WILLI BAUM

FIRST EDITION

Code 8044

The Carnegie Council Series

The following publications are available from Jossey-Bass Publishers.

The Federal Role in Postsecondary
Education: Unfinished Business,
1975–1980
*The Carnegie Council on Policy
Studies in Higher Education* (1975)

More Than Survival: Prospects for
Higher Education in a Period
of Uncertainty
*The Carnegie Foundation for the
Advancement of Teaching* (1975)

Making Affirmative Action Work
in Higher Education: An Analysis
of Institutional and Federal
Policies with Recommendations
*The Carnegie Council on Policy
Studies in Higher Education* (1975)

Presidents Confront Reality: From
Edifice Complex to University
Without Walls
*Lyman A. Glenny, John R. Shea,
Janet H. Ruyle, Kathryn H. Freschi*
(1976)

Progress and Problems in Medical
and Dental Education: Federal
Support Versus Federal Control
*The Carnegie Council on Policy
Studies in Higher Education* (1976)

Faculty Bargaining in Public
Higher Education: A Report and
Two Essays
*The Carnegie Council on Policy
Studies in Higher Education,
Joseph W. Garbarino, David E.
Feller, Matthew W. Finkin* (1977)

Low or No Tuition: The Feasibility
of a National Policy for the
First Two Years of College
*The Carnegie Council on Policy
Studies in Higher Education* (1975)

Managing Multicampus Systems:
Effective Administration in an
Unsteady State
Eugene C. Lee, Frank M. Bowen
(1975)

Challenges Past, Challenges
Present: An Analysis of
American Higher Education
Since 1930
David D. Henry (1975)

The States and Higher Education:
A Proud Past and a Vital Future
*The Carnegie Foundation for the
Advancement of Teaching* (1976)

Education Leaves for Employees:
European Experience
for American Consideration
*Konrad von Moltke,
Norbert Schneevoigt* (1977)

Investment in Learning: The
Individual and Social Value of
American Higher Education
*Howard R. Bowen
with the collaboration of Peter
Clecak, Jacqueline Powers Doud,
Gordon K. Douglass* (1977)

Contents

*The meaning of cost in higher
education • Unit cost • Educational
and noneducational expenditures • The
long run: societal determinants of cost •
The short run: institutional
determinants of cost • The revenue
theory of cost summarized • The "laws"
of higher educational costs •
Institutional autonomy • Conclusions*

*Professional industries • Aggregate
costs • Educational costs per student •
Structural changes that influenced the*

FOREWORD

The Carnegie series on higher education (1969–1980) began with Howard Bowen, and it is appropriate that it should end with him. For he is the preeminent economist writing about higher education, and, also, was a good friend and supporter of the Carnegie review from start to finish. His study on *The Finance of Higher Education* (1968b) was one of the first two publications in the Carnegie series, along with a study by William G. Bowen on *The Economics of the Major Private Universities* (1968). The current book and one by David Riesman *On Higher Education* (in press) are the last two.

In between, he contributed *Efficiency in Liberal Education* (1971) with Gordon K. Douglass (one of the best sellers in the Carnegie series); and *Investment in Learning* (1977), the most useful volume ever written on the benefits of higher education. He also acted as adviser on a number of Carnegie reports, particularly *The States and Private Higher Education* (1977) and *Three Thousand Futures* (1980).

The Costs of Higher Education is a companion volume to *Investment in Learning*. It treats costs as the former volume did benefits. Once again, it evidences throughout the careful scholarship of Howard Bowen in assembling the facts and his good judgment in evaluating their implications.

Each reader will have his or her own favorite passages. A few of mine are: (1) Bowen's explanation of the "revenue theory of costs" — that costs are determined by revenues: "Each institution raises all the money it can" and it "spends all it raises"; (2) his analysis of how and why costs in higher education rise faster than costs generally; (3) the history of the rise and fall of faculty compensation; (4) his discussion of "socially imposed costs" of higher education, which he estimates at 7 to 8 percent of total costs; and (5) the section on the enormous cost differentials per student-credit-hour among institutions—including differentials of two to one among what appear to be quite comparable institutions. I also particularly like his analysis of how institutions with higher expenditures per student spend their extra funds, Chapter Nine's examination of the economies and diseconomies of scale, the discussion of the deterioration of the financial situation of higher education in the 1970s, and his study of financial deficits of underfinanced institutions. Bowen notes that the period ahead may make possible the raising of quality, as the quantity of students may go down, at no greater or not much greater total cost to society.

As he always does, Howard Bowen places a very high value on the contributions of higher education and calls attention to the constructive possibilities even in difficult situations. He is the supreme defender of higher education and the supreme optimist about its future. I agree in full with the defense. I have some doubts about the level of optimism. My optimistic hope is that higher education, over the next twenty years, may maintain its current level of quality. The possibility that higher education can raise quality substantially by restoring all the losses of the 1970s and by raising significantly the comparative level of financing of the least well financed institutions is very heartening, but it seems to me to be an unlikely realization. The battle ahead, as I see it, is to maintain current quality. My optimism leads me to think that this battle will be won. The chances of winning it are helped by the more sanguine aspirations of Bowen that raise hopes within higher education and offset the exceedingly negative projections by the planning and coordinating agencies of most of the fifty states. Whatever happens, Howard Bowen has once again provided the definitive volume on a highly important subject. It should be of great interest to all trustees, all administrators, and all students of higher education.

Clark Kerr
Chairperson
Carnegie Council
on Policy Studies
in Higher Education
1974–1980

Preface

What should American colleges and universities spend to educate their students? This is the basic question addressed in this book. It is a question faced by governing boards and administrative leaders for their particular institutions, it is confronted by public officials and donors as they ponder appropriations for higher education, and it is even considered by students and their families as they decide which colleges and universities to attend. Could the higher educational system operate satisfactorily with less money per student? Should it be supported more generously? Or is it financed at about the "right" level from the standpoint of the public interest? Words like "should" and "right" are normative. They denote concepts such as warranted, legitimate, or reasonable. Questions such as these resist final and definitive answers. In the end, the answers to such normative questions involve technical judgment and moral principle. But it is possible to proceed some distance on fairly firm ground: to gather information about expenditure trends, to explore the competitive position of higher education in relevant markets for faculty and staff, to trace changes in the prices of purchased goods and services, to track increases in costs imposed by governmental mandates and social pressures, and to inquire into other factors affecting expenditures. It is also possible to assemble information on the remarkable differences among institutions in their operational costs and thus to reach inferences on the levels of expenditure that may be necessary or warranted. These investigations are the main agenda of this book. Along the way, it is hoped that the study will provide fresh insights into the characteristics and operations of the American higher educational system and that the journey will prove to be as significant as the destination.

The fortunes of American higher education have fluctuated widely over the past fifty years. Colleges and universities, individually and collectively, have been affected profoundly by the great events of the era, events such as the Great Depression of the 1930s, three major wars, the Cold War, the space race symbolized by the launching of Sputnik, demographic fluctuations, and intermittent inflation. In the whole half-century, it is hard to find even a five-year period that can be described as normal or stable. The events of these turbulent years did lead to periods of unprecedented development in higher education, but they also produced long years of stagnation and discouragement.

Recently, in the 1970s, higher education has been through one of the episodes of stagnation complicated by rapid inflation. And in the early 1980s it is entering a period of profound uncertainty due partly to the impending decline in the number of eighteen-year-olds and partly to the unsettled state of the nation and the world. Unresolved questions abound: How should the system respond to the coming decline in the number of persons of conventional college age? How can it overcome the inadequate secondary preparation of many of its students? How can it strike a satisfactory balance between reasonable government regulation and essential institutional autonomy? In what ways can the spirit of affirmative action be nurtured in an era of restricted resources and concern about reverse discrimination? How can the quality of American higher education be improved, not only for its traditional students but especially for the growing numbers of low-income youth, part-time commuters, and adult learners? All these questions have financial dimensions. Thus, the most all-embracing question is: How much money may be needed to operate the American system of higher education at a reasonable level? It is with this question that the present study is concerned.

The study focuses on *institutional expenditures for the education of students*. The educational function includes not only direct instruction but also student services, that part of student financial aid paid from institutional funds, and such portions of other institutional costs as may properly be allocated to the education and welfare of students. Of course, there are some technical problems involved in separating the costs of the educational function from those of other functions of higher education. The procedures used are described in detail, partly in appendices. In general, the intent is to isolate the educational costs of institutions from expenses related to organized research, public service, auxiliary enterprises, teaching hospitals, student financial aid from sources other than the colleges and universities, and expenses of families connected with the attendance of students. The expenditures are not excluded because they are unimportant. Rather, they are left out to limit the study to manageable proportions and to facilitate comparisons among institutions.

The book is in three parts. Following an introductory chapter on the determinants of cost, Part One examines long-term trends in these costs. Part Two looks at the costs of individual institutions and the budgetary allocations of these costs, with special attention to the effects of institutional affluence and size upon expenditure patterns. Part Three contains the conclusions and commentary on institutional and public policy.

Some of the words and phrases that are important in a study of the costs of higher education have numerous meanings or shades of meaning. It is desirable, therefore, to define the more frequently used terms precisely and to use them consistently according to the meanings assigned to them. The definitions are presented in the glossary.

Acknowledgments

Many persons contributed directly or indirectly to the preparation of this book. I acknowledge with deep appreciation the support of the Exxon Education Foundation and the Ford Foundation—both of whom contributed to the financing of the study. I owe a special debt for the advice and encouragement of officials of these foundations, especially Frederick de W. Bolman, Robert L. Payton and Steven Cahn of Exxon, and Fred E. Crossland of Ford.

Several persons were especially helpful in connection with particular parts of the study. Peggy Heim of the Teachers Insurance and Annuity Associations gave valuable advice and assistance in connection with Chapter Three on Faculty and Staff Compensation and arranged for publication of detailed statistics and analysis to supplement that chapter. Important data for Chapter Eight on Institutional Affluence and Educational Outcomes were provided by C. Robert Pace and Oscar Porter of the University of California at Los Angeles, Kim Cameron of the University of Wisconsin, Aubrey Forrest of the American College Testing Program, and Louis Benezet of the State University of New York at Stony Brook. Helpful data and analysis for Part Two on the Costs of Individual Institutions were provided by Kristine Dillon of the University of Southern California, W. John Minter of John Minter Associates, Inc., and Susan Selhorst of Pomona College. Carl Kaysen of the Sloan Commission on Government and Higher Education was extremely helpful in the planning and criticism of Chapter Four on Socially Imposed Costs of Higher Education.

I recognize the important contributions of Peter Clecak of the University of California at Irvine, Gordon Douglass of Pomona College, Jack Schuster of Claremont Graduate School, Lewis Solmon of the Higher Education Reserch Institute, Verne Stadtman of the Carnegie Foundation for the Advancement of Teaching, and my son, Thomas Bowen of California State University at Fresno. These persons read the manuscript, offered many valuable suggestions, and saved me from some flagrant errors.

Many people were helpful without their knowing it. I refer to June O'Neill, whose book, *Resource Use in Higher Education* (1971), is the classic study of higher educational costs; to D. Kent Halstead of the National Institute of Education, who is the author of the *Higher Education Price Index*; and also to the many scholars and statisticians at the National Center for Education Statistics in the U.S. Department of Education who collect and disseminate basic statistics of increasing relevance, scope, and reliability.

I take pleasure in acknowledging the continuing encouragement and support of several cherished friends: Clark Kerr of the University of California at Berkeley, Joseph Platt of Claremont University Center, and Barbara and George Susens of Crestone, Colorado, who helped to create ideal working conditions in a remote and beautiful setting. I wish to thank my colleague, Dorothy Pearson of Claremont Graduate School, for many contributions to the study and for making my office run smoothly.

Finally, I should like to recognize the unfailing encouragement and support of my wife, Lois Bowen, who has lived through my professional endeavors with exceptional tolerance, patience, and good humor.

Claremont, California   Howard R. Bowen
November, 1980

The Author

Howard R. Bowen is R. Stanton Avery Professor of Economics and Education at Claremont Graduate School. A native of Spokane, Washington, he attended Washington State University, received the Ph.D. degree in economics from the University of Iowa (1935), and was a postdoctoral student at Cambridge University and the London School of Economics (1937–1938). He is an economist who in recent years has specialized in the economics of higher education.

His career has included service in business, government, and higher education. Bowen was chief economist of the Joint Committee on Internal Revenue Taxation of the U.S. Congress (1942–1945) and economist of the Irving Trust Company, a Wall Street bank (1945–1947). He has taught at the University of Iowa, Williams College, and Claremont Graduate School. He served as dean of the Business School at the University of Illinois and as president or chancellor of three institutions: Grinnell College (1955–1964), the University of Iowa (1964–1969), and Claremont University Center (1970–1974).

Bowen has served on the boards of many organizations and is currently a director or trustee of Grinnell College, Claremont University Center, Bankers Life Company, Teachers Insurance and Annuity Association, Higher Education Research Institute, and *The Journal of Higher Education*. He has been president of the American Finance Association, the American Association for Higher Education, the Association for the Study of Higher Education, and the Western Economic Association and chairman of the National Citizens' Committee for Tax Revision and Reduction (1963) and of the National Commission on Technology, Automation, and Economic Progress. He is a member of the National Academy of Education. Bowen has been a member of foreign missions to Japan, Thailand, and Yugoslavia. His numerous honorary degrees and awards include special awards for educational leadership presented by the National Council of Independent Colleges and Universities, the New York Association of Colleges and Universities, and *Change* magazine.

Howard Bowen is the author or coauthor of ten books and many articles and pamphlets. Among his books are *Toward Social Economy* (1948, reprinted 1977), *Social Responsibilities of the Businessman* (1953), *Graduate Education in Economics* (1954), *Automation and Economic Progress* (1966), *The Finance of Higher Education* (1969), *Efficiency in Liberal Education* (1971), and *Investment in Learning* (1977).

Glossary

Academic Support: Programs, services, and offices that facilitate or enhance the instructional program; for example, offices of academic deans, libraries, museums, computer centers, media centers, testing centers, demonstration schools, and course and curriculum development programs.

Affluence, Institutional: A college's or university's financial status as measured by educational expenditure per student unit.

Assets: *See* Capital.

Auxiliary Enterprises: Services operated by colleges and universities, often funded by special student fees or sales; for example, residence halls, student unions, and bookstores.

Capital: Durable assets owned by a college or university such as land, buildings, and heavy equipment. Often called *physical capital* or *plant.*

Capital Expenditures: Outlays to acquire durable assets such as land, buildings, and major equipment.

Compensation: Combined salaries and fringe benefits for faculty or staff. *Fringe benefits* include insurance premiums, provision for retirement, tuition remission, use of recreational facilities, and other benefits available to employees that are paid for by a college or university.

Comprehensive Universities and Colleges: State colleges with an enrollment of 1,500 or more and private colleges with an enrollment of 1,000 or more that offer a liberal arts program and at least one professional or occupational program, such as teacher training or nursing.

Coefficient of Correlation: *See* Correlation.

Coefficient of Regression: *See* Regression.

Correlation: The process of establishing the degree of relationship between two variables (or among several variables). The relationship may be positive or negative. The degree of correlation is measured by a *coefficient of correlation* ranging from 0 to +1.0 or from 0 to –1.0 where 0 represents absence of correlation and +1.0 represents perfect positive. and –1.0 perfect negative correlation.

Cost: Expenditure by a college or university to acquire the services of land, labor, or capital, to purchase goods and services, or to provide student financial aid. For most purposes, *cost* is synonymous with *expenditure, outlay,* or *payment.* More accurately and fundamentally, *cost* refers to the opportunities sacrificed by reason of such expenditures.

Current Expenditures: Expenditures of a college or university for current operations, as distinguished from capital expenditures.

Deflation: *See* Price Index Numbers.

Departmental Research: Research conducted within an academic department and financed by the department from its annual budget, as distinguished from organized or separately budgeted research.

Educational Expenditures: That part of educational and general expenditures of colleges and universities connected with the instruction and welfare of students. Includes expenditures for instruction and departmental research, student services, scholarships and fellowships paid from institutional funds, and a prorated share of expenditures for academic support, institutional support, and operation and maintenance of plant. Excludes all direct and indirect expenditures for organized research and public service.

Educational and General Expenditures: Current expenditures of colleges and universities devoted to instruction and departmental research, organized research and public service, and administration exclusive of expenditures for auxiliary enterprises, teaching hospitals, and independent governmental research laboratories. Educational and general expenditures includes instruction and departmental research, organized research and public service, student services, scholarships and fellowships paid from institutional funds, academic support, institutional support, operation and maintenance of plant, and mandatory transfers.

Endowment: Monies accumulated by a college or university in a permanent fund that is invested to produce income to help meet institutional expenses.

Expenditures: *See* Capital Expenditures, Current Expenditures, Educational Expenditures, and Educational and General Expenditures.

Fringe Benefits: *See* Compensation.

Full-Time Equivalent: A unit for counting students or faculty members. Full-time persons are each counted as one and part-time persons as appropriate fractions of one; for example, two half-time persons or four quarter-time persons equal one full-time equivalent.

Higher Education: Education beyond the secondary level and conducted in accredited institutions usually known as colleges and universities. Collectively, the "higher educational system" refers to all these institutions combined.

Index Numbers: *See* Price Index Numbers.

Institutional Affluence: *See* Affluence.

Institutional Support: Expenditures for general administration including governing board, president's office, business management, accounting and finance, personnel administration, public relations, and development.

Instruction and Departmental Research: Activities related directly to instruction such as faculty compensation, office and laboratory supplies, repairs of educational equipment, administration of academic departments, and clerical and technical assistance to faculty.

Liability: A debt payable immediately or in the future.

Liberal Arts College: An institution devoted primarily to liberal education.

Mandatory Transfers: Transfers from current funds mainly for the amortization of debt.

Opportunity Cost: *See* Cost.

Outcomes: Results flowing from higher education in the form of changes in students or changes in society.

Plant: *See* Capital.

Plant, Operation and Maintenance of: Expenditures for the maintenance and repairs of buildings and major equipment, insurance, fuel, and utilities.

Price Index Numbers: A series of numbers expressing changes in the general level of prices relative to a base period. Price index numbers are often used to "deflate" statistics which are influenced by price level changes, that is, to remove the effects of price level changes so that "real" change independent of price fluctuations may be observed.

Purchased Goods and Services: Goods and services (other than capital goods) purchased from outside vendors by colleges and universities. Includes such items as books, typewriters, building materials for plant maintenance, and legal services.

Regression: The process of establishing the average amount of change in one variable associated with change in another variable. Visually, regression is shown by a curve; mathematically it is expressed by two or more constants establishing the position of the curve.

Research and Doctorate-Granting Universities: Major universities that awarded at least twenty doctoral degrees in 1973-74.

Resources: A general economic term referring to the basic means of production: labor, land, and capital. Also often used to include purchased goods and services used in production.

Revenue: Income to colleges and universities from any source.

Salaries: Payments to faculty or staff for services rendered, exclusive of fringe benefits.

Scholarships and Fellowships: Student financial aid paid from institutional funds including both restricted and unrestricted funds but not including aid which is exchanged for student work.

Student Services: Functions of colleges and universities related to the general welfare of students such as registrar's office, admissions, financial aid administration, student health, psychological counseling, career counseling, vocational placement, and student activities.

Student Unit: A unit developed in this study for measuring the instructional load of colleges and universities. The number of student units in any institution is equal to the number of full-time-equivalent students adjusted for the academic level of the students. In accomplishing this adjustment, weights are asigned to several classifications of students based on the estimated cost of education for each classification. The weights assigned are: freshmen and sophomores 1.0, juniors and seniors 1.5, first-year graduate students 2.1, advanced professional students 2.5, and advanced graduate students 3.0.

Unit Cost: Cost or expenditures per student unit.

For Lois Schilling Bowen

THE COSTS OF HIGHER EDUCATION

How Much Do Colleges and Universities
Spend per Student and
How Much Should They Spend?

A REPORT PREPARED WITH THE SUPPORT
OF THE EXXON EDUCATION FOUNDATION
AND THE FORD FOUNDATION
AND ISSUED BY THE CARNEGIE COUNCIL
ON POLICY STUDIES IN HIGHER EDUCATION

1

What Determines the Costs of Higher Education?

The biography of an American family is written in its canceled checks. A family's life-style as well as its day-to-day events and problems are evidenced by its check stubs: Every birth, marriage, change of residence, change of career, educational decision, illness, and death is recorded there. Similarly, the budget and expenditures of a college or university reveal a great deal about its activities, achievements, and vicissitudes. This book is mainly a study of the behavior of colleges and universities individually and collectively as seen through their financial records.

This first chapter is concerned with the factors that determine the costs of American colleges and universities for educating their students. Some of the determinants operate through society. Others operate through individual institutions. Therefore, both societal and institutional factors—as well as their relationship—are considered.

The Meaning of Cost in Higher Education

In our thoroughly monetized economy, costs usually appear in the form of expenditures of money. They are payments made to acquire goods and services. For example, as consumers we refer to the cost of a new automobile as the amount of money we must pay for it; producers of automobiles refer to cost as the amount of money paid for the thousands of workers, materials, and services needed to produce automobiles. Similarly, the costs of colleges and universities are usually money payments to acquire the resources needed to operate the institutions. They include cash outlays for the wages and salaries of personnel, the purchase of goods and services, student financial aid, and the acquisition or use of plant and equipment.

The real costs, however, lie beneath the money payments. The products or outcomes of higher education are obtained through the use of scarce resources. These resources consist partly of labor, capital, and land that are employed within the institutions. And they consist partly of goods, services, plant, and equipment purchased from outside vendors. These purchased items are, however, also the product of labor, capital, and land employed by outsiders. Thus, all the expenditures of higher education reduce ultimately to payments for the services of scarce resources.

These same resources, however, could be allocated to alternative purposes. The real cost of higher education, then, consists of the benefits that might have been realized from these resources, but were sacrificed, because these resources were committed to higher education. These alternative benefits might have been in the form of consumer goods—such as food, gasoline, or tennis rackets—and social goods—such as highways, police protection, or environmental improvement. These are the kinds of benefits that are sacrificed when resources are devoted to higher education. These sacrificed opportunities represent the real costs, or, as they are sometimes called, the *opportunity costs.*

Whenever one suggests that more resources should be devoted to higher education, the underlying assumption is that the additional resources so used will produce a greater return than the same resources devoted to other purposes. Or when it is suggested that the resources employed in higher education should be cut back, the implication is that the same resources would produce a greater return if applied to an alternative use. So when one considers how much of the nation's resources should be devoted to higher education, there is an implicit comparison of the benefits that could be obtained from increments of other goods.

As indicated, the costs of higher education are ordinarily expressed in money, which serves reasonably well for the purpose of measuring the relative benefits from different uses of resources. But in some cases, costs expressed in money can lead us astray. For example, in a time of widespread unemployment, the real cost of an increment of higher education may be relatively small because those employed in higher education, either as staff or students, may have no immediate alternative jobs. Similarly, at a time of temporary decline in enrollments due to demographic changes, such as the decline in the early 1950s or the decline widely predicted for the 1980s, higher education may develop idle capacity in both plant and staff. The cost of putting this capacity to work by encouraging increased enrollments or improving educational quality may be negligible if the resources devoted to higher education could not be readily transferred to other productive uses. Also, cost is not adequately measured by money when it takes the form of a deterioration of assets through lack of maintenance or replacement. When this happens, costs are being incurred even though no money payments are being made. The subject of undermaintenance of assets is so important that parts of Chapters Five and Ten will be devoted to it. For these reasons, one must beware of measuring costs solely in terms of money: costs, rather, should be thought of as opportunity costs of the resources employed. Generally, however, money is a reasonably good measure of cost and most of the discussion in this book will be conducted in monetary terms.

Since inflation has become rampant, it is scarcely necessary to mention that when money costs are being compared over time, cost data must be adjusted for changes in the value of the dollar. This adjustment is accomplished with the use of index numbers reflecting changes in the general level of prices. Unfortunately, no price index ever is completely appropriate for the purpose, and these adjustments inevitably introduce distortions.

Unit Cost

It is not difficult to calculate the total annual dollar cost of operating a college or university. All that is needed is to add up all the expenditures—making sure to include only the costs that are properly allocated to the year in question. But, even when adjusted for changes in the value of the dollar, this total is not meaningful for comparisons over time or among institutions unless it is related to the number of units of service rendered. For example, if the total expenditures of a typical college or university in 1970 and in 1980 were compared, much of the increased cost would be explained simply by the growth

of the enterprise over the decade. The cost per unit of service might
not have increased at all. But there is a further complication: if the
expenditures of two institutions were compared, one of which serves
2,000 students and the other 20,000 students, the difference in expenditures would be explained largely by the contrast in enrollment.
Useful cost comparisons, either over time or among institutions,
require that expenditures be related to the number of units of service
rendered. Given such units, it is then possible to compute cost per
unit and thus to make meaningful comparisons.

Traditionally, what passed as cost per unit was computed simply by adding up total institutional expenditures for all purposes and
dividing by the number of students. The result was called "cost per
student." This method of rough approximation had the virtue of
simplicity and worked reasonably well when the education of full-
time resident undergraduate students was the predominent business
of colleges and universities. However, with the increasing differentiation of institutions by functions—some with substantial expenditures for research, public service, and auxiliary enterprises, and others
confining their missions largely to the education of undergraduate
commuter students—this rough and ready method of computing unit
cost became largely untenable, except for comparisons of institutions
having similar missions and student bodies. It became necessary to
separate educational expenditures from outlays for noninstructional
purposes. Only the remainder—after deduction of expenditures for
research, public service, and auxiliary enterprises—could be regarded
as expenditures for the education of students and properly related to
number of students.

But the counting of number of students also had its complications. Some students attend part-time and others full-time. To
estimate the effective number of students the concept of "full-time-
equivalent student" was devised. With this concept, the number of
students was computed by counting full-time students as one each
and counting part-time students as a fraction of one according to the
number of credit hours for which they are enrolled. But students differ
also as to academic level. Some are beginning freshmen and sophomores, some are juniors and seniors, some are advanced graduate and
professional students. Costs tend to be higher as students advance up
the academic ladder. The educational cost per student therefore tends

to be greater in institutions with high proportions of advanced students than in institutions with high proportions of beginners. To standardize the units in which teaching loads are measured, heavier weights must be assigned to advanced students than to beginners. For example, in the present study, doctoral candidates are assigned three times as much weight as entering freshmen. Thus, to obtain a satisfactory measure of the teaching load of an institution it is necessary to express the enrollment in full-time equivalents weighted according to the academic level of students. The resulting adjusted enrollment is expressed in what I shall call "student units"—each unit being the equivalent of one full-time freshman or sophomore student. The unit cost of any institution can then be calculated by dividing the educational expenditures by the number of student units. Theoretically at least, the educational costs of institutions of all types—from community colleges to major universities—may thus be reduced to the same units and compared.

In a study of institutional costs, it would have been desirable to include the costs of organized research and public service, as well as educational costs, because research and public service are integral and important functions of colleges and universities. To include them, however, would have required units in which the products of research and public service could be measured. Unfortunately, these two activities do not lend themselves to measurement in discrete units. There is simply no known way, except through the broad general judgment of experts, to measure the output of an institution's organized research or public service program. Cost studies, therefore, are usually confined to the educational function for which a tenable measuring unit is available. This unit is a full-time-equivalent student with appropriate adjustment for academic level. The present study is no exception.

Admittedly, the student unit is not an ideal measure of the outputs of the educational process. The student is an input, a resource employed, not an output. The outputs of higher education are results. For individuals, they are mainly learning and personal development; for society, they are mainly advancement of the culture and economic growth. These are the true outcomes in terms of which unit costs ideally should be calculated. But our knowledge of outcomes is so feeble, and even if we had the knowledge, our ability to quantify outcomes would be so limited, that it would be hopeless to count costs in terms of the true outcomes. (Some efforts to relate costs and outcomes are described in Chapters Six and Eight.) Therefore, we resort to the expedient of using adjusted number of students as a proxy for the true outcomes. It is an expedient that can be tolerated but not commended. One may hope that as more is learned about the true outcomes, we can do better than merely compute "cost per student unit." Meanwhile, students are our only reliable indicators of the amount of education being conducted and the only tolerable base for establishing unit costs.

Educational and Noneducational Expenditures

To launch the study of actual costs, I shall present estimates of the combined expenditures of America's colleges and universities in a single year. Table 1 shows the percentage distribution of expenditures by broad functions and by recipient groups for 1974-75. This table may be thought of as representing either the entire American higher educational system or a single college or university. The data are expressed as percentages because the proportions of expenditure in various categories remain fairly constant from year to year whereas the dollar amounts change rapidly with inflation. Table 1 was of necessity constructed by piecing together information from scattered sources; the resulting figures are only estimates but they convey a general view of the way higher educational dollars are spent.

Note that only 33.1 percent of total expenditures are spent directly for instruction and departmental research. When to this 33.1 percent are added student services, scholarships and fellowships, and a *pro rata* share of academic support, institutional support, and operations and maintenance of plant, the percentage that may be allocated to the education of students is 58.9 percent of total expenditures. This 58.9 percent is the part of higher educational expenditures with which this book is concerned. It excludes organized research and public service, auxiliary enterprises, and teaching hospitals—which together account for the balance, 41.1 percent of the total.

Departmental research is distinguished from organized research and public service. Departmental research is the ordinary part-time research that professors pursue as part of their regular work. It is regarded as an essential ingredient of teaching excellence and there-

Expenditures classified according to recipients (expressed as a percentage of total expenditures)

Expenditures classified by administrative divisions	Employees: salaries, wages, and fringe benefits					Vendors: purchased goods and services (current)			Students: financial aid	Capital costs	Total
	Faculty	Other professional staff	Administrative staff	Other workers	Subtotal	Equipment and books	Other	Subtotal			
Education											
Direct expenditures for instruction and departmental research	23.8%	1.5%	—	1.1%	26.4%	0.7%	1.7%	2.4%	—	4.3%	33.1%
Student services	—	—	2.2	1.0	3.2	—	0.3	0.3	—	1.0	4.5
Scholarships and fellowships	—	—	—	—	—	—	—	—	3.5	—	3.5
Academic support	—	—	1.8	1.5	3.3	0.6	0.1	0.7	—	0.9	4.9
Institutional support	—	—	1.2	1.6	2.8	0.4	2.4	2.8	—	0.7	6.3
Operation and maintenance of plant	—	—	0.4	3.7	4.1	0.3	1.7	2.0	—	0.5	6.6
Subtotal	23.8	1.5	5.6	8.9	39.8	2.0	6.2	8.2	3.5	7.4	58.9
Organized research and public service											
Direct expenditures	1.5	4.0	—	1.9	7.4	0.8	2.0	2.8	—	1.5	11.7
Academic support	—	—	0.6	0.5	1.1	0.2	0.1	0.3	—	0.3	1.7
Institutional support	—	—	0.4	0.6	1.0	0.2	0.8	1.0	—	0.2	2.2
Operation and maintenance of plant	—	—	0.1	1.3	1.4	0.1	0.6	0.7	—	0.2	2.3
Subtotal	1.5	4.0	1.1	4.3	10.9	1.3	3.5	4.8	—	2.2	17.9
Auxiliary enterprises	—	—	0.4	2.3	2.7	1.2	6.1	7.3	—	6.3	16.3
Teaching hospitals	—	1.5	0.2	2.3	4.0	0.5	1.2	1.7	—	1.2	6.9
Total	25.3	7.0	7.3	17.8	57.4	5.0	17.0	22.0	3.5	17.1	100.0

Note: See Appendix A for sources and methods used in deriving these estimates.

fore chargeable to education. Organized research and public service, on the other hand, are less closely linked with education and are separately funded and separately budgeted. (See Appendix C.)

The bottom row of Table 1 shows the distribution of expenditures by recipient groups. All the expenditures of higher education are paid out to staff as wages or salaries, to outside vendors for the purchase of goods and services, to students for financial aid, and to outside vendors and contractors for the purchase of capital goods such as buildings and equipment. The breakdown of expenditures by recipient groups is for many purposes more revealing than the customary classification by functions and this classification will be used to some extent in this study. However, expenditure data are seldom gathered in this way and so the figures in the table are only informed guesses and not accurate amounts. (As an aside, I would recommend that institutions analyze their expenditure data and construct their budgets by recipient groups as well as by functional categories and that the National Center for Education Statistics routinely collect data by recipient groups as well as functional categories.)

As indicated in the bottom row of Table 1, staff compensation accounts for 57.4 percent of total expenditures. This percentage is lower than that usually cited because the total expenditure, of which this figure is a percentage, includes capital costs as well as current operating expenditures. When staff compensation is expressed as a percentage of *current* expenditures excluding capital costs, the figure rises to 69 percent (Millett, 1952, pp. 115–116).

As shown in the top row of Table 1, about one-quarter (26.4 percent) of the total expenditures are for compensation of the people directly engaged in instruction and departmental research. This portion may be thought of as the front-line expenditure to deliver the basic service colleges and universities were created to provide, namely, the education of students. This 26.4 percent is less than half the total expenditures for education which amount to 58.9 percent of the grand total of all expenditures (row seven of right-hand column). The other educational expenditures amounting to 32.5 percent[1] may be

---

[1]Total educational expenditures of 58.9 percent of the grand total (row seven of right-hand column in Table 1) minus percentage paid to employees engaged in education of 26.4.

thought of as backup or supportive services. Just as an army needs large amounts of personnel, facilities, services to sustain the front-line troops, so colleges and universities need substantial behind-the-lines support to assist the work of the faculty and other front-line staff. The backup expenditures are intended to create the general institutional environment in which the basic service can flourish.

The distinction between "front-line" and "backup" expenditures is by no means precise. The environment created by the backup expenditures may have direct educational effects. For example, student counseling and recreational activities may be influential in shaping the character and aspirations of students. Cultural programs may awaken and develop artistic sensitivity and humane inclinations. Student housing and dining may be a vehicle for meaningful discussion and for valuable experience in human relations. The physical plant through its beauty and careful maintenance may create a serene environment favorable to deep thoughts and high ideals. Even the character of the administration may influence the educative and scholarly capacity of institutions. A college or university is a community whose every part is a potential instrument of learning. Effectiveness in higher education calls for the use of every part of the institution to form an academic community of maximum influence upon its students.

Though all parts of an institution may contribute directly or indirectly to the fulfillment of its purposes, the relative proportions of academic resources devoted to front-line and to backup functions is a matter to which educational leaders cannot be indifferent. The basic educational purposes of colleges and universities are achieved through the work of the people directly engaged in education. That only a quarter of total higher educational expenditures is paid for the compensation of these people is a matter of concern. Indeed, it is a matter of growing concern because, as will be indicated in Chapter Seven, the proportion of resources devoted to the front-line functions has been decreasing over recent decades. Given the constraint of fixed total resources, it cannot be denied that every addition to backup expenditures—every additional clerk, accountant, affirmative action officer, gardener, or security guard or every additional air conditioning system or landscape improvement—may be at the expense of front-line staff. No one would expect a college or university, any more

than an army, to operate without behind-the-lines support, yet the
trends in this ratio over time may be an important barometer of the
progress and health of higher education. Indeed, the ratio of front-
line to backup expenditures may be a revealing index of efficiency in
higher education.

The Long Run: Societal Determinants of Cost

The educational expenditures of higher educational institutions in
the aggregate are ultimately determined by the amount of money our
society is willing to devote to them. However, no single social
decision-making authority provides the resources for higher education or regulates the flow of these resources. The sources of funds are
widely diffused. They include tuitions and fees paid by millions of
students and their families; gifts from numerous donors; endowment
income controlled by the governing boards of the institutions; and
public appropriations of fifty separate states and several territories,
many local authorities, and the federal government. The collective
decisions of all these people, organizations, and public authorities
determine the amount of money available for higher education. This
amount in turn determines the total sum that can be spent, or the
aggregate cost, of the colleges and universities.

The broad general characteristics of the higher educational
system also are determined by "society." Those who provide the funds
all exercise some influence over the scope and organization of the
higher educational system and also over its technologies or modes of
operation. They influence such characteristics as the number and
qualifications of students admitted; the relative emphasis on vocational and liberal studies; the number, types, sizes, and geographic
locations of the institutions; and even the modes of instruction as
determined by the ratio of students to faculty. "Society" as represented by the several sources of funds usually does not regulate the higher
educational system in detail and leaves much scope for the institutions individually. Yet, through widely diffused decisions about the
missions and the allocation of funds, considerable influence is exerted over the broad general characteristics of the higher educational
system.

These societal decisions are strongly influenced by tradition. At
any given moment, concepts of what higher education "ought to be

like" have evolved from the past and are accepted widely as part of the general culture. Examples of such concepts are: that colleges and universities should be physically spacious and architecturally beautiful, that they should provide enough staff to give attention and guidance to students individually, that they should extend opportunity to less-privileged social classes, that they should be more or less removed from detailed governmental control, or that they should charge tuitions as low as feasible. These concepts are never universally accepted and are always slowly evolving. For example, in recent decades, controversy has swirled about admissions policies, faculty teaching loads, and tuition. The unsettled questions about what higher education ought to be in the future are the substance of ongoing public debates about higher education. At any given time, however, the general public tends to hold a set of concepts that define the system and influence decisions about the amount of funds to be devoted to it.

Changes in the amount of funds that the public is willing to allocate to higher education ordinarily occur by small annual increments or decrements. In the past, as higher education has grown, the allocation has usually increased each year. In a possible future stable or declining state, the public may favor decreases. Each increment in expenditure involves an opportunity cost, that is, to allocate additional resources to higher education requires that some amount of another good or goods, which could have been obtained with the same resources, must be forfeited. These sacrifices are the incremental costs of higher education. For example, a small increment in funds devoted to higher education might require a family to decrease personal consumption in another area or might require a state government to forgo a low-priority public project. As successive increments are added for education, they require the abandonment of progressively more important alternative projects. The incremental growth of higher education, relative to other industries, results in a successively increasing opportunity cost. Conversely, each successive decrement of higher education allows increases in the amount of other goods and produces declining opportunity cost, because it allows resources to be used for alternative opportunities of successively lower priority.

An increment of expenditure for higher educational institutions may have either or both of two purposes. It may finance an expansion of the number of students in attendance, or it may be intended to enhance the quality of the service rendered, for example, by raising the ratio of faculty to students or by improving facilities and equipment. Of course, not every addition to cost that is intended to enhance quality will improve the performance of higher education, any more than every increase in private consumption adds to the quality of life. The trade-offs between quality and quantity at any given time are determined by the prevailing ideals for higher education held by those who support colleges and universities.

The cost per student unit results from three societal decisions that reflect the combined influence of the many persons and public authorities who control the flow of funds to higher education. These three decisions pertain to: the total amount to be spent on higher education, the number of units of service to be provided, and the level of quality.

Societal decisions about higher educational institutions are affected not only by cost but also by expectations of benefits to be received from higher education. Higher education, like all other forms of production, is subject to diminishing returns. As expenditures increase, each incremental addition to expenditure may yield fewer or lesser benefits. For example, successive improvements in quality—distinction of faculty, richer faculty-student ratios, elaboration of equipment, additional library resources, architectural refinement—may have a diminishing effect on outcomes until a point is reached at which they have no effect or a negative effect on performance. As higher education expands, it may attract less qualified and less motivated students, which also may eventually bring about reductions in incremental outcomes. Tendencies toward diminishing returns means that as higher education expands, the incremental returns decline and that the amount people are willing to pay for additional units of higher education correspondingly tends to fall.

The tendencies of opportunity costs to rise and benefits to fall, as expenditures increase, are illustrated in Figure 1 by an upward-sloping cost curve (CC) and a downward-sloping benefit or demand curve (DD). The point at which the cost curve (CC) intersects the benefit curve (DD) defines the equilibrium position, the amount of

Figure 1. Schematic Diagram of demand and cost for higher education

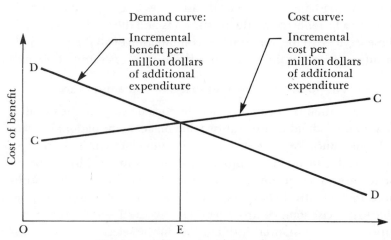

Demand curve: Incremental benefit per million dollars of additional expenditure

Cost curve: Incremental cost per million dollars of additional expenditure

Cost of benefit

Total expenditures for higher education

expenditure (OE) at which the incremental benefits are equal to the incremental costs (Solmon, 1980). Deviation from this point indicates that higher education is overextended (costs exceed benefits) or that it is underdeveloped (benefits exceed costs).

The two curves are by no means stationary, and the equilibrium position can change. A society may value the returns to higher education more at some times than at others. For example, after the USSR launched Sputnik, the American public called for increased expenditures for education; the demand curve exhibited a sizable, sudden upward shift. In the 1970s, however, the demand curve seems to have shifted downward because of an imminent decline in the number of high school graduates or, possibly, a general decline in the public's valuation of education. The cost curve also may shift upward or downward. For example, the urgency of alternative uses of resources may increase, thus raising the cost curve, as when resources must be diverted to national defense or to environmental purposes. Or the urgency of alternative uses of resources may decline as when unemployment frees resources that could be diverted into higher education at minimal opportunity cost.

The interaction of demand and cost, as conceived by "society" at any given time, determines total expenditures or the amount of resources to be allocated to the operation of higher educational institutions. At the same time, societal influences also affect the kinds of service to be rendered by the institutions and the level of quality of these services. In the long run, the combination of all these decisions or influences determines the expenditure or cost per unit of service.

The Short Run: Institutional Determinants of Cost

The determinants of cost also may be considered from the point of view of the individual institutions that make up the national system of higher education. They must, of course, operate within the context of societal demand and supply. They are constrained by the broad preferences and decisions underlying societal choices. But the institutions individually do have considerable freedom of action. They are able to exercise some control over their separate destinies. Most institutions exert substantial influence upon the selection of their students, the educational programs they provide, the relative emphasis they place on quantity and quality of services, and the technologies they employ. In these ways, each institution may determine to some extent the share of the higher educational "market" it serves. Each institution also may discover and cultivate new social needs for higher education not previously recognized, for example, by reaching out to adults or minority groups, or by offering new programs of vocational training. Moreover, each can engage in promotional activities akin to selling, advertising, public relations, and lobbying. In these ways, individual institutions—each pursuing its own interests—may in the aggregate affect the societal demand for higher education.

Each institution endeavors to fulfill its own purposes within the constraints set by the social milieu and the competition of other colleges and universities. These purposes vary among institutions. They may include providing needed services for particular clienteles, raising the quality of service, achieving financial security, and enhancing the institutional reputation. It must be said that reputation ranks high among the purposes of most institutions. As an institution pursues its own interests, operating within the given constraints, it seeks a special niche for itself. The niche may be defined partly by location, by size, by type of clientele, by type of programs, and by level of "quality." The particular niches of the many institutions may vary widely. Some may offer two-year and others four-year programs of instruction, some may cater only to undergraduates and others may have highly developed graduate and professional study. Some may confine themselves strictly to liberal education and others may have elaborate vocational programs. In the competitive race, some institutions may be in the ascendancy and others may be slipping. If some social needs are not being met, new institutions may be established to fill these niches. If some institutions persist in trying to occupy niches for which there is insufficient need, they will disappear.

One of the most striking findings of this study is that institutions of higher education spend their money in very different ways and experience widely different costs per student. The societal influences bearing upon higher education do not enforce standardized patterns in the way institutions are conducted—even among institutions with essentially similar missions. Colleges and universities have no strong incentive to cut costs in quest of profit because they do not seek profit. They are not forced by competition to lower costs in order to survive. This is so partly because they are subsidized by government and philanthropy and partly because they are shielded from competition by geographic location and by differentiation of services. It is so also because institutions know little about the relationship between their expenditures and their educational outcomes, and it is easy to drift into the comfortable belief that increased expenditures will automatically produce commensurately greater outcomes. Under these conditions, the unit costs of operating colleges or universities are set more largely by the amount of money institutions are able to raise per unit of service rendered than by the inherent technical requirements of conducting their work. Within wide limits, institutions can adjust to whatever amount of money they are able to raise. When resources are increased, they find uses for the new funds, and unit costs go up. When resources are decreased, they express keen regret and they protest, but in the end they accept the inevitable, and unit costs go down. This set of generalizations might be called the *revenue theory of cost;* attention is now directed to this theory.

Institutions doubtless are constrained by vague, but nevertheless effective, lower and upper limits to unit cost. The floor is set by prevailing societal concepts of what a college or university ought to be like, by the willingness or unwillingness of students to attend institutions of various characteristics, by the mandate of funding agencies, and by the standards set by accrediting bodies, licensing agencies, and professional societies. In order to function, each institution must attain some bare minimum of funds per unit of service. Otherwise it is not a member of the higher educational community— either because it is not recognized as such or because it does not survive. A ceiling on unit costs is set by aversion to ridiculous waste on the part of institutional leaders and their constituencies. However, as institutions become increasingly affluent, they rarely reject additional funds. Nor do they typically increase unit costs without limit. Rather, they are likely to allow enrollments to grow, take on new and expensive educational programs, expand their research and public service activities, add physical plant, or accumulate endowments.

In explaining the unit cost of higher education, sometimes educators argue that it is determined by the *needs* of institutions. To conduct education of a satisfactory quality, it is said, a certain ratio of faculty to students, or an appropriate salary scale, or funds to pay increased Social Security taxes are needed. This line of argument is common to educators as they plead the case for increased revenues or fend off potential revenue cuts. Because higher education is conducted at so many different levels of expenditures and with so many different allocations of resources, however, there is no precise need that can be objectively defined and defended.

The needs which educators present to legislators and donors are arguments in favor of increased funding, not causes of increased cost. They are often sensible and persuasive arguments but, as every educator knows, they do not automatically bring about increases in unit costs. If arguments persuade and revenues are increased, then costs will rise. But they will rise because revenues grew, not merely because of newly perceived needs. For example, increased energy prices or the demand to expand women's athletics do not automatically bring about increases in appropriations, gifts, or tuitions. The persuasion of educators is, however, one influence on the amount of funds society allocates to higher education. Each educator intends only to influence donors, legislators, and others to be more generous to his or her own institutions; but the combined persuasive effort of all educators may be to increase the total flow of funds to higher education and therefore to increase total expenditures and unit costs.

The obverse of the "needs" argument is the "efficiency" argument. Those who wish to cut the educational costs of institutions often advance proposals for improving the efficiency of operations. A whole array of proposals is offered, for example, to adopt the techniques of modern management, to operate institutions year around, to use classrooms more intensively, to lower the faculty-student ratio, to cut telephone and utility bills. All of these and many more might reduce costs, but they would do so only if revenues were cut commensurately. If revenues were not so reduced, any saving would simply be expended elsewhere in the institution and no net saving would occur. Unit costs are determined not by changes in efficiency but by changes in revenues.

Institutional adjustments to meet perceived needs or to improve efficiency, even though they do not alter overall unit costs, may change the internal allocation of resources and thus alter the overall performance of the institution. It may be possible to meet a need, such as career counseling, by shifting resources from an obsolete academic department without bringing about any increase in overall unit cost. Or it may be possible through improvements in efficiency, for example by simplifying the curriculum, to save resources which can then be shifted to other urgent uses. Given the enrollment of an institution, whether meeting needs or improving efficiency will raise or lower overall unit cost will depend on the amount of revenues. If revenues are changed, there will be a change in overall unit cost, otherwise not. To say that identifying new needs will not raise costs or that achieving efficiency will not lower costs unless revenues rise or fall accordingly does not imply that it is not important or even urgent to meet needs or to improve efficiency. It means only that unit cost will not be affected unless there are corresponding changes in revenue.

The Revenue Theory of Cost Summarized

The basic concept underlying the revenue theory of cost is that an institution's educational cost per student unit is determined by the revenues available for educational purposes. Given the enrollment, cost per student unit is directly proportional to these revenues. In most institutions, public or private, educational revenues are closely related to enrollment. In most public institutions, educational revenues are derived largely from tuitions and from state appropriations based on "enrollment driven" formulas. In most private institutions, educational revenues come mainly from tuitions. The situation is more complicated in the elite private institutions which potentially have considerable control over the internal allocation of revenues to education and research and over enrollment. But even they depend on tuitions as the major source of revenue available for educational purposes.

On the whole, unit cost is determined neither by rigid technological requirements of delivering educational services nor by some abstract standard of need. It is determined rather by the revenue available for education that can be raised per student unit. Technology and need affect unit cost only as they influence those who control revenues and enrollments.

Given an institution's enrollment, whoever or whatever controls the flow of educational revenue to that institution will determine the unit cost. This control, however, tends to be diffused because revenues are derived from several sources: federal, state, and local appropriations, tuitions, gifts and grants from private individuals and corporations, endowment, and sales of goods and services. Since an institution usually tries to maximize revenues from all sources, one can say that unit costs are determined by the amount of money the institution is able to raise, and that no single person or organization is fully in control of unit costs. In most institutions, the control lies mainly in the hands of state governments as reflected in their willingness to vote appropriations and of students as reflected in their willingness to attend and to pay tuitions. Insofar as institutions have other outside sources of revenue or have endowment income, control is to that extent more widely diffused.

The revenue theory of educational cost is subject to an important qualification. It is a *short-run* theory. It describes what happens practically from year to year in most institutions. In the long run, of course, the amount of revenue institutions receive from public appropriations, gifts and grants, and tuitions will be influenced by such factors as changes in social attitudes toward the value of higher education, by changes in educational technologies that affect resource requirements, by changes in the labor market affecting wages and salaries, by changes in the prices of purchased goods and services, by changes in competitive conditions within the higher educational community, and by any other factors that may affect the willingness of legislators and donors to provide funds and the willingness of students and their families to pay tuitions. Nevertheless, at any given time, the unit cost of education is determined by the amount of revenues currently available for education relative to enrollment. This statement is more than a tautology. It expresses the fundamental fact that unit cost is determined by hard dollars of revenue and only indirectly and remotely by considerations of need, technology, efficiency, and market wages and prices.

The "Laws" of Higher Educational Costs

From the revenue theory of cost, it is possible to deduce a set of closely interrelated "laws" pertaining to unit costs in colleges and universities. These laws describe the incentives and the behavior of higher educational institutions as they conduct their activities from year to year.

A basic assumption underlying these laws is that the size, type, and mission of each institution is given—having been determined by the unique events of its history. Institutions, of course, change— sometimes drastically. Yet in any short span of years, the great majority have settled into a pattern. Their mission and their enrollment are well established.

Given this assumption, certain laws of higher educational costs may be derived (Bowen, 1970):

1. The dominant goals of institutions are educational excellence, prestige, and influence.

    The "excellence" or "quality" of institutions are commonly judged by such criteria as faculty-student ratios, faculty salaries, number of Ph.D.s on the faculty, number of books in the library, range of facilities and equipment, and academic qualifications of students. These criteria are resource inputs most of which cost money, not outcomes flowing from the educational process. The true outcomes in the form of learning and personal development of students are on the whole unexamined and only vaguely discerned.

2. In quest of excellence, prestige, and influence, there is virtually no
   limit to the amount of money an institution could spend for seemingly fruitful educational ends.

   Whatever level of expenditure is attained is seldom considered
   enough. Institutions tend, therefore, to spend up to the very
   limit of their means. As a result, the financial problems of rich
   institutions are about as severe as those of all but the most
   impoverished institutions. This is especially so because whatever expenditures are once admitted into the budget become
   long-term commitments from which it is difficult ever to
   withdraw.

3. Each institution raises all the money it can.

   No college or university ever admits to having enough money
   and all try to increase their resources without limit.

4. Each institution spends all it raises.

   Many institutions, however, accumulate reserves and endowments. These "savings" are derived primarily from gifts designated for endowment and not from voluntary allocations of
   current income. In most institutions, the accumulations are of
   negligible amount. The few institutions that become very affluent, however, are able to save substantial amounts and
   accumulate significant endowments.

5. The cumulative effect of the preceding four laws is toward ever-
   increasing expenditure.

   The incentives inherent in the goals of excellence, prestige,
   and influence are not counteracted within the higher educational system by incentives leading to parsimony or efficiency.
   The question of what *ought* higher education to cost—what is
   the minimal amount needed to provide services of acceptable
   quality—does not enter the process except as it is imposed from
   the outside. The higher educational system itself provides no
   guidance of a kind that weighs costs and benefits in terms of
   the public interest. The duty of setting limits thus falls, by
   default, upon those who provide the money, mostly legislators
   and students and their families.

Laws similar to these are applicable to many kinds of
not-for-profit organizations other than higher education, such as

hospitals, churches, schools, museums, and, not least, governmental agencies. The people committed to these organizations—trustees, administrators, professional persons, and workers—generally share the goals of excellence, prestige, and influence. They have in common a sense of limitless horizons. The field in which they work is to them so vital to human welfare that no effort or resources should be spared. In most cases, this means that the services rendered to each client should be as perfect and complete as possible. Indeed, the sharing of these goals is the very definition of organizational morale, and the success of any organization is dependent upon the commitment of its members to these goals. These aspirations are always tinged with the personal ambitions of the administrators and professional workers involved. This is not all bad. If institutions individually were not ambitious, they would be lethargic, unimaginative, and unresponsive to social needs. However, there is nothing in these aspirations and motives that restrains unit cost. From the point of view of institutions, higher unit cost is better almost without qualification. Yet there must be some limit on not-for-profit institutions and governmental agencies including colleges and universities. In the public interest, the economic principle of equi-marginal returns to all areas of expenditure must somehow come into play. According to this principle, the final dollar spent for higher education should yield a return equal to the final dollar spent for health services, national defense, elementary education, environmental improvement, private family consumption, or any other purpose. Yet there are few within higher education, or other not-for-profit organizations, whose purview is the broad public interest. There are only advocates whose purposes and motives are described in the five "laws" of cost.

It is, of course, the political process that we usually depend upon to work out the flow of funds to various fields according to the equi-marginal principle. In the case of higher education, however, no single public agency is responsible for the financing. Funds flow from the federal government, fifty state governments, several territorial governments, and hundreds of local governments. Funds are derived also from tuitions and other fees paid by millions of students and their families, from gifts and grants donated by thousands of donors, and from the income on endowments held by the institutions. The many persons who finance higher education do not

speak with a single voice in their estimation of the marginal benefits
to be derived from it. Even the fifty states differ widely in their support
of higher education. Thus, the allocation of funds to higher education is singularly dependent upon the efforts of the institutions. Each
one operates with a sort of hunting license which enables it to gather
funds wherever it can find them and to obtain the maximum amount
possible. The costs, then, are determined by success in overall fund-
raising and they vary widely among institutions.

The hunting licenses vary among institutions in scope and
flexibility. For example, most state institutions are largely dependent
upon state appropriations and tuitions and rely only marginally on
gifts, grants, and endowment income. Most community colleges derive their funds mainly from appropriations of state and local government. Most private institutions are financed mainly by tuitions.
Many private and public institutions, however, draw upon varied
sources of support. All, however, are free to exert influence on whatever financial sources are accessible to them. They seek appropriations by lobbying and by public relations efforts, they try to maximize
tuitions through various admissions and public relations techniques,
they assiduously cultivate gifts, and they try to increase endowment
income through successful investment policy. All are attempting to
increase revenues from whatever sources are available to them. In the
end their costs are affected by the degree of their success in
fund-raising.

The unit costs of particular institutions are thus determined in
large part by the amount of money they are able to raise, not necessarily by some rational determination of the minimal amount needed to
provide services of acceptable quality. There are Cadillac institutions
and Pinto institutions and all gradations between. Just as Cadillacs
and Pintos both provide acceptable transportation, albeit with differing degrees of comfort and prestige, so rich and poor institutions may
both provide acceptable education, likewise with differing degrees of
excellence and prestige.

There is waste associated with competition among colleges and
universities just as there is competitive waste among business firms in
the free enterprise system. For example, individual institutions often
spend money to enhance their reputations, to attract donors, or to
raise the calibre of students attending. Expenditures for such pur-

poses, though they may help to advance the status of some institutions vis a vis their competitors, do not add much to the overall outcomes of higher education. They are basically moves in a zero sum game. They force competitors to make similar expenditures with the result that all the players are worse off while their relative positions remain about unchanged. There are costs of institutional autonomy in higher education just as there are costs of free enterprise in private business. In the case of higher education, one of the functions of various multi-campus universities or governmental coordinating agencies is to minimize these expenses of competition and to guide the development of the higher educational system through centralized planning. However, it is doubtful whether central planning is superior to institutional initiative and whether the savings achieved through central planning are not obtained at a high cost in loss of local initiative, flexibility, social responsiveness—not to mention erosion of academic freedom.

Institutional Autonomy

One of the most vexing problems of higher education is to balance the need for control of costs with the need for institutional autonomy. Institutional autonomy is widely acknowledged to be essential to maintaining professional responsibility for academic decisions and to academic freedom in thought and expression. On the other hand, the financing of colleges and universities, especially when public funds are used, cannot be wholly open-ended. There must be some control over costs such that marginal returns to higher education are balanced against marginal returns to other uses of public monies. Even in private institutions that use little or no public funds, governing boards have a responsibility to keep expenditures within reason, relative to those in other parts of the national economy.

In order to bring costs under control, some legislators, state coordinating bodies, boards of trustees, and other governing bodies have tried to regulate educational activities and expenditures in great detail. From this effort have evolved line-item appropriations and detailed supervision by state boards and central offices of multi-campus universities. Excessively detailed financial control brings about a false efficiency and threatens institutional autonomy in academic decisions. For the small sums saved, the much greater efficiency flowing from local initiative and common sense is constrained and discouraged.

The revenue theory of costs suggests that when public agencies or governing boards wish to control costs, they need do only two things: first, to establish in broad general terms the basic scope and mission of the institutions for which they are responsible, and second, to set the total amount of money to be available to each institution each year. With these parameters given for each institution, both total and unit costs will be determined. The individual institutions through their internal decision-making processes can then allocate resources to meet local needs and to protect freedom of thought and expression. The state agencies and governing boards will then be freed from supervision of budgetary line items and they are freed from involvement with supervision of the professional aspects of instruction and research. They may wish to be generally informed on these matters and in particular to make sure that each institution is adhering to its mission. But these goals do not require detailed control of institutional operations. Broad general observation and post-audits are sufficient. To exercise cost control, state agencies and governing boards are obliged to decide only the level of educational revenues in light of the established mission and enrollment of each institution. (Clark, 1978; Harcleroad, 1975).

Such decisions may be based upon simulation studies, comparisons with other institutions, and formulas that take into account enrollments, salary levels, staffing ratios, cost of purchased goods and services, and capital requirements. In the end, however, these decisions are inevitably reached through the political process. Whatever these decisions may turn out to be, they are the ultimate determinants of both total expenditures and unit costs.

Conclusions

The pattern of American higher education, as it has evolved over three centuries, is part of the national culture. Questions about who should be educated, how the education should be conducted, what level of quality should be maintained, how the system should be organized, what institutions should be responsible for research and public service—all these questions—are largely settled through widely accepted concepts about what higher education should be like.

These concepts are at times controversial. They evolve over time. Yet there exists in society at any moment a substantial body of widely-accepted views about higher education.

The services of the institutions of higher education, like most products or services, are subject to increasing unit costs and to diminishing unit benefits as expenditures increase. In the long run, societal decisions about total expenditures will tend toward an equilibrium at which incremental cost per dollar of expenditure equals incremental benefit per dollar of expenditure, that is, at the point of intersection between the cost curve and the demand curve (see Figure 1). Both the cost curve and the demand curve shift from time to time and it is with these shifts that changes in the level of spending occur.

Individual institutions operate within the context of societal decisions concerning total expenditures. Institutions may differ in their responses to the environment in which they operate and they may fare differently. But they are constrained by the societal environment and also by the competition among them. However, their combined activities may affect societal demands for higher education as when they discover new needs or new clienteles or when they launch effective public relations campaigns; and their combined activities may affect overall costs, as when they find ways to reduce expenses or discover ways to enhance outcomes that justify increased costs. Thus, there is constant interplay between societal influences and institutional influences in determining total expenditures. In the long run, however, the broad societal influences are predominant; institutions must accept the parameters laid down by society.

To recognize societal influences on higher educational expenditures does not suggest that somewhere there is a central authority that consciously and overtly articulates public attitudes or regulates the entire higher educational system of the United States. Obviously, there is no such authority. Rather, it suggests that higher education is a relatively stable feature of the culture, that those who control the flow of funds to higher education—students and their families, other users, donors, legislators, and trustees—hold roughly similar concepts of what higher education should be like, and that these concepts provide the context within which the institutions operate and determine both total expenditures and cost per unit of service. As Lord

Keynes once said, however, "In the long run, we are all dead." In the short run, which may be very long indeed, costs per student unit for individual colleges and universities are determined by the amount of money they can raise for educational purposes relative to the number of students they are serving.

Part One

National Trends in
Higher Educational Costs

The four chapters in this part are focused on longitudinal changes in the unit cost of higher education over long periods of time and on the factors responsible for these changes. Chapter Two describes long-term trends in unit cost; Chapter Three deals with faculty and staff compensation as a major element of cost; Chapter Four is an analysis of costs that have been socially imposed as the nation has tried to protect and enhance social welfare; and Chapter Five is concerned mainly with undermaintenance of assets.

This section treats the higher educational system as a whole, not individual institutions or subgroups of institutions. Therefore, the longitudinal trends presented reflect not only changes over time in existing institutions but also substantial changes in the structure of the system. For example, the period under review witnessed the transformation of normal schools into state colleges and universities, the creation of hundreds of community colleges, the expansion of the public sector relative to the private sector, great increases in the size of most institutions, and shifts in the proportions of students served by different types of institutions. All of these structural changes, as well as internal changes in particular institutions, affected cost trends.

This section will be followed by a parallel section in which the same questions will be approached cross-sectionally through a study of a sample of institutions viewed in a single year. Near the end of the book the findings from the longitudinal and cross-sectional studies will be assembled and reviewed. There these questions will be addressed: (1) How did higher education fare in the decade of the 1970s? (2) In the national public interest, what would be a reasonable level of cost in 1979-80? and (3) By how much did the higher educational system fall short of that "reasonable level" of cost in 1979-80?

Any analyst of higher education is handicapped by the unavailability and inadequacy of data. One must splice together bits and pieces, fill in gaps, use price indexes not wholly appropriate to the subject, and in many cases make some informed guesses. In these chapters, and throughout the rest of the book, I have stretched available statistical resources to the outer limits—I hope not irresponsibly. For detailed descriptions of data, sources, and methods used in Part One, see Appendix B.

2

Long-Term Trends

It is widely believed that the costs of higher education per student have increased steadily over many years and that there is something inevitable about this trend. As will be shown in this chapter, this belief is probably not well founded. Although aggregate costs in current dollars have increased steadily over many years, when these costs are adjusted for inflation, growth in enrollments, and changes in the composition of student bodies, one discovers that during some long periods instructional costs per student remained steady or declined. As is well known, unit costs rose rapidly during the 1950s and 1960s when the nation poured vast sums of new money into higher education, but this era appears to have been highly exceptional.

Higher education, nevertheless, seems to have more difficulty than many other industries—especially those producing physical products such as automobiles, television sets, or food—in achieving improvements in productivity through changes in technology. Many such industries are able to raise regularly the real wages and salaries of their workers and still hold cost per unit of product about level (in constant dollars). Although some of the alleged feats of improved productivity are achieved at the cost of deterioration in product quality or customer convenience, many industries have made great strides in holding down unit costs. Striking examples in recent decades include the electronic industry and commerical agriculture. (It is well to remember that higher education plays an important part in such technological progress). Yet, those institutions of higher education that have been able to hold their unit cost steady have done so largely at the expense of their workers who have received smaller pay increments than their counterparts in other employments.

Professional Industries

It is often argued that sluggish gains in productivity are common to all service industries of which higher education is a notable example. But, in fact, some service industries are quite adept at improving their productivity so as to allow substantial increases in wages and salaries without raising costs (in constant dollars). For example, many financial institutions such as banks, insurance companies, and brokerage houses reduce clerical and accounting costs through the use of computers. Similarly, the costs of long-distance telephone service are held down through radical automation. It is simply not true that the problem of sluggish gains in productivity is characteristic of all service industries.

It is not hard, however, to identify industries that are plagued by slow gains in productivity. Some are producers of physical goods, for example, building construction and book publishing; others are in the service sector—barber and beauty service, shoe repair, laundry and dry cleaning, luxury hotels and restaurants, and postal service.

Another set of industries faced with slow gains in productivity is a subgroup of the service sector, the *professional industries* such as health services, legal services, consulting services, research and development, architecture, engineering, the creative arts, the performing arts, museums, libraries, botanical and zoological gardens, churches, social welfare institutions, elementary and secondary education, and many branches of government. Higher education is one of these. These industries have three characteristics that set them apart from most other sectors of the economy. First, these industries are based on an intellectual or esthetic foundation and require of the practitioners exceptional skill that can be developed only through long study and experience. Second, the professional industries are deeply involved in the advancement of human well-being and the cultivation of the civic, cultural, religious, and intellectual life of the nation. These industries touch some of the most critical and sensitive aspects of peoples' personal lives. They gather about them, therefore, an aura of high importance and even of sanctity. They tend to be steeped in tradition and to be influenced by long-standing and influential ethical codes and laws. Third, the performance of the services of the professional industries usually requires that practitioners be physically in the presence of the clients. Rendering the service usually involves communication of knowledge or exercise of special skill for the direct benefit of the individuals or groups being served. The need for this personal relationship usually places limits on the scale at which the service can be performed and on the ability to cut costs through mass production. For example, health services require the presence and attention of physicians and nurses, legal counsel is based on the personal attention of lawyers, religious work calls for the presence of clergymen, a symphony concert demands the presence of about 100 musicians, instruction requires the presence and attention of teachers, and research demands the time of scientists and scholars.

These three characteristics in combination undoubtedly inhibit technological changes in the professional industries and prevent these industries from achieving the kind, of cost stability or cost reduction common to other industries. Cost-saving technologies are hard to achieve without shortcutting the training of professional people, without impairing personal communications that are deemed essential to the service, and without disturbing valued traditions. At stake is the advancement of human welfare and the cultural development of the nation. Indeed, the practitioners of these professions characteristically assume that it is their duty to improve the quality of the services they render within the existing technology and thus by inference to increase unit cost. Given all these conditions, the professional industries tend to be sluggish in the achievement of increased productivity of a kind that would hold real costs steady or even cut real costs.

This sluggishness produces either of two results. On the one hand, if wages and salaries in a given professional industry are increased to meet the competition of the more progressive sectors of the economy, then the cost of producing professional services in that industry will tend to rise relative to the cost of producing goods in the more progressive industries. On the other hand, if the cost of production in a professional industry is held constant, then wages and salaries in that industry will tend to fall relative to those in more progressive industries. The actual cost of professional industries depends on their ability to raise money from whatever sources are available. If it is able to raise enough money to finance increases in wages and salaries, employee compensation will rise and the cost of the product will increase. But if it cannot procure the money to finance competitive increases in the pay of its workers, then the cost of the product will remain constant and wages and salaries will fall. Or as an intermediate possibility, if the industry can raise enough money to increase wages and salaries some but not enough to make them competitive, the compensation of workers and the cost of the product will be increased moderately. The critical factor that determines the result is the amount of money the industry is able to raise. Changes in the amount of available funds may affect the quantity and quality of service rendered as well as the compensation of workers. But the compensation of workers tends to be an item of high priority in the budgets of most professional industries and is strongly affected by changes in the flow of funds.

In the case of higher education, the typical condition has been the intermediate one. Higher education has generally been able to raise enough money to increase wages and salaries moderately but not enough to keep them competitive with compensation in the more progressive industries. This situation changed drastically in the 1950s and 1960s when societal demands for higher education enabled colleges and universities to raise vast sums of new money. Funds were sufficient to allow increases in real wages and salaries at a rate even faster than that in the technologically more progressive industries and, at the same time, to allow increased enrollment, expanded research and improved quality. Under these conditions, unit costs rose dramatically. In the 1970s, however, the nation became relatively less generous with higher education, and academic wages and salaries moved ahead more slowly than wages and salaries in the more progressive industries. (For discussions of the cost behavior of the professional industries, see Baumol and W. G. Bowen, 1966; W. G. Bowen, 1968; Baumol and Marcus, 1973; Blaug, 1976.)

The special characteristics of the professional industries do not exclude all reductions in unit costs. For example, the performing arts use recordings, films, and videotapes to reach larger audiences (though they have achieved little if any cost-cutting for live performances). Health services use nurses' aides, various specialized technicians, telephone consultation, automated tests, and paramedical ambulance personnel; the legal system to some degree employs legal aides and adopts streamlined procedures for divorce and small claims. Libraries save storage costs through miniaturization of periodicals and other materials. Some public schools use teacher aides. Similarly, some colleges and universities increase the average size of classes; some substitute junior faculty for senior faculty or part-time faculty for full-time faculty; some offer courses "taught" by books, films, radio, television, or computers in place of faculty; some have adopted various systems of independent study; some economize on building space; and some delete expensive programs. There are many ways to cut costs in all the professional industries, higher education among them. Indeed, in the cost of higher education at least, virtually every conceivable way of cutting costs has been adopted by some institution somewhere. It is interesting and perhaps revealing, however, that films have been available for seventy-five years, radio and sound films for fifty years, television and computers for twenty-five years, yet these have not made a pronounced impact on the institutions of higher education (though they have had an important role in informal education and in certain kinds of vocational training). In addition to the numerous attempts at cost reduction within institutions, new types of institutions such as community colleges and state colleges have been introduced with the expectation that they would be less costly than traditional universities and liberal arts colleges. Despite these many attempts, higher education as a whole—along with most other professional industries—has not achieved much by way of cost-cutting. Many educators maintain that the new technologies are not always less costly than the old ways. Many also maintain that even those technologies that are less costly, if used indiscriminantly, would damage quality of programs in the short run or quality of faculty and staff in the long run. Critics claim that the higher educational establishment is rigid and tradition-bound and is, in effect, sabotaging possible gains in efficiency. The truth may lie somewhere between. A fact that bears on the question of productivity is that the cost of education per student unit is lower in some institutions than in others. It is not clear, in every case, that institutions with lesser unit cost are purveying education having lesser outcomes than institutions with higher unit cost, or that differences in cost are commensurate with the differences in outcomes. Thus there may indeed be room for improvements in productivity—either by increasing outcomes or reducing costs—in at least some parts of the higher educational system. These matters will be discussed in detail in Part Two of this book.

In the remainder of this chapter, actual cost trends in higher education will be traced over almost a half-century from 1929–30 to 1975–76. The text of this chapter presents main conclusions without detailed description of the statistics and their sources. (Readers interested in statistical details are referred to Appendix B.)

Aggregate Costs

To begin the exploration of trends, it may be useful to consider expenditures of American colleges and universities for all purposes— education, research, public service, auxiliary enterprises, and teaching hospitals—and then to concentrate on educational costs, which are the main concern of this book. Aggregate expenditures of American colleges and universities for all purposes have increased at a spectacular rate over most of the period since World War II. The record of this phenomenal growth is shown in Tables 2 and 3. Between 1929–30 and 1975–76, total expenditures for all purposes including capital increased from $632 millions to $43,605 millions, an increase of sixty-nine times over forty-six years, or an average annual rate of increase of 9.6 percent. These are the figures people often have in mind when they refer to the explosive growth of higher educational costs or when they assert that higher educational costs have been out of control.

Actually, much of the growth was due to a vast expansion of enrollment and to an accelerating decline in the value of the dollar. As shown in Table 2, the number of students expressed in full-time equivalents increased from 890,000 to 8,481,000 between 1929–30 and 1975–76. Also, during the same period, the purchasing power of the dollar declined as the Consumer Price Index rose from 50.3 to 165.9 (1967=100). Expenditures, when expressed per student and in constant dollars, increased on the average by only about 1.4 percent a year. This was still a formidable rate of growth. At this rate, real cost per student would double every fifty years. But it was not the runaway condition that sometimes has been alleged.

The annual rate of growth in aggregate expenditures per student (in constant 1967 dollars), as shown in Table 3, was anything but constant throughout the period 1929–30 to 1976–77. It grew very

Table 2. Aggregate expenditures for all purposes and related data, all U.S. colleges and universities, 1929–30 to 1975–76

	1929–30	1939–40	1949–50	1959–60	1969–70	1975–76
Expenditures (current dollars)						
Current expenditures (millions)[a]	$ 507	$ 675	$2,246	$5,601	$21,043	$38,903
Capital expenditures (millions)[a]	125	84	417	1,315	4,233	4,702
Total (millions)	632	759	2,663	6,916	25,276	43,605
Total as percentage of gross national product	0.7%	0.8%	1.0%	1.4%	2.6%	2.7%
Expenditures (constant 1967 dollars)[b]						
Total (millions)	$1,428	$1,900	$3,812	$7,961	$22,214	$25,895
Per full-time-equivalent student[c]	1,605	1,581	1,777	2,869	3,516	3,053
Total full-time-equivalent enrollment (thousands)[c]	890	1,202	2,145	2,775	6,319	8,481
Gross national product (billions of current dollars)	96.8	95.4	272.1	496.3	959.0	1,614.5
Consumer Price Index (1967 = 100)	50.3	41.8	71.8	88.0	113.1	165.9
Index of construction and equipment prices (1967 = 100)[b]	29.8	29.5	61.0	82.4	117.3	192.3

[a] These data from National Center for Education Statistics, *Digest of Education Statistics*, 1978, pp. 184–185.

[b] Current fund expenditures deflated on the basis of the Consumer Price Index of the U.S. Department of Labor: capital expenditures deflated on the basis of an index of construction and equipment prices. See Appendix B, Table 40.

[c] For data on full-time-equivalent students, see Appendix B, Table 41.

Table 3. Changes in aggregate expenditures for all purposes, all U.S. colleges and universities, 1929–30 to 1975–76

	Average annual percentage of change			
	from 1929–30 to 1949–50	from 1949–50 to 1969–70	from 1969–70 to 1975–76	from 1929–30 to 1975–76
Total current and capital expenditures (current dollars)	7.5%	11.9%	9.5%	9.6%
Total current and capital expenditures (constant 1967 dollars)	5.0	9.2	2.6	6.5
Current and capital expenditures per full-time-equivalent student (constant 1967 dollars)	0.5	3.5	-2.3	1.4

Note: Data calculated on the basis of data presented in Table 2.

slowly in the 1930s and 1940s, it surged ahead in the "golden years" of the 1950s and 1960s, but declined during the 1970s. When all these facts are taken into account, the past rate of growth in cost was much less awesome than ordinarily supposed. The data hardly support the notion that higher educational costs rise steadily and inevitably over time. There is no doubt, however, that cost per student was substantially higher at the end of the period than at the beginning. In 1929–30 aggregate current expenditure per student (in 1967 dollars) was $1,605; in 1975–76 it was $3,053, an increase of 90 percent.

As a consequence of rising total expenditures, higher education's share of the gross national product (GNP) has grown. As shown in Table 2, total expenditures of higher education, as a percentage of the GNP, increased over the years from 1929–30 to 1975–76 from 0.7 percent to 2.7 percent. This increase meant that higher education had to reach out for new sources of revenues. It could not simply draw from the same old sources to obtain needed increases from general economic growth, and so it has pressed hard for additions to the traditional appropriations, gifts, and tuitions and has sought out new sources in the form of government grants, student loan plans, annual giving programs, and the like. A traditional function of educational leaders has been to persuade various elements of society to provide the funds for higher education's ever-expanding "needs." However, in the first half of the 1970s, higher educational expenditures as a precentage of GNP rose very slowly. Indeed, if in the 1980s there should be a fall in enrollments or even a slowing of enrollment growth, higher education's share of the GNP might actually begin to decline.

The rise in expenditures per student during the past half-century often has been attributed to many factors outside institutional control. For example, higher education was required to participate in various costly labor programs such as Social Security, minimum wage, workmen's compensation, collective bargaining, and affirmative action. Technological and scientific advancement demanded ever more expensive computers, electron microscopes, nuclear accelerators, and other elaborate equipment. The proliferation of knowledge called for increased acquisition of library books and journals, and the prices of these materials escalated rapidly. New academic programs were needed to reflect changing social and politi-

cal conditions, for example, urban studies, ethnic studies, computer science, and Chinese language. The entry of large numbers of students from low-income families resulted in expanded student aid and remedial programs. The prices of fuel, utilities, postage, and many other purchased items escalated rapidly. One could go on indefinitely listing the ingredients of rising higher educational costs. In explaining the rise, however, it is well to remember that expenditures could increase only to the extent that society was willing to provide the money. Ultimately, total expenditures were controlled by the amount of revenue higher education managed to acquire.

Educational Costs per Student

This section concentrates on long-term trends in costs connected solely with education. The objective is to isolate those institutional costs that properly can be ascribed to the education of students and then to compute cost per student in constant dollars. In this way, the effects upon costs of factors extraneous to education may be removed and trends in costs related to the education of students may be identified. From these calculations, conclusions may be drawn as to whether American higher education, in its main business of educating students, has experienced significant increases or decreases in cost over time. Table 4 shows educational expenditures by all U.S. colleges and universities from 1929–30 to 1977–78.

Table 4 indicates that educational costs per student have not risen steadily year after year. When expressed in constant dollars, they have held steady or declined over long periods, for example, during the period 1929–30 to 1949–50, and also during the 1970s. Only in the golden years of the 1950s and 1960s did unit costs increase. They rose during this period precisely because society was willing to pour rapidly increasing resources into higher education. In a sense, the public and their leaders wanted instructional costs to go up. They wanted the colleges and universities to pay better salaries, to add new buildings and equipment, and to develop larger libraries. The cost increases of the 1950s and 1960s were in no sense evidence of the inevitability of rising instructional expenditures per student, and the experience in other periods strongly suggests that higher education is capable of stable or slightly declining costs per student. This fact does not necessarily imply, however, that declining costs in the 1930s and

Table 4. Expenditures for education per full-time-equivalent student, all U.S. institutions of higher education, by decades, 1929-30 to 1977-78

	1929-30	1939-40	1949-50	1959-60	1969-70	1977-78
Educational expenditures per FTE student						
In current dollars	452	409	704	1,275	2,245	3,646
In constant (1967) dollars[a]	1,030	1,027	1,008	1,467	1,973	1,902
In constant (1967) dollars[a] with FTE enrollment adjusted for changes in the distribution of students by academic level	814	786	751	1,084	1,413	1,373
		1929-30 to 1949-50		1949-50 to 1969-70		1969-70 to 1977-78
Average annual rates of change in educational expenditures per FTE student adjusted for changes in the distribution of students by academic level, in constant (1967) dollars		−0.40%		+3.21%		−0.36%

Note: Expenditures include operating and capital expenditures. For sources of data, see Appendix B, Tables 39, 40, and 41.

[a] Deflated using a two-year moving average of the Consumer Price Index of the U.S. Bureau of Labor Statistics and an index of construction and equipment prices described in Appendix B, Table 40.

1940s or in the 1970s were in the public interest. But the available data do indicate that historically educational costs did hold steady, or even decline, over long periods of time.

When enrollments are expressed in "student units" by adjusting to take account of the increasing proportion of advanced students, the increase in cost per student over the period from 1929–30 to 1977–78 is considerably less than when unadjusted enrollment figures are used (see Table 4). This finding suggests that the expansion of relatively expensive graduate and advanced professional study was a significant element in the overall growth of educational costs per student unit.

The trends of educational expenditures per student are illustrated in Figure 2. It shows a steady and accelerating rise in expenditures per student in current dollars. But when the same data are adjusted for inflation, and for the changing composition of the student body, the pattern is quite different. From 1929–30 to 1949–50, and again from 1969–70 to 1977–78, expenditures per student were about level, actually declining slightly. The only period of increase was the special era of 1949–50 to 1969–70.

The results presented in Table 4 and Figure 2 were checked by deflating the data on current operating expenditures using the Higher Education Price Index[1] instead of the Consumer Price Index. This did not change the pattern significantly except that it tended to depress the rate of growth in cost per student during the prosperous years 1949–50 to 1969–70. This was so because the index is heavily weighted with salaries, which increased sharply during that period.

Structural Changes That Influenced the Trend of Costs

The trend of unit cost over the period from 1929–30 to 1977–78, as shown in Table 4, was affected by an important structural change in the higher educational system, namely, a great increase in the proportion of total enrollments in the public sector. In 1929–30 the public sector served about half the nation's students, whereas in 1977–78 it accounted for almost four-fifths of them. Because costs per student are about 30 percent lower in public than in private institutions (see Chapter Six), this shift had the effect of lowering the average cost per

[1]Prepared by D. Kent Halstead of the U.S. National Institute of Education. See Appendix B, Table 40.

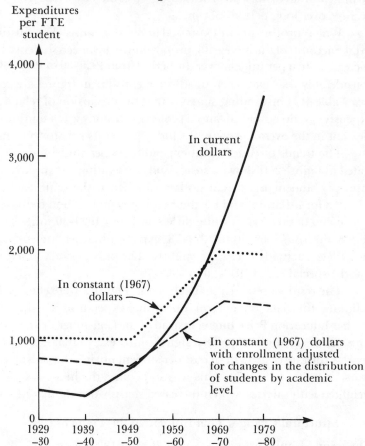

Figure 2. Education Expenditures per full-time equivalent (FTE) student, all U.S. institutions of higher education, 1929–30 to 1977–78

student. In 1977–78, cost per student unit probably was about 8 percent lower than it would have been if this relative shift toward public colleges and universities had not taken place. Apparently, a significant source of economy during the period under review was the change in the public-private makeup of the higher educational system. The possibility cannot be ignored, however, that if the public sector had not grown relatively, the private sector might have supplied an abundance of low-cost institutions.

One result of this massive shift from the private to the public sector was a pronounced increase in the ratio of students to faculty.

Generally, this ratio was higher in public than in private institutions. The extent of this increase is shown in Table 5 where two sets of ratios are presented. In one set, the number of students and faculty are expressed conventionally as simple full-time equivalents without adjustment; in the other set, numbers of students are expressed in "student units" with heavier weights assigned to advanced students than to beginning students, and numbers of faculty are adjusted to include only full-time-equivalent persons engaged in educational functions (excluding those engaged in organized research and public service).

The student-faculty ratios derived from the unadjusted number of full-time-equivalent students follow a slowly rising trend, but with substantially lower ratios in the two decades of the golden years and with an increase during the 1970s. In contrast, the student-faculty ratios based on the adjusted number of students produced a quite different result: a strongly upward trend in student-faculty ratio over most of the period from 1929–30 to 1969–70. The increasing proportion of students at the graduate and advanced professional level tended to increase the number of student units institutions served, and the increasing proportion of faculty engaged in organized research and public service tended to decrease the proportion of faculty engaged in education.

It is often asserted that the relative growth of public two-year colleges had the effect of restraining average unit costs. Actually, this change had only a slight effect because the average cost per student unit in public two-year colleges was not far different from that in public four-year institutions. The median cost per student unit in 1977–78 was $2,020 in public research and doctorate-granting universities, $2,025 in public comprehensive universities and colleges, and $1,959 in public two-year colleges (see Chapter Six).

Escalation of Unit Costs: Higher Education Compared with Other Goods and Services

Everyone knows that the expenditures per student of higher educational institutions are higher today than they were several decades ago. But anyone who operates a household, or must maintain an automobile, or needs medical care, or travels knows that higher education is not the only good or service that has become more costly.

Table 5. Student-faculty ratios, all U.S. institutions of higher education, 1929–30 to 1977–78

	1929–30	1939–40	1949–50	1959–60	1969–70	1977–78
Number of full-time-equivalent (FTE) students (in thousands)[a]						
Unadjusted FTE	890	1,202	2,145	2,775	6,319	8,560
Adjusted FTE	1,127	1,570	2,876	3,756	8,822	11,855
Number of full-time-equivalent faculty (in thousands)[b]	66	89	152	229	477	599
Ratio of students to faculty[c]						
Unadjusted student FTE	13.5	13.5	14.1	12.1	13.3	14.3
Adjusted student FTE	17.1	17.6	18.9	16.4	18.5	19.8

[a] For basic data and sources, see Appendix B. Adjusted FTE assigns heavier weights to advanced students than to freshmen and sophomores.

[b] Includes only faculty engaged in educational functions, not those engaged in organized research or public service. Estimated by the author drawing upon the following sources: U.S. Bureau of the Census, *Historical Statistics of the United States*, vol. 1, pp. 382–383; National Center for Education Statistics, *Digest of Educational Statistics*, 1978, pp. 94, 95, 98; National Center for Education Statistics, *Projections of Education Statistics*, 1964, p. 25; 1968, p. 56; 1970, p. 47; 1973, p. 72; 1976, p. 68; 1977, p. 56; 1978, p. 68.

[c] Number of full-time-equivalent students divided by number of full-time-equivalent faculty.

Table 6 compares cost trends for higher education with those for other goods and services. The comparative data are shown in the form of index numbers, with 1950 as the base year, reflecting prices or costs in current dollars. Expenditures of colleges and universities per student (in current dollars) were over five times higher in 1978 than in 1950. This rate of increase was surpassed by several other services. For example, the per pupil cost of elementary and secondary schools increased nearly sevenfold; government costs, as reflected in per capita purchases of goods and services, increased tenfold; and hospital expenses per patient day were seventeen times higher. However, prices in general rose less steeply than higher educational costs per student. The Consumer Price Index stood at 271 in 1978—less than three times what it had been in 1950. The prices of some manufactured products increased much less than that. For example, the price of new automobiles increased by a mere 84 percent, the price of prescriptions and drugs by 49 percent, and the price of television sets actually declined. Even the comprehensive cost of medical care rose considerably less than the cost of higher education. From these data, one can only conclude that since 1950 higher education has been among the industries experiencing relatively rapid escalation of costs—but it has not been the only or the worst offender in this respect.

A closer comparison of higher education with other professional and other industries, however, reveals that its pattern of cost escalation has been quite different from that of the others. As shown in Table 7, its pattern of cost behavior was in three stages: from 1930–50 expenditures per student declined slowly; from 1950 to 1970, its costs surged ahead rapidly; then after 1970, its costs lapsed back into slow decline. By contrast, other comparable industries showed consistent patterns of increases in expenditures per unit throughout the entire period. Moreover, even in the 1950s and 1960s, their rate of increase greatly exceeded that of higher education.

Why did higher education exhibit a pattern so different from other industries—especially from other professional industries? It appears that over long periods, higher educational expenditures per student, when expressed in constant dollars, remained about level. The surge of expenditures during the 1950s and 1960s was apparently a unique event that lifted costs per student in constant dollars to a new

Table 6. Prices or expenditures per unit of service, higher education and selected other commodities and services, 1930–1978 (prices expressed as index numbers that reflect current dollars; 1950 = 100.)

	1930	1940	1950	1960	1970	1976	1977	1978
Higher educational institutions								
Expenditures for education per full-time-equivalent student[a]	64	58	100	181	319	429	483	518
Public elementary and secondary schools								
Expenditures per pupil in average daily attendance[b]	42	41	100	182	369	656	688	—
Medical and related services								
All medical care items[c]	—	69	100	147	225	345	—	409
Physicians' fees[c]	—	—	100	139	220	341	—	404
Prescriptions[c]	—	—	100	118	117	142	—	149
Semiprivate hospital room rates[c]	—	—	100	189	480	886	—	1,097
All hospitals: total expense per patient day[d]	—	—	100	206	676	1,750	—	—
Churches: contributions per member[d]	—	—	100[i]	134	178	254	274	—
Government								
Purchases of goods and services per capita: federal, state, and local[d]	25	37	100	261	569	939	1,026	—
U.S. Congress: expenditures per U.S. resident[e]	—	—	100	189	370	924	1,203	—
Postal rate: one-ounce first class letter[f]	100	100	100	133	200	433	500	500
Hotels and motels: room rates[g]	—	—	100[i]	132	192	274	299	—
Publications: average retail prices[g]								
Hard cover books[g]	—	—	100[i]	128	286	426	471	—
Periodicals[g]	—	—	100[i]	132	258	557	609	—
Consumer Price Index (1950 = 100)[h]								
All items	69	58	100	123	161	236	252	271
Food (at home)	—	—	100	115	147	231	—	271
Apparel	—	—	100[i]	111	144	180	—	192
Home ownership costs	—	—	100[i]	115	171	256	—	303
Rent for housing	—	80	100	130	156	205	218	233
New automobiles	—	56	100	125	129	163	—	184
Television sets	—	—	100	81	64	66	—	65

[a] Expenditures from Table 4.
[b] U.S. Bureau of the Census, *Historical Statistics of the United States*, 1975, vol. 1, pp. 373–374; National Center for Education Statistics, *Digest of Education Statistics*, 1978, p. 73.
[c] U.S. Bureau of Labor Statistics, Consumer Price Index.
[d] U.S. Bureau of the Census, *Statistical Abstract of the United States*, various issues.
[e] Estimated by the author from various sources, for examples, U.S. Bureau of the Census, *Statistical Abstract of the United States*, 1976, p. 232; 1978, p.263.
[f] U.S. Bureau of the Census, *Historical Statistics of the United States*, 1975, vol. 2, p. 807; U.S. Bureau of the Census, *Statistical Abstract of the United States*, 1977, p. 575.
[g] *Statistical Abstract of the United States*, various issues.
[h] U.S. Bureau of Labor Statistics, Consumer Price Index.
[i] Estimated by author.

Table 7. Average anual changes in prices or expenditures per unit of service, higher education and selected other groups of commodities or services

	Percentage of change in constant dollars		
	1930–1950	*1950–1970*	*1970–1978*
Higher educational institutions: expenditures for education per adjusted student unit	–0.40%	+3.21%	-0.36%
Elementary and secondary schools: expenditures per pupil in average daily attendance	+2.50	+4.23	+2.54 [a]
Federal, state, and local government: purchases of goods and services per capita	+5.24	+6.51	+2.05
All hospitals: total expense per patient day	—	+7.44	+9.95 [b]

Note: For sources, see Table 6.

[a] Change between 1970 and 1977.
[b] Change between 1970 and 1976.

and unprecedented plateau from which the higher educational system is now slowly receding.

Conclusions

The exploration of long-term trends in the expenditures of American higher education reveals six important conclusions—some rather surprising.

First, aggregate higher educational expenditures for all purposes grew prodigiously at the rate of 9.6 percent per annum over the nearly half-century since 1929–30. This growth was enough to double the amount every seven years. Expenditures were sixty-nine times as high in 1975–76 as in 1929–30. But most of this growth was due to a vast expansion of enrollment and to the declining value of the dollar. When expenditures are expressed per student and in constant dollars, the annual rate of growth over the period since 1929–30 was only 1.4 percent. This is not a negligible growth rate, but it is not a runaway condition.

Second, the figures on aggregate expenditures include outlays for organized research, public service, auxiliary enterprises, and other purposes not directly related to the education of students. An effort was made to isolate the educational expenditures and to compute the amount of these expenditures per student in constant dollars. The long-term trend of educational expenditures so defined was not one of uninterrupted growth. Rather there were three distinct stages. In the first stage, covering the period from 1929–30 to 1949–50, cost per student declined slightly; in the second stage, 1949–50 to 1969–70, there was rapid growth; in the third stage, during the 1970s, cost per student again slowly declined. The average annual percentage of change during the three stages was:

1929–30 to 1949–50	−0.40%
1949–50 to 1969–70	+3.21
1969–70 to 1977–78	−0.36

As these figures show, educational costs have declined slowly over long periods of time. Only during the golden years of the 1950s and 1960s was there a pronounced and prolonged rate of increase. That period was a special episode when the nation wished to improve as well as expand higher education and deliberately provided the money to make possible a big increase in unit cost. That episode came to an end in the early 1970s, and during the 1970s cost per student declined slowly as funds became insufficient to hold the level attained at the end of the golden years.

Third, during the past half-century, the enrollment of public institutions has expanded more rapidly than that of private institutions. Public institutions, on the whole, operate at a lower cost per student than their private counterparts. Therefore, this relative increase in public enrollment offset some of the factors tending to push average expenditures per student upward. Had this relative growth of the public sector not occurred, unit cost might have been 8 percent higher in 1977–78 than it actually was—that is to say, the increase in unit cost since 1929–30 might have been 77 percent instead of the actual 69 percent. By 1980, however, the public sector had become so dominant that future savings from its relative growth will likely be small.

Fourth, a comparison of the trend of unit costs in higher education and that of other industries reveals that the rate of growth was greater than that in most of the goods-producing sector and some of the service sector but less than that in some of the non-profit professional industries such as elementary and secondary education, government, and hospitals.

Fifth, higher education has experienced a unique three-stage pattern in unit costs: slightly declining costs from 1929–30 to 1949–50, explosive increases from 1949–50 to 1969–70, and again slightly declining costs from 1969–70 to 1979–80. This three-stage pattern seems not to have been shared by other industries, most of which experienced more steady cost increases over long periods. In particular, higher education seems to be almost alone among the various industries in its present trend toward slowly falling unit costs (expressed in constant dollars). Higher education appears to be losing in its effort to stay even with inflation.

Sixth, the trend of unit costs in higher education is powerfully influenced by levels of faculty and staff compensation. What appears as a decline in cost per student may have been achieved only by a decline in the real wages of those employed in higher education; and conversely what seems to be a rise in cost may consist largely of an increase in real wages. The effect of employee compensation on cost per student will be considered in the next chapter.

3

Faculty and Staff Compensation

In 1976–77, American colleges and universities employed for all purposes—including education, research, public service, auxiliary enterprises, teaching hospitals, and all other functions—nearly 1.9 million persons in almost 1.6 million full-time-equivalent positions (see Table 8). As noted in Chapter One, the payroll to compensate these persons amounted to about 57.4 percent of total expenditures for all purposes, or about $26 billion. How well paid are the faculty members, administrators, and general service workers who are employed in higher education? In the public interest, what rates of compensation should be paid to these people to ensure quality in higher education? These questions are addressed in this chapter. In answering these questions, one must review long-term trends in compensation and compare trends in higher education with those in other industries. In organizing this review, the author prepared a study of academic compensation that presents detailed statistical data. Only the findings and conclusions of that study are presented here; those who wish to review the data are referred to that study (see Bowen, 1978a).

Throughout most of this book, educational costs are distinguished from noneducational ones. In the discussion of pay rates, this distinction is unnecessary. Within each college or university, the compensation of various categories of workers tends to be about the same regardless of the particular function or functions in which they are engaged. The rate of pay, for example, of faculty, secretaries,

Table 8. Numbers of persons employed in American higher education, 1976–77 (in thousands)

	Full-time	Part-time	Total number of persons	Full-time-equivalents	
				Number	Percentage of total employees
Instructional faculty	469	333	802	591	38
Executive, administrative, and managerial staff	98	4	102	100	6
Other professional persons	152	28	180	165	11
Nonprofessional persons	645	161	806	710	45
Total	1,364	526	1,890	1,566	100%

Source: National Center for Education Statistics, Digest of Education Statistics 1977–78, 1978, p. 95.

plumbers, or computer specialists are the same for people engaged in work related to education, to research, to auxiliary enterprises, or to a combination of these functions.

In this chapter, the words *salary* and *compensation* are used frequently. *Salary* refers to a direct payment for services rendered and excludes fringe benefits paid by the employer; *compensation* refers to the sum of salary and fringe benefits paid by the employer. As fringe benefits have become an increasing part of the real income of employees and the real labor cost of employers, the distinction becomes increasingly important. A recent study indicates that fringe benefits paid for by colleges and universities average 18.7 percent of their payroll, or $2,371 a year for each full-time-equivalent employee (Cook and Zucchi, 1979, p. 2).

Compensation Policy

Institutions' policies regarding rates of remuneration for academic workers may be viewed from various standpoints. Those who must pay the costs—taxpayers, donors, students, and parents of students—view faculty and staff pay as a major cost of operating colleges and universities. Their interest would seem to lie in the direction of holding down rates of compensation. For faculty and staff, compensation is a major source of income and of personal reward and recognition. Their interest, naturally, lies in the direction of higher levels of compensation. Governing boards, administrators, and others who are responsible for particular institutions, view salaries as the chief means of attracting and retaining qualified faculty and staff. They tend to favor high levels of compensation as a means of raising the quality and distinction of their institutions—though they must balance personnel costs against other needs. Legislative bodies, state coordinating commissions, federal bureaus concerned with education, other broadly representative groups, and disinterested observers presumably consider compensation rates in relation to the broad public interest. They weigh the needs and demands of higher education against those of other parts of the economy and seek a balance between rates of compensation in higher education and in other industries and occupations. This chapter discusses compensation from the point of view of the public interest.

In purchasing most items, colleges and universities have no policies regarding price. They simply pay market prices for goods or services of particular specifications. They may bargain in some cases, and they may compromise on the specifications of goods and services they purchase, but they are bound by general market prices. In the case of wages, salaries, and fringe benefits of faculty and staff, the situation is different.

There are no fixed market rates of compensation for professors of history, registrars, or secretaries—as there are fixed prices for food or building materials. The levels or scales of compensation that are set year after year are the result of fairly conscious policy decisions made, in part, by the persons who provide the funding—students, legislative bodies, donors. Collectively they determine the amount of money available to institutions, and therefore they have considerable influence over so dominant a budgetary item as rates of compensation for faculty and staff. These decisions are also made, in part, by institutions as they set their budgetary priorities within the limits of their available funds and within the boundaries of their budgetary autonomy. When those who control higher educational funding are stingy, institutions may be forced to freeze or reduce salaries. When those who control the funds are more generous, institutions may be able to grant handsome raises. Institutions that place a high priority on faculty and staff compensation may economize on staff size, library development, or student aid in order to grant the largest possible pay raises. Other institutions favor other priorities at the expense of salaries.

To be sure, the policy makers who determine rates of compensation must acknowledge that if faculty and staff are underpaid, higher education will in coming years be unable to attract and retain employees of "adequate" capability. The policy makers also must recognize that if faculty and staff are overpaid, higher education will attract more than its necessary share of talent, and money will be wasted. The movement of workers in and out of the educational labor market, however, is slow and does not respond quickly to changes in compensation. Most faculty and professional staff in higher education have chosen their work because of deep-seated preferences, they have invested themselves in lengthy training, and they continue because of strong loyalties. Although individuals may move quite readily from one college or university to another, few move readily from higher education to other industries, such as manufacturing, retailing, or banking. Thus temporary increases or decreases in salaries, wages, and fringe benefits do not trigger large movements of workers either into or out of higher education. Furthermore, there is a degree of potential flexibility from year to year in the compensation rates paid workers, a flexibility that does not exist, at least to the same extent, for commodities and services purchased on the general market.

In the long run, however, prevailing academic pay scales affect the power of higher education to attract and retain workers. As compensation rates fall, there are limits to the strength of preferences and loyalties. In the long run, underpaid workers will be attracted away to other industries and prospective new workers will seek their fortunes elsewhere. Academic workers are not without mobility—even though they are slow to exercise it. Most administrators and general service workers can find comparable employment outside of academe. Most faculty in professional fields such as business, law, engineering, and medicine can easily find employment outside. And many faculty in the traditional sciences and arts—natural scientists, economists, psychologists, for example, have alternative employment opportunities. There are few faculty in fields so esoteric or specializations so narrow that they have no mobility. Conversely, as compensation rates rise, outward mobility will be discouraged, increasing numbers of young persons will be attracted to careers in higher education, and substantial numbers of persons employed in other industries will be tempted to switch to academic work. These shifts, however, take time and leave room for policy decisions affecting compensation in the short run—a length of time which may span many years.

In another way, the compensation rates for academic workers are flexible and give rise to conscious policy in their determination. There is no required level of salaries, wages, and fringe benefits that must be maintained in order to staff higher education even in the long run. Within reasonable limits, higher education can be staffed fully at various compensation levels. If compensation is low, the capability of the people attracted and retained will on the whole be relatively modest; if the level of compensation is more generous, their capability generally will be higher. This does not mean that no capable people will be attracted or held at low rates of compensation or that no one but geniuses will be employed if compensation is high. Rather it means that at the margin, as economists say, the degree of capability will vary according to the level of compensation. The relationship of pay scales to capability raises two important policy questions: How capable do the workers in academe need to be? What level of compensation is necessary over the long run to attract and hold faculty and staff of adequate capability? Similar questions can be asked about commodities and services purchased from outside vendors. Just as administrators may ask how competent their institution's professors should be, they also decide what type of computer to purchase, what quality of stationery to order, and what grade of fuel oil to burn. However, the quality of faculty and staff is much more critical to the institution's function than that of purchased goods.

There is no simple answer to these questions but they do get answered from time to time. For example, in the early 1950s, a time when higher education was clearly underfinanced, a national consensus was reached to the effect that academic compensation rates were so low that they failed to attract and hold faculty and staff of adequate capability. At that time, the nation set out to raise academic pay scales. As a result of these efforts, the rates of compensation in higher education improved steadily throughout the 1950s and 1960s. Since 1970 rates of compensation have been slipping though they remain tolerable compared with compensation in other industries. At present, the opinion that higher educational faculty and staff are overpaid is often heard in legislative quarters. Current funding policies tend to constrain pay increases. Most institutional leaders, however, are striving to increase salaries, wages, and fringe benefits, but often they can do so only at the expense of other services, such as building maintenance, library acquisitions, and student services.

Compensation policy is also influenced by the weak market position of most academic personnel, especially faculty and administrators. An unusually large number of qualified people are competing in the market, while a possible decline in enrollments is expected, and the finances of many institutions are precarious. Should the nation take advantage of this weak market to slow the rate of increase of faculty and staff compensation? Few legislators or administrators advocate this strategem and, in general, the institutions appear by their actions to oppose it. However, the weak market is clearly a factor that influences policy.

The next four sections of this chapter trace the long-term trends in compensation and compare compensation in academe and that in other industries. The final section returns to this basic policy question about academic compensation and offers recommendations.

Long-Term Trends in the Pay of Faculty and Staff

As the first step in the factual review, information was assembled about the historical trends in the remuneration of faculty and staff in order to analyze the effects of economic and social conditions upon the pay of faculty and staff—with special emphasis on the effects of inflation which is a dominant factor today. Annual data were gathered on average faculty salaries and compensation for the period from 1903–04 to the present. These are shown in Figure 3. Since trends in faculty compensation were found to be quite similar for the several faculty ranks and for administrators as well, no special study of each subgroup was necessary. Unfortunately, however, there were no usable historical data on general service workers such as secretaries, clerks, and physical plant employees.

The period since 1902–04 may be divided into twelve distinct episodes, each defined by prevailing economic conditions at the time. Table 9 describes these episodes and shows what happened to faculty compensation during each one. The table and the related discussion refer exclusively to average faculty compensation expressed in constant dollars.

Table 9 shows that World War II was a major watershed in the evolution of faculty compensation. Consider first the eight episodes in the period prior to World War II (1903–04 to 1942–43):

1. In the three periods of orderly economic growth and stable prices (1903–04 to 1913–14, 1922–23 to 1929–30 and 1934–35 to 1939–40), faculty compensation increased steadily but slowly at 1.0 to 1.5 percent a year.
2. In the two periods of rapid inflation (1913–14 to 1919–20 and 1939–40 to 1942–43), pay raises failed to keep pace with inflation and

Table 9. Twelve episodes in the history of faculty compensation, 1903–04 to 1977–78

Periods	Conditions in the national economy: Description and average annual percentage change in consumer price index		Trend of constant dollar faculty compensation and average annual percentage change	
1903–04 to 1913–14	Steady economic growth; stables prices	+ 1.03%	Steady slow advance	+ 1.09%
1913–14 to 1919–20	War; rapid economic growth; rapid inflation	+11.00	Sharp decline	– 5.29
1919–20 to 1922–23	Depression and deflation	– 3.20	Rapid advance	+10.75
1922–23 to 1929–30	Steady economic growth; stable prices	0	Steady slow advance	+ 1.42
1929–30 to 1931–32	Crisis; early stages of Great Depression; deflation	– 7.59	Rapid advance	+ 8.92
1931–32 to 1934–35	Deep depression; continued deflation	– 2.12	Moderate decline	– 2.87
1934–35 to 1939–40	Slow recovery; stable prices	+ 0.58	Steady slow advance	+ 1.45
1939–40 to 1942–43	Rapid recovery; rapid inflation	+ 6.36	Sharp decline	– 4.93
1942–43 to 1945–46	World War II; rapid economic growth; substantial inflation	+ 3.77	Substantial advance	+ 2.95
1945–46 to 1951–52	Korean War; erratic economic growth; rapid inflation	+ 5.77	Slow decline	– 0.91
1951–52 to 1969–70	Steady economic growth; slow but accelerating inflation	+ 2.04	Steady rapid advance	+ 3.61
1969–70 to 1977–78	Slow and erratic economic growth; rapid inflation	+ 6.70	Stable with slow downward trend	– 1.05

Note: Average annual percentage changes represent compounded growth rates.

Source: Bowen, 1978a, pp. 64–69.

Figure 3. Average full-time faculty salaries and compensation, all ranks and all
U.S. institutions of higher education, 1903–04 through 1976–77

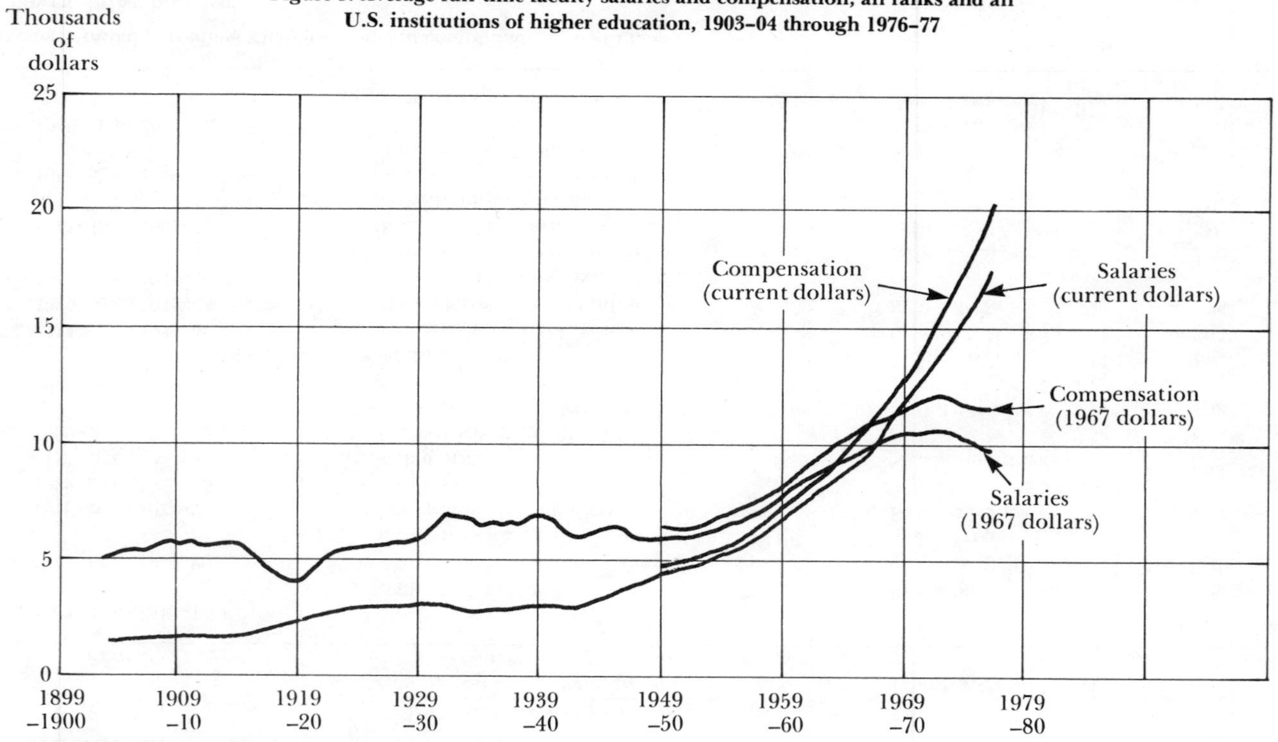

Source: Bowen, 1978a, p. 21.

faculty compensation in constant dollars declined sharply at the rate of about 5 percent a year.

3. In the three deflationary periods (1919–20 to 1922–23, 1929–30 to 1931–32, and 1931–32 to 1934–35), the response of faculty compensation was mixed. In the first two, it increased sharply at the rate of 9 to 11 percent a year because current-dollar compensation held fairly steady while the price level plummeted. But when the Great Depression took hold in 1931–32 to 1934–35, compensation fell even faster than the price level, and the net decline was at the rate of nearly 3 percent a year.

This pattern changed at the beginning of World War II.

1. In the one period of orderly economic growth and reasonably stable prices (1951–52 to 1969–70), compensation increased by about 3.6 percent a year—as compared with 1.0 to 1.5 percent in comparable prewar periods.
2. In the three periods of rapid inflation (1942–43 to 1945–46, 1945–46 to 1951–52, and from 1969–70 on), faculty compensation did not decline drastically in the prewar manner. During World War II (1942–43 to 1945–46), when inflation was substantial even though held in check by price controls, compensation increased by nearly 3 percent a year. And during the two later periods of acute inflation (1945–46 to 1951–52 and 1969–70 to the present), compensation declined only slowly—in the most recent episode at a rate just above 1 percent a year.
3. There were no episodes of deflation in the period after 1942–43.

Clearly, something changed around the beginning of World War II. Since then, during periods of economic stability and growth, the rate of increase in compensation has been greater than formerly. And since then, inflation has not triggered serious setbacks in faculty compensation. Indeed, during the entire period 1942–43 to 1976–77, the average rate of increase in faculty compensation was about 2 percent a year; whereas in the period 1903–04 to 1942–43 it had been a mere 0.5 percent a year. How does one explain the differences?

The explanation undoubtedly lies in a marked change in public attitudes toward higher education (H. R. Bowen, 1968a). During

World War II or just after, Americans began to see college attendance not merely as a privilege for a small minority but as an opportunity for all youth. Moreover, the Great Depression and World War II brought about a new appreciation of higher education as a source of economic productivity and national power. These attitudes led to the creation of the GI Bill and, in turn, were greatly reinforced by the striking success of that law. During the 1950s, the educational achievements of the USSR—symbolized by the launching of Sputnik—also strengthened public concern for higher education. Corporations and government noted the potential benefits of research and development and recognized the need for educated people to assume managerial and technical positions. Moreover, the high postwar birth rate assured a large college-age population in the 1960s and 1970s. Higher education would have to expand dramatically to meet increased demand. In this atmosphere, the nation recognized that faculty compensation would have to be raised if the academic profession were to attract and retain adequate talent.

Thus, during the postwar period, higher education obtained from various interested sources the financing necessary to improve faculty compensation. Parents became more interested in higher education and were willing to pay tuitions. Private donors and foundations were increasingly generous in their support of higher education. State legislators approved large appropriations, and the federal government entered the field with increased determination and funding, as manifested by the Higher Education Facilities Act of 1963 and the Higher Education Act of 1965. Academic leaders, too, realized the need for higher compensation to retain capable faculty members and to recruit new people for academic positions.

Though support of higher education had grown stronger since 1942, the effect of new attitudes and initiatives became apparent around 1951–52. Beginning in that year, faculty compensation (in constant dollars) increased at an average annual rate of 3.61 percent and continued at that rate until 1969–70 when rapid inflation set in. But even after 1969–70, the efforts of colleges and universities, sustained by public concern for the academic enterprise, were sufficient to maintain compensation (in constant dollars) at nearly the 1969–70 level and to prevent inflation from seriously eroding the gains of previous years. However, during the years of double-digit inflation,

1974 and 1979, academic compensation fell considerably behind the cost of living. Nevertheless, much of the financial stress among institutions of higher education since 1969–70 has been caused by their determined effort to increase faculty compensation at least on par with inflation and to avoid the decline in real earnings that occurred in prewar inflationary periods. Maintaining faculty compensation has necessarily slowed institutional progress in other respects.

The basic trend in faculty salaries has been more closely linked to public attitudes about the value of higher education than to market demand, as indicated by enrollments, or to market supply, as indicated by numbers of new Ph.D.'s and other indicators. The turning point in the rate of growth of faculty compensation occurred around 1942–43 precisely when enrollments were declining at the onset of World War II. The acceleration of this growth around 1951–52 coincided exactly with an enrollment trough following the departure of the GIs and preceding the arrival of the postwar baby generation. Moreover, the decline in faculty compensation since 1969–70 has been moderate, about one percent a year, despite a slowing of the growth in enrollment and a rapidly increasing supply of persons qualified for college teaching.

Comparative Trends in Compensation

The next step in the factual review was to compare progress in the compensation of faculty and staff in higher education with the growth in compensation for other elements of the national labor force. For this purpose, a mass of data on earnings of various groups was assembled and analyzed (see Bowen, 1978a, pp. 20–34, 73–83). A sampling of these data is presented in Table 10. The data are all expressed in current dollars. There was no need to adjust them for price level changes since all groups were faced with similar costs of living. The findings are briefly summarized in the following paragraphs.

1904–1930. The rate of growth of academic pay was substantially lower than that for almost all other occupational groups for which data were available. One exception was federal civilian employees who fared even less well. Whereas, faculty pay increased during this period at the rate of 3.19 percent a year, the pay of most other groups

Table 10. Average annual percentage increases in compensation or salary, college and university faculties compared with broad occupational groups, 1904 to 1978

	1904–1930	1930–1952	1952–1961	1961–1970	1970–1978	1904–1978
Colleges and universities[a]						
Faculty (compensation)	3.19%	2.19%	5.41%	6.03%	5.89%	3.79%
Faculty (salaries)	3.14	2.08	5.21	5.58	5.48	3.62
Other sectors of the labor force						
All civilian full-time employees (compensation)	4.17	4.42	4.46	5.23	7.79	4.79
Full-time employees in manufacturing (compensation)	4.02	4.57	4.53	4.84	8.01	4.80
Telephone and telegraph employees (salaries)	4.51	4.14	5.13	4.66	9.67[d]	4.91[e]
Workers paid union hourly wage rates						
Building trades	6.21[b]	3.36	4.40	5.67	7.65[d]	4.99[c]
Printing trades	5.64[b]	3.96	3.19	4.27	7.99[d]	4.71[e]
Truck drivers and helpers	—	—	5.12	5.11	9.01[d]	—
Workers paid the legal minimum wage	—	7.93[c]	4.85	3.74	6.51	—
Consumer Price Index	2.40	2.13	1.34	2.94	6.70	2.71

[a]Data for colleges and universities refer to academic years ending in the designated calendar years.

[b]1914 to 1930.

[c]1940 to 1952.

[d]To 1976 only. The comparable figure for higher education is 6.17 percent.

[e]To 1976 only.

Source: Bowen, 1978a, pp. 64–69, 74–75.

increased by annual percentages averaging from 3.50 to 6.21 percent. The percentage for all civilian full-time employees in all occupations was 4.17.

1930–1952. The relative progress of academic pay was less in this period than in the years 1904–1930. Academic pay was increasing at a rate of slightly over 2 percent a year. Most other groups were enjoying average annual increases of 2.5 to 4.5 percent—though federal professional and administrative employees were gaining less rapidly than academic workers. The rate of increase in compensation for all civilian employees was 4.42 percent. In view of these disparities extending over long periods of time, it is little wonder that academic people were discouraged in the early 1950s and that the inadequacy of academic salaries was widely acknowledged.

1952–1961. The situation changed abruptly in this period. It was a time of new appreciation of science and learning as major ingredients of national economic growth and power. During these years, it was recognized widely that enrollments in higher education should grow relatively and absolutely to include a larger percentage of young adults, as well as the horde of postwar babies soon to be ready for college. Improvement of academic salaries became a major national objective. Under these conditions, faculty salaries rose by 5.21 percent a year and faculty compensation by 5.41 percent a year (which indicates the growing importance of fringe supplements). The rates of increase for other groups ranged mostly from 2.75 percent to 5.25 percent, the figure for all civilian employees being 4.46 percent. Only a few groups received raises larger than those in higher education, among them state and local government employees, lawyers, physicians, engineers, and members of Congress. Clearly, academic people were near the head of the procession in the annual rate of pay raises.

1961–1970. The situation was mixed but the gains in higher education were ahead of those for workers in most other occupations and industries. The compensation of academic faculty and staff increased by 6.03 percent annually as compared to 5.23 percent for compensation of all civilian full-time employees. The comparative growth of compensation in higher education was somewhat slower than in the preceding period, but it could not be said that higher education was falling behind.

1970–1978. The situation changed drastically. The rate of increase in academic compensation was substantially below that of most other groups: an annual increase of 5.89 percent compared with 7.79 percent for all civilian full-time employees—leaving a gap of nearly 2 percentage points. However, the gap was somewhat less between faculty and other professional and white-collar workers (see Table 11). In these comparisons, the most frequent difference is only 1 percentage point. On the basis of these and similar figures, one might generalize that between 1970 and 1978 the average annual increase in faculty compensation of 5.89 percent compared with average annual increases of roughly 7 to 8 percent for other groups, leaving a gap of from 1 to 2 percentage points.

When all the periods are combined, and comparisons made for the entire period between 1904 and 1975, it becomes clear that the periods of relative academic prosperity during 1952–1961 and 1961–1970 were not sufficient to offset the losses for the periods of 1904–1930, 1930–1952, and 1970–1978. Between 1904 and 1974, faculty compensation increased on the average at an annual rate of 3.79 percent, where-whereas compensation of all civilian full-time employees increased at an average rate of 4.79 percent, a difference of one percentage point a year. The comparability of the data over such a long period may be imprecise, and conclusions about relative progress in rates of pay must be accepted with caution. However, in the brief period since 1970, compensation in higher education clearly failed to keep pace with the consumer prices or with compensation in the rest of the economy. Moreover, as the pace of inflation accelerated in 1978 and 1979, the disparity increased. Average faculty compensation in 1978–79 increased at a rate of 6.0 percent, whereas the Consumer Price Index increased 9.4 percent. In 1979–80, the rate of inflation was even higher, and it is likely that the disparity between academic compensation and the cost of living widened. These conclusions are generally applicable to the compensation of academic administrators as well as of faculty because, as indicated earlier, the trend of administrative compensation tends to run parallel to that of faculty compensation.

Table 11. Average annual percentage increases in compensation
or salary, college and university faculties compared with selected
occupational groups, 1970 and after

	1970 to 1976	1970 to 1977	1970 to 1978
Colleges and universities[a]			
Faculty compensation	6.17%	6.15%	5.89%
Faculty salaries	5.53	5.52	5.48
All civilian full-time employees (compensation)[b]	7.63	7.66	7.79
Selected professional and administrative positions in private industry (salaries)[c]			
Accountants	6.40		
Attorneys	5.51		
Directors of personnel	6.48		
Chemists	6.28		
Engineers	6.09		
Civilian full-time workers in the federal government (salaries)[d]			
All employees		8.05	
Civil Service employees on the general schedule		5.63	
Scientific personnel	6.51		
Engineers	6.38		
Health officers	7.80		
Nurses	7.46		
State and local government employees (salaries)[e]			
All employees		6.43	
City employees (except education)		6.95	
Teachers		6.43	
Scientists and engineers (salaries)[f]			
Employed by federal government		9.24	
Employed by business and industry		8.68	
All scientists and engineers		7.94	

[a] Bowen, 1978a, p. 67.
[b] Bowen, 1978a, p. 74.
[c] Bowen, 1978a, p. 83.
[d] U.S. Bureau of the Census, *Statistical Abstract of the United States*, 1978, pp. 282, 632.
[e] U.S. Bureau of the Census, *Statistical Abstract of the United States*, 1978, pp. 154, 318, 321.
[f] Scientific Manpower Commission, 1971, p. 22; 1979, p. 32.

Comparative Compensation in 1976-77

In comparing the compensation of academic people with that of other groups of workers, the present situation is perhaps more significant than past trends. How are faculty, administrators, and general service workers paid *today* relative to persons in other industries and occupations? (see Bowen, 1978a, pp. 35-38, 84-99).

As compared with most American workers, faculty and administrators in higher education are relatively highly paid. Their average annual compensation in 1976-77 ranged between $20,000 and $30,000, depending on the nature of their work and the length of their annual contracts. In contrast, the average compensation of all civilian workers was $13,300; of public elementary secondary teachers $12,800; and of all federal civilian workers on the Civil Service General Schedule $16,700. However, 1969 census data on salaries of male workers presents a somewhat less favorable comparison. When women are excluded from the salary data, academic administrators are still near the top among professional occupations, faculty on calendar year contracts are in a relatively good position, but faculty on academic year contracts are considerably below the average for all professional and technical workers.

Salaries of engineers and scientists employed in the federal government and private business are on the average a quarter more than those paid by four-year institutions of higher education—even when academic year salaries are adjusted to a calendar year basis. Salaries of scientists and engineers in higher education are roughly comparable to those in state government and in hospitals. In general, higher educational pay scales are roughly similar to those in hospitals.

Salary comparisons of professional people employed by business and academic faculty on calendar year appointments show that, on the whole, business pays more, and this difference is especially marked in the lower ranks. Similar comparisons of professional people employed by the federal government and academic faculty on calendar year appointments show that the overall differences are not great, but that the federal government pays somewhat more in the lower and upper ranks and a bit less in the middle ranks. It is noteworthy that academic salaries in the upper professional ranks for persons on calendar year appointments begin to overlap with those of important business executives in substantial companies. However, administrators' salaries in higher education are from half to two thirds of the salaries of those occupying comparable jobs in businesses of comparable size.

Faculty members on academic year appointments earn 20 to 30 percent less than their counterparts in business who are employed the year round, and 10 to 20 percent less than their opposite numbers in the federal government. Finally, physical plant workers in higher education are paid wages that are at least 10 percent lower than the wages paid to comparable workers in business.

The conclusion from these findings is that faculty salaries for year-round appointees are relatively good, though on the whole considerably lower than those in business and perhaps a bit lower than those in the federal government. But the disparities are not shockingly great. The position of the majority of faculty, who are on academic year appointments, however, is not so favorable. If they are regarded as full-time workers who happen to be paid on an archaic nine- or ten-month schedule, they are clearly underpaid compared to persons doing comparable work in the federal government and in business. In contrast, if they are regarded as part-time employees, then their rate of pay may be construed to be about as good as that of colleagues who have calendar year appointments. The salaries of administrators in higher education are drastically lower than those in business, even for comparable jobs in organizations of similar size. The wages of physical plant workers in higher education are about 10 percent lower than those for comparable employees in business.

Nonmonetary Benefits and Outside Earnings

Before reaching conclusions about relative earnings in higher education and those in other industries, nonmonetary benefits and outside earnings must be taken into account. (See Bowen 1978a, pp. 59–63.) These are modest for most academic administrators and general service employees, significant for faculty on calendar year contracts, and substantial for faculty on academic year contracts.

Among the many nonmonetary benefits are the following (those marked with an asterisk are often available to administrators and general service workers as well as to faculty):

* Tuition remission for the employee and his or her family
* Access to sports facilities, such as golf courses, tennis courts, and gymnasiums
* Subsidized housing
  Tenure
  Substantial freedom and flexibility in daily schedule
  Long vacations
  Subsidized sabbatical leaves
  Membership in the academic community

These benefits are widely, but by no means universally, available. Although their value depends on individuals' preferences, certainly they are of sufficient value to most academic employees to offset some part of any disparity between their pay and the pay of persons in other occupations.

In addition to the above-mentioned personal benefits, faculty often receive professional benefits, for example, the use of facilities that may contribute little to the educational services of the institution but that provide convenience and comfort for the faculty. Many institutions offer their faculties library resources, laboratory equipment, and support staff that serve the specialized interests of the professors and are not required by their instructional duties. These costly benefits are an inducement for professors to join particular institutions or to remain there, and may be regarded as part of total compensation. Admittedly, to distinguish between facilities that serve institutional objectives and those that serve the special needs of professors is often difficult.

Perhaps more important than these nonmonetary benefits are the opportunities for faculty members to earn outside income, not only after hours or during vacations, but even during periods of regular work. (Administrators and general service workers have far fewer such opportunities.) The main sources of these outside earnings are summer or part-time teaching, consulting, research, private practice fees, royalties from inventions, royalties from writing, sale of works of art, lecture fees, and miscellaneous "moonlighting." Dunham, Wright, and Chandler (1966) report that outside income is earned by 74 percent of faculty members on academic year appointments and by 51 percent of those on calendar year appointments in four-year institutions. (See also, Carnegie Commission on Higher Education, 1972, and *Chronicle of Higher Education*, October 15, 1979.) In the aggregate, outside earnings amount to 19 percent of base salaries for faculty on academic year appointments and 11 percent for those on calendar year appointments. Ladd (1978) reports that 83 percent of all faculty receive some outside earnings and that their average earnings equal 15 percent of their base salary. Outside earnings are not distributed equitably among all ranks or among all disciplines, but in total they are substantial and compensate for some disparities between academic employees and their counterparts in nonacademic fields.

Substantial nonmonetary benefits and outside income place faculty in a strong position relative to comparable workers in other industries. Faculty on calendar year appointments may be earning more than their counterparts in business and government when their nonmonetary benefits and outside earnings, which average 11 percent of base salary, are taken into account. Similarly, the overall position of faculty on academic year appointments may be comparatively good when their nonmonetary advantages and outside earnings, which average 19 percent of base salary, are considered. Another indication that faculty remuneration may be not too inequitable is the notable absence of any exodus from the profession and the number of people who are willing to enter when jobs are available. The compensation of administrators and general service workers, however, is not signficantly supplemented by nonmonetary benefits and outside income.

Recommendations for Future Policy

The experience of the past several decades has shown that the level of faculty compensation has been heavily influenced by conscious public attitudes and conscious policy toward higher education. Faculty compensation increased significantly in the 1950s and 1960s as the public recognized higher education as critical to national welfare and progress and deemed compensation too low to attract professionals of appropriate talents. Those supplying the funds to higher education and the leaders of the institutions succeeded in their determined effort to make faculty compensation competitive with that of talented people in other industries and occupations. By the late 1960s, the position of faculty (including salaries, fringe benefits, nonmonetary benefits, and outside income) was almost certainly equal or superior to that of persons in comparable nonacademic jobs. Not surprisingly, a large number of capable people sought entry to the academic profession. At about that time, however, public attitudes toward higher education changed. Student unrest, rising costs, congestion in the job market for graduates, the shift of public attention toward competing priorities, and the need to control inflation all contributed to disenchantment.

Under these conditions, the institutions faced a gradual but persistent financial squeeze, and faculty compensation began slowly to lose parity with the pay of workers in other industries and occupations. Nevertheless, colleges and universities almost uniformly continued to place high priority on faculty compensation, often at the sacrifice of plant maintenance, student services, new programs, financial reserves, and general institutional advancement. As a result, faculty compensation almost kept up with inflation (except in the years of double-digit inflation) even if it did not match the gains in salary by workers who received productivity increases in addition to cost-of-living increases. This record is in sharp contrast to past episodes of inflation, which were uniformly accompanied by sharp declines in the real earnings of faculty. In spite of great efforts, however, faculty have trailed behind other groups in recent years— though the economic position of faculty today is still relatively good.

The critical issue is to determine what future compensation policy will be in the broad public interest. One's recommendation regarding future compensation policy depends basically on one's judgment as to what level of competence is needed, in the public interest, to staff higher education. If one judges that the present staff is overqualified, one would favor slower rates of increase in compensation; if one feels that the present staff is none too qualified, one might favor increases greater than those in comparable occupations and industries; if one feels that the present staff is adequately but not excessively qualified, one might favor increases proportionate to those in other occupations and industries.

We can thus compare three alternative policies. (1) Lower the priority now granted faculty compensation in favor of other priorities (either inside or outside higher education). The rate of growth of faculty compensation could be slowed to take advantage of the undoubted market weakness of the academic profession. This policy would almost certainly cause faculty compensation (in constant dollars) to fall absolutely as well as relatively. (2) Continue the present policy whereby faculty compensation does not quite keep pace with the cost of living and increases at a slower rate than average compensation in the rest of the economy. This policy would cause faculty compensation to fall slowly and steadily behind the overall economy and would slowly undermine its competitive position. (3) Increase faculty compensation to keep pace with earnings in other sectors of the labor force. This policy would require average annual increases perhaps of 0.5 to 1.0 percent greater than increases in the Consumer Price Index.

Clearly, the temptation for institutions to adopt the first option is very great and could become greater should their financial positions worsen. Those who supply educational revenues are also tempted to hold salaries down by refusing to allocate funds to pay for salary increases. Indeed, it would be possible to "solve" temporarily the financial problems of higher education simply by slowing the rate of growth of faculty compensation, for example, by placing a freeze on faculty salaries or even by imposing cuts. Given higher education's recent financial position, it is remarkable that this temptation has been resisted. The surprise is not that faculty compensation has failed to keep pace with pay in other industries and occupations; it is rather that faculty compensation has fared so well in view of historical patterns and the present weak market.

Several phenomena contributed to the surprisingly strong performance of faculty compensation. One is that the public disenchantment with higher education has been less profound than often alleged. Many studies show that both students and alumni overwhelmingly indicate satisfaction with their college experience and that a vast majority of parents want their children to attend college (Bowen, 1977). Other attitudes that support increases in faculty compensation include the general wish to treat fairly professionals who happened into a weak bargaining position, the desire to avoid undermining faculty morale, and the hope of forestalling collective bargaining. The pressure to raise the pay of minorities and women has also enhanced support for increased academic compensation.

More important than these factors, though, is the belief, both on and off the campus, that the improvement in relative compensation during the 1950s and 1960s resulted in the attraction and retention of capable and well-trained professionals, that such progress is in the broad public interest, and that it should not be sacrificed to financial expediency. The public and the academic community share the fear that a continued deterioration in the relative economic position of faculty would eventually discourage able people from entering the academic profession, and thus the quality of higher education would gradually decline.

Many argue that higher education need not be concerned about disparities in compensation because it is entering a period of falling demand and will not need to hire many faculty members—especially since the present faculty lack easy mobility. This argument is not wholly convincing, for it is not inevitable that the demand for higher education will decline. The number of potential students of all ages is still quite large. More important, it is not true that faculty members lack mobility—though many do not wish to move or are not aware of the opportunities before them. Most faculty in professional fields can readily move to other industries, and many in the natural sciences and social sciences are capable of changing careers and often do. Moreover, even those in the humanities can find new careers in business, journalism, and government.

Even if we assume that steady or declining enrollments are likely and that faculty are not very mobile, the academic community will still need to recruit many new people in the next several decades. About 27 percent of all faculty are over fifty years of age (Bayer, 1973; Dunham, Wright, and Chandler, 1966; Minter and Bowen, 1980).[1] Thus, allowing for mortality, some early retirement, and some transfers to other occupations, at least one third of all faculty will have to be replaced within the next fifteen to twenty years—even if the retirement age is raised to seventy. About 57 percent of the present

---

[1]The distribution of faculty by age in a representative sample of 135 private colleges in 1979–80 (Minter and Bowen, 1980) was as follows: twenty to twenty-nine, 11 percent; thirty to thirty-nine, 35 percent; forty to forty-nine, 27 percent; fifty to fifty-nine, 19 percent; sixty and over, 8 percent. Inferences about age of faculty can also be drawn from data on the years in which highest degrees were received (National Center for Education Statistics, 1968, p. 96).

faculty are over forty years of age. Again allowing for mortality, early retirement, and mobility, at least two thirds of the faculty will have to be replaced in the next twenty-five to thirty years. Should faculty compensation fall significantly, the number of faculty retiring early and leaving education for other occupations would increase, and the problem of securing competent people would be compounded. If enrollment grows, as is at least possible in the 1980s, and likely in the 1990s, the need for faculty will further increase. No one doubts that all available faculty positions could be filled at lower relative compensation than now obtains, but they probably could not be filled with people who have the vigor and competence of those recruited in recent decades.

The second policy alternative, namely, to allow the present trend to continue, would bring about slow deterioration rather than sharp cuts. Faculty compensation has been increasing at an annual rate of about 6 percent, whereas the compensation of various other occupational groups has increased at an annual rate of about 7 to 8 percent. This difference, which represents the rate of deterioration for faculty, if maintained for a decade would have a substantial effect, and over two decades it would be catastrophic. This policy was followed from the turn of the century to 1952; to reinstate it would eventually subject faculty to the depressed position they experienced after World War II.

The third option is to raise the annual rate of faculty compensation so that it approaches or matches the average rate for workers in other industries and occupations. This is the policy I would recommend. The strong financial and moral support for higher education provided by our society during the 1950s and the 1960s, support that made higher education attractive to capable people, was a sound investment in the public interest. Although this support did not ameliorate all the problems of society or even resolve all the problems of higher education, it did give the nation a large cadre of talented and well-trained people to serve our colleges and universities during a time of enormous demand for education by various clienteles and to serve our society in a turbulent and uncertain era.

The compensation of academic people in 1979–80, although behind that of other industries, is sufficient, on the average, to protect this investment. But to continue to protect it will require that in the

1980s and 1990s the growth of academic compensation must maintain parity, or approximate parity, with compensation for the general labor force. I say "nearly keep pace" because the secular upward trend of earnings for highly educated people may, however, be less rapid than those for less-educated people. The number of highly educated people is increasing more rapidly than the number of less-educated people, and the relative earnings of the better-educated may therefore be slowly declining. In the years ahead, the annual growth of faculty compensation might reasonably be just above the annual increases in the Consumer Price Index (CPI) and just below the annual increases in the compensation for all civilian full-time employees. Had such a policy been in effect in the 1970s, when the CPI increased at about 6.7 percent annually and compensation of all civilian workers increased at 7.8 percent, faculty compensation would have risen approximately 7.25 percent annually, whereas the actual rate was 5.89 percent. If faculty compensation continues to lag behind the CPI, the highly productive investment in higher education that was made in the 1950s and 1960s will be forfeited.

A word is in order about nonmonetary income and outside earnings of faculty. If institutions could maintain compensation for faculty on a par with that of the civilian labor force, they could curtail many of the privileges and perquisites faculty now receive. Many of these benefits were instituted at a time when faculty were grossly underpaid. But if faculty compensation continues to decline relative to nonacademic salaries, the justification for various nonmonetary benefits increases apace. The same holds for outside earnings, indeed the arguments for allowing fairly generous outside earnings is even stronger. The opportunity to earn outside income encourages faculty members to take part in the affairs of the world, to gain practical experience in their professional fields, and to become proficient in their disciplines. This opportunity also offers a special incentive to ambitious persons because it provides the chance within the academic profession to earn substantial amounts and even in a few cases to get rich. In other words, it removes the ceiling on earnings that are attainable within the academic profession and, thus, strengthens the incentives for adventurous and imaginative people to enter the profession. Moreover, outside work is an antidote to the boredom that afflicts many faculty people in midcareer. There are, of course, disadvantages to outside employment: some faculty neglect their academic duties, some lose their loyalty to their institutions, some misuse their professional status in the public arena. But on the whole, to have faculty involved in affairs external to higher education is socially advantageous and a constructive way to ease disparities between the compensation of faculty and of persons in other occupations.

Compensation of Administrators and General Service Workers

The earnings of academic administrators are reasonably comparable with those of administrators in hospitals and government but far below those of business executives in comparable jobs within organizations of similar size (Bowen, 1978a, pp. 44–57). For instance, the earnings of presidents or chancellors of colleges and universities are less than half those of chief executive officers in private business; the salaries of admissions and development officers—the "sales executives" of higher education—are far below those of sales managers in industry, and so on for the entire roster of administrative officers. Yet, the administration of a college or university is no less difficult and entails no less responsibility than the management of a company of similar size. Given these circumstances, the following questions must be considered: Would colleges and universities be more successful over a period of time if they paid higher salaries to their administrators? Would they attract and retain more capable and better-prepared people? Would these people perform with greater energy and dedication? Would the higher costs be returned in greater efficiency? Clearly, higher education now attracts many capable and dedicated administrators, and one might argue that higher salaries for administrators would attract people who were not necessarily dedicated to education. In my opinion, however, a gradual upgrading of administrative salaries, on a highly selective basis, would be sound policy for higher education.

Limited data show the wages and salaries of general service workers to average some 10 percent below those for comparable jobs in private business (Bowen, 1978a, p. 58). Some or all of this differential may be justified by the relatively pleasant working conditions and steady employment colleges and universities offer. Some colleges and universities, however, do pay union scale wages, even though they offer more steady employment than is available elsewhere.

Conclusions

On the average, faculty compensation (including nonmonetary income and outside earnings) relative to earnings in other occupations and industries was reasonably good as late as 1978–79. Administrative compensation is roughly comparable to that in government or hospitals, but far less than that in business. The average compensation of general service workers is probably lower in higher education than in other parts of the economy.

Faculty and administrative compensation is declining relative to compensation in other industries and occupations. This slow relative attrition of compensation threatens to impair higher education's future soundness. Policies are needed to bring about near parity between the rates of growth in compensation in higher education and those in other occupations and industries. Faculty compensation should increase at least at an average rate between that of the cost of living and the average compensation for all civilian workers.

As indicated in Chapter Two, cost per student declined slowly between 1929–30 and 1949–50 and again during the 1970s. This decline in cost undoubtedly was made possible by the sluggishness of faculty and staff compensation during the same periods. Similarly, the increase in unit costs from 1949–50 to 1969–70 was largely a result of the increase in staff compensation during that period. The relationship between cost per student and faculty compensation is a close one, as shown by the following figures.

| | *Average Annual Percentage Change in:* | |
	Cost per student (in constant dollars)	*Faculty rate of compensation (in constant dollars)*
1929–30 to 1949–50	−0.40%	+0.29%
1949–50 to 1969–70	+3.21	+3.13
1969–70 to 1977–78	−0.36	−0.53

Currently the salary goals of most institutions are (1) to keep up with other academic institutions, and (2) to keep pace with the cost of living. These goals are not sufficient. If persistently followed, they will ensure that the compensation of academic workers will become steadily less competitive in relation to the rates of pay prevailing in the general labor force.

4

Socially Imposed Costs of Higher Education

This chapter is concerned with cost increases imposed on colleges and universities through informal social pressure or governmental mandate. The great bulk of these costs relate to the pay, fringe benefits, and working conditions of employees; for example, compliance with Social Security and pension programs, minimum wage laws, occupational safety regulations, and the like. Other significant socially imposed costs, however, are not related to employees; for example, the costs of special minority programs for students, provision of information to public agencies, or pollution abatement. All these costs add to an educational institution's total cost of "doing business."

Such socially imposed costs are not new. For more than a century, legislators have sought to protect workers, consumers, and the general public by mandating regulations and standards for virtually all businesses, nonprofit organizations, municipal and state agencies, and even agencies of the federal government. In recent decades, however, the pace of new regulatory demands has accelerated, and higher education has been increasingly affected by the costs of compliance. Educators have voiced great concern about both the cost of these demands and about their effect on academic freedom.

Note: This chapter is based on a paper given by the author as the David D. Henry Lecture at the University of Illinois on April 24, 1978, and published by the university (Bowen, 1978b). The original research was supported by the Alfred P. Sloan Foundation.

The informal social pressures and government mandates with which organizations, including colleges and universities, are faced include:

- Personal security: protection of workers against unemployment, illness, accident, old age, premature death, and protection of individual privacy
- Work standards: prescribed standards for wages, hours, working conditions, and collective bargaining
- Personal opportunity: access for all persons to education, work, public facilities, and cultural amenities without discrimination on the basis of sex, race, religion, or physical handicap
- Participation and due process: equitable, open decision making in the conduct of affairs with individuals participating in organizational decisions that affect them
- Public information
- Environmental protection

In addition, most industries are subject to particular socially imposed costs related to their special circumstances. For example, railroads are subject to rate regulation and labor standards, automobile companies to requirements relating to fuel consumption and pollution, and multinational companies to the requirements of U.S. foreign policy. Similarly, colleges and universities are subject to special costs connected with the emancipation of youth, federal grants and contracts, teaching hospitals and clinics, and tax reform.

Organizations of all kinds, including higher education, have responded to these social demands in three ways: (1) by voluntarily adjusting to the new conditions on the basis of self-interest or social responsibility; (2) by altering their behavior in ways forced upon them by social pressure in the form of collective bargaining, community opinion, mass protest, and threat of governmental action; and (3) by changing their behavior in conformity with specific governmental laws and regulations. Governmental laws and regulations in turn have been responses to these same social demands. Thus, basic social change—not merely the arbitrary or whimsical decisions of government—lies at the root of much of the behavioral modification of organizations. The path of causation is illustrated in the following diagram:

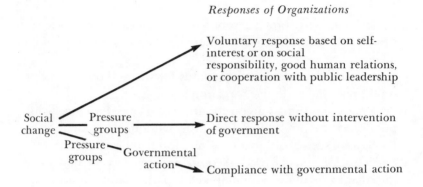

Responses of Organizations

Voluntary response based on self-interest or on social responsibility, good human relations, or cooperation with public leadership

Direct response without intervention of government

Compliance with governmental action

Social change — Pressure groups

Pressure groups — Governmental action

The changed behavior of organizations, and any associated increases in costs, are ultimately due to social change—sometimes mediated through government and sometimes not. Governmental programs and regulations are thus seen as part of a more fundamental social process. This chapter is concerned with all socially imposed costs, not merely with those in which government happens to be involved.

Some Conceptual Issues

Analysis of the effects of socially imposed costs on higher education raises several basic conceptual issues.

First, social change of the kinds under consideration may raise cost, lower cost, raise income, lower income, or have no effect on either cost or income. The frequent assumption that such social change always will raise cost surely is false. For example, when an organization responds to social demands regarding the conditions of work, the morale or the health or the job satisfaction of workers may be enhanced and, as a result, productivity may be raised and cost lowered. Even when this effect is not immediately noticeable within the particular organization, improved working conditions may in the long run bring about a rise in productivity for the whole society (eventually including the particular organization). Comparably, a change in tax laws intended to enhance the fairness of the tax system may reduce philanthropic contributions and thus lower the income of nonprofit organizations, an effect tantamount to an increase in cost. Socially imposed costs thus include positive and negative effects on both costs and income in the long run. Furthermore, in evaluating the cost of a change in public policy, one must consider not only the costs of a particular activity or program but also the cost of not implementing it. For example, if the workers of the nation are demanding universal health insurance, their morale and productivity might fall if their demand is rejected. Meeting the demand, then, may be said to increase productivity and lower cost, compared with what it would have been with rejection but not compared with past performance. However, in a different psychological climate, adopting universal health insurance might raise morale and increase productivity compared with past performance. The effect on cost may be relative to the psychological climate.

Second, socially imposed costs may be usefully divided into two groups: (1) costs for actual program operations, and (2) costs associated with compliance or information. For example, one may distinguish between the cost of Social Security taxes and the cost of record keeping, the cost of operating an ethnic studies program and the cost of providing statistical information on minority enrollments, the cost of improving facilities and the cost of preparing compliance reports, the cost of increasing the faculty-student ratio as suggested by an accreditation team and the cost of preparing an institutional self-study. These distinctions may break down when pressed too far, but they are important because much of the furor about social costs pertains to costs of compliance or of gathering and supplying information rather than to program costs which in the aggregate are much greater.

Third, the analysis must specify the period of time over which socially imposed costs are to be measured. In the literature, there is a good deal of carelessness about this matter. In a sense, all costs of higher education are socially imposed in that all were, at one time or another, instituted in response to the needs and demands of society. When identifying costs recently imposed, one must clearly indicate the period of time under consideration and distinguish between capital costs and recurrent operating costs, and between initial costs and continuing recurrent costs. For example, some of the costs of the

Occupational Safety and Health Act (OSHA) are one-time capital
costs that seem very large but are less overpowering if amortized over
the life of the capital improvements. Whereas a program that has low
initial costs but continuous operating costs—for example, a new
women's intercollegiate athletics program—may over a period of
years be far more costly than OSHA. Similarly, in many cases, the
costs of compliance or of supplying statistical data are relatively high
in the first year, when new procedures and new computer programs
must be adopted and employees must be trained, but become much
lower in later years once the procedures have become routine.

Fourth, the analysis must distinguish between social demands
that increase costs and those that affect priorities. When social or
governmental intervention imposes new programs and activities
upon organizations, the organizations do not necessarily incur increased aggregate costs. Such intervention may merely change the
priorities of the organizations, causing a substitution of new programs or activities for old ones, with total costs unchanged. For
example, if higher education had not been required to meet the costs
of compliance with the Employment Retirement Income Security Act
(ERISA), the introduction of ethnic studies, and the implementation
of affirmative action, institutions might have spent the same amount
of money to raise faculty-student ratios, expand libraries, or build new
sports arenas. The amount of money available to spend would not
necessarily have been greater because of the imposed social costs.
Similarly, when administrators and faculty members are called upon
to assemble statistics, prepare reports, entertain site visitors, negotiate, lobby, or read governmental regulations, these activities may
not increase aggregate expenditures but may merely divert staff time
and energy from accustomed work to new tasks. These new demands
may change the priorities but not necessarily increase aggregate costs.
One then must ask whether the new priorities involve an improvement or a deterioration in the efficiency of the organization viewed
from the standpoint of the broad public interest.

Consideration of these four conceptual issues suggests caution
in rushing to the conclusion that every social pressure or governmental regulation raises cost or reduces efficiency. The probabilities,
nevertheless, are high that the combined net effect of these social
changes indeed has been to raise costs of traditional services or to

change priorities in ways that impair efficiency of conventional operations. When these social changes are viewed in a broader context, however, they may mean that in recent decades the majority of the American people have chosen to devote an increasing share of the national product to security, health, participation, due process, equality, privacy, consumer protection, and the like, while devoting a smaller share to conventional goods and services. Americans have apparently chosen a more secure, a more humane, and a more informed world in place of a more affluent world. This is not necessarily a bad choice—though not everyone agrees—but the consequence is a significant change in the composition of the national product. However, our conventional social accounting does not include these new goods relating to security, opportunity, due process, and so on, as part of the national product. The cost of producing these goods is assigned to the production of ordinary goods and services and shows up as reduced efficiency or impaired productivity in the production of these ordinary goods and services rather than as legitimate costs that yield distinctive and useful, albeit intangible, products.

These costs are akin to taxes. To finance them, organizations must either increase their revenues or make offsetting reductions in regular costs. They may increase revenues by raising the prices of the ordinary goods and services they produce. Or they may reduce their regular costs by lowering the range or quality of goods and services produced. In either of these cases, costs are shifted forward to consumers. Nonprofit organizations may shift some or all of the cost forward to consumers by raising tuitions and fees. Or they may shift them forward to philanthropists and taxpayers by obtaining increased amounts of gifts or appropriations which might otherwise have been directed to other purposes. On the other hand, organizations may shift some or all of the new costs backward to workers by paying wages and salaries lower than would otherwise prevail. It is often argued that payroll taxes and other fringe benefits paid for by employers are shifted in the long run to workers in the form of lower wages. This conclusion has been based on the assumption that real labor costs (including wages, salaries, and fringe benefits) are limited by the net productivity of workers. The question of the precise shifting and incidence of taxes and related charges is far from settled. Since most members of the population are both workers and consumers, it may not make much practical difference whether the shifting is backward to workers or forward to consumers. But to the extent that the shifting is forward to consumers, and in my judgment a large part of it does go in this direction, it is likely that some of the increases in the general price indexes that we call inflation are due to socially imposed costs passed on to consumers, in the form of higher prices or reduced quality of product, or to taxpayers and philanthropists through increased appropriations and more generous gifts.

To the extent that the new costs are shifted to consumers in the form of higher prices, they affect the general price indexes, accelerating the rate of increase in these indexes. Some of the so-called "inflation," then, is almost certainly due to cost increases generated by social demands. Strictly, these costs should not be registered in the price indexes because they are incurred for the purpose of producing important social values such as personal security, job satisfaction, participation, environmental improvement, and all the rest. But since these values are not counted statistically in the national product, they show up as higher prices for ordinary goods and services with which they are jointly produced. It is not known to what extent the price indexes have been biased upward because of these social costs. But it is certain that the effect has been substantial, and that the true rate of inflation derived from monetary and fiscal factors has been substantially less than usually supposed.

Because some socially imposed costs become incorporated in the general price indexes, it is necessary in estimating social costs to avoid the error of deflating expenditures on the basis of a general price index and then considering the social costs as part of the deflated expenditures. Rather, at least some part of social costs must be considered as part of the expenditures reflected in the rising price indexes.

The Special Position of Higher Education

Up to this point, I have discussed socially imposed costs in general as applied to all sectors of the economy, colleges and universities being only one class of organizations affected. I shall now consider the special position of colleges and universities.

Higher education became subject to some of the newer socially imposed costs later than other industries. For example, higher education was exempted from some of the earlier programs such as Social

Security, minimum wage laws, and collective bargaining legislation, and was brought in only after many years. More recently, however, higher education has come to be regarded for purposes of social legislation as no different from other industries, and in the newer programs, it has been included from the start. As a result, higher education has had to adjust to the many socially imposed costs over a shorter period of time than other industries. This problem has been exacerbated because the cost and inconvenience of social programs is often greatest during the first year of the program, as noted earlier.

Higher education, like other nonprofit organizations, frequently has more difficulty than profit-making enterprises in recovering social costs. Whereas profit-making enterprises are financed almost wholly from the sale of their products in the market, colleges and universities receive only part of their income from tuition and fees and the rest from appropriations, gifts, and investment income. For higher educational institutions to finance increased social costs, they must usually enlist the aid of legislators and donors as well as raise prices in the form of tuitions and fees. If they are unsuccessful in these efforts, then their only recourse is to absorb at least some of the costs within their budgets at the expense of the range or quality of their programs. In this case, the social costs are indeed shifted to consumers but through deterioration of programs, a way that is seldom acceptable to educators. This is not to say that profit-making enterprises always can shift new social costs instantly through higher prices to consumers, but only that their power to do so may be greater than that of higher education (Van Alstyne and Coldren, 1976).

Higher education differs from business in that it is largely tax exempt. This special status cuts two ways. On the one hand, higher education receives a hidden subsidy in the form of general governmental services for which it does not pay. This may justify government in expecting colleges and universities to bear some social costs or to serve in partnership with government in some costly research and training programs. On the other hand, tax exemption means that higher education is not able to deduct socially imposed costs from taxable income, as private business can do. Colleges and universities must bear the whole cost rather than about half the cost as in the case of private companies of comparable size.

Though the special conditions within higher education may put it at some disadvantage in comparison with profit-making business, the differences are not very pronounced. On the basis of the differences mentioned, it would be hard to make a case that higher education should receive special treatment except the obvious and important one that its funding sources should take socially imposed costs into account in setting the amount of appropriations and gifts. There is, however, one additional difference that stands alone because of its central importance. This is the special need of colleges and universities for freedom from governmental controls and social pressures. Profit-making enterprises are, of course, as concerned as any other organizations to protect their freedom of decision and action. As centers of teaching and research, however, colleges and universities have an additional interest in autonomy because of their responsibility to protect freedom of thought from encroachments either of interest groups or of government. For this reason, the sensitivity and the resistance of the higher educational community to some forms of external pressure and control are likely to be greater than the resistance of profit-making enterprises—and properly so.

Specific Socially Imposed Costs in Higher Education

In this section I shall try to identify the principal sources of socially imposed costs that have affected higher education in the decades of the 1960s and the 1970s and comment briefly on them. At this point, I shall not try to distinguish between costs related to the education of students and those related to research, public service, auxiliary enterprises, and other noneducational functions. In a later section, I present some rough estimates of the amount of these costs and allocate them between educational and noneducational functions.

Personal Security. The increasing concern in our society for the protection of individuals against such hazards of life as unemployment, illness, accident, old age, and premature death has resulted in many informal influences on organizations to adopt practices that will enhance personal security. It has also resulted in a flood of federal and state legislation requiring organizations to provide for the personal security of their workers. Most of these programs or practices involve substantial costs for the benefits afforded employees (and, in some cases, students) and for the expenses of compliance. Special federal legislation and regulations include:

- Social Security Act of 1935, as amended, providing retirement pensions, survivors' insurance, disability insurance, unemployment compensation, and health insurance
- Occupational Safety and Health Act of 1970 (OSHA)
- Employment Retirement Income Security Act of 1974 (ERISA)
- Legislation regarding radiation safety and protection of human and animal subjects used in research and teaching

State and local legislation and regulations include:

- Workmen's Compensation
- Building codes for protection against fire, flood, earthquake, panic, and other natural or social disasters
- Rules and inspections relating to public health and health care services
- Requirements regarding retirement, occupational health and safety, unemployment compensation, and the like—some of which duplicate federal programs

Lastly, certain institutional practices result from informal social influences. Such practices include the provision of fringe benefits in the form of pensions, health and disability insurance, life insurance, and severance pay; the granting of tenure and other long-term employment contracts; and the adoption of procedures making termination of employment legally and practically difficult.

Work Standards. Over the years, prevailing standards for wages, hours, and other employment conditions have steadily risen. The nation has chosen to reap part of its increased productivity in higher wages, shorter hours, and improved working conditions. These changes, though basically derived from widespread and insistent social demands and reflected in generally accepted standards of employment conditions, have often been codified by legislative mandate. Higher education has long been affected by social demands for improved work standards but has only recently become subject to the principal legislation concerning work standards. The three major pieces of legislation that now apply to colleges and universities are the National Labor Relations Act of 1935 (as frequently amended), which guarantees the right of workers to organize, to bargain collectively, and to strike, and formulates rules governing collective bargaining; the Fair Labor Standards Act of 1938 (as frequently amended), which legislates minimum wages, maximum hours, time-and-a-half for overtime work, and similar standards; and the Equal Pay Act of 1963, which holds that employees doing similar work receive equal pay regardless of the employee's sex. In addition, numerous state laws regulate various aspects of working conditions.

Collective bargaining is, with few exceptions, fairly new to higher education, but it probably has already had a substantial effect on costs. Collective bargaining may not, in the long run, raise the level of real wages in the overall economy, but it probably does raise the wages of particular groups. Colleges and universities have a long record of paying less than prevailing wages to their nonacademic employees. They have been able to do so, in part, by offering steady employment; by providing pleasant and humane working conditions; by exploiting captive workers such as students, wives of students, and faculty wives; by placing workers under less pressure than is customary in private industry; and by providing special fringe benefits (for example, reduced tuition or tickets to public events). The widespread unionization of nonacademic employees probably has raised their wages and thus increased higher educational costs. In the case of faculty members, there is some doubt as to whether collective bargaining has raised compensation overall, though it may have done so in particular institutions. However, the effect of collective bargaining may be considerable over time—especially in preventing the decline in real earnings that might otherwise accompany the weakening demand for faculty and administrative staff.

The minimum wage and overtime compensation laws have undoubtedly raised higher educational costs. Their effect has been to increase labor costs without necessarily increasing productivity or decreasing fringe benefits. The secular trend toward higher standards for working conditions other than wages and hours has also undoubtedly raised costs in higher education.

Personal Opportunity. Recently our society has expressed increasing concern about equal access for all persons to education, work, public facilities, and cultural amenities without discrimination on the basis of race, national origin, religion, sex, physical and mental handicap, age, personal appearance, or life-style. This concern has prompted voluntary changes in policy by colleges and universities, strong informal pressures on them, and much legislation and many judicial rulings that affect higher education.

Because higher education is often a prerequisite for social mobility for disadvantaged groups and a strategic point of access to the mainstream of American society, colleges and universities have been focal points in the struggle for personal opportunity and human equality. Their role has been more significant in the areas of student recruitment and special educational programs than in the area of employment practices. To some degree, higher education's commitment to equal opportunity antedated both the intense social pressure and governmental programs of the past three decades. However, without the pressure—informal and governmental—it is doubtful that they would have extended themselves as much as they have.

The efforts of colleges and universities to respond to social demands for equal personal opportunity have involved substantial costs—especially in recruiting and admitting students, supplying student aid, and providing special programs and facilities. Some of these costs may level off; for example, the costs of recruiting minority students may decline as institutions develop networks of minority alumni who can assist in the recruitment process. Other costs take the form of capital investments, but most are recurrent and increasing. Complying with various governmental programs involves expenditures for data collection, report preparation, and legal services. Also, dealing with campus unrest associated with minority issues has involved significant time and effort on the part of faculty and administrative officers.

Public programs have undoubtedly supplied a large part of the funds for student aid. Nevertheless, social pressures on institutions have required them to stretch their resources for student aid and also to bear significant administrative or matching costs connected with public student aid.

Two new areas of federal intervention with substantial cost implications are in the initial stages. One is the extension of affirmative action to student admissions and the other is providing facilities to accommodate handicapped students. The costs resulting from these two initiatives is likely to be very high, and it remains to be seen how these costs will be financed.

Specific federal legislation and regulations that concern personal opportunity include:

- Affirmative Action: Executive Order 11246 of 1965, as amended in 1967, which prohibits discrimination on the basis of sex
- Employment Act of 1967, which prohibits discrimination on the basis of age
- Title VII of the Civil Rights Act of 1964, as amended by the Equal Employment Opportunity Act of 1972, which prohibits discrimination in employment practices on the basis of sex, race, creed, or national origin
- Title IX of the Educational Amendments of 1972, which bars discrimination on the basis of sex in educational policies, programs, and employment practices
- Financial aid to students programs, which include a variety of grants, loans, and work-study programs, some of which require institutional matching funds or substantial administrative costs
- Internal Revenue Service regulations that concern discrimination in employment and in student admissions
- Various judicial decisions that affect employment, student admissions, and educational practices

State and local legislation and regulations in some states and municipalities outlaw discrimination in student admissions or in employment, or mandate open admissions or special provisions for minorities. Finally, informal social influence has encouraged colleges and universities in active recruitment of minorities, women, the handicapped, and others; and to provide special remedial programs, counseling, curriculums, facilities, and financial aid for them. These innovations were often adopted as institutions carried out their newly perceived social responsibilities or reacted to informal, but often intense, pressures.

Participation, Openness, Due Process, and Privacy. A prominent characteristic of contemporary society is the rejection of paternalism, arbitrary decision making, and secrecy in the conduct of affairs. As a corollary, there is a strong demand for the participation of individuals in organizational decisions that affect them. Business, educational institutions, churches, political parties, and government have all been persuaded or forced to adopt more open and democratic decision-making processes. Closely related to the demand for wide participation is a new insistence on due process in decisions that affect individuals. In the present climate of opinion, most organizations find it expedient or mandatory to reach decisions about individuals by open procedures that include provisions for appeal and review. This is especially so because decisions often lead to litigation, and courts have tended increasingly to review organizational decisions not only on the basis of substance but also of procedure. Indeed, the mandate for due process comes largely from judicial decisions rather than from legislative actions.

The principal legislation on these matters includes the First Amendment to the Constitution, as continuously reinterpreted; the Wagner Act of 1935, as frequently amended and interpreted, which guarantees the rights of workers to organize, to bargain collectively, and to strike, and formulates rules governing collective bargaining; and various federal and state laws that prohibit secrecy in the conduct of public business. Other sanctions derive primarily from informal social pressure and judicial decision.

The demands for participation, openness, and due process have deeply affected governance and decision making within higher education. They have strengthened the influence of students, faculty, and nonacademic staff in the affairs of colleges and universities. They have compelled institutions to adopt policies that foster consultation, greater attention to the codification of rules, and the elaboration of formal procedures. They have given rise to pressure groups among faculty, students, and employees; to new tactics for exerting pressure, including picketing, strikes, publicity, and demonstrations; to the establishment of the office of ombudsman; to formal grievance procedures; to formal procedures for reaching decisions about individuals; and to frequent litigation. Thus the new demands for participation, openness, and due process have required institutions to expend much time, effort, and money to revise their decision-making processes, establish formal procedures, settle specific complaints, engage legal counsel, and defend law suits.

Closely related to these matters has been an increasing interest in the protection of individual privacy. The traditional limitation on the search of private premises has been extended to restrictions on covert surveillance and to limitations on the use of credit and financial records, medical histories, criminal records, letters of recommendation, identity cards, and identity numbers.

These developments have profound significance for higher education. Colleges and universities keep records on employees and they also accumulate detailed records on students. The student records contain information on academic performance, campus work, personal behavior, and health; faculty members and administrators add to these records by conferring awards and prizes and by writing letters of recommendation. These records are shared with other educational institutions, prospective employers including the armed services, and law enforcement agencies. Often these records have had a bearing on crucial educational decisions such as admissions, promotion, retention, the awarding of degrees, transfer to other institutions, etc. In the present climate of opinion, and especially since the enactment of the Family Educational Rights and Privacy Act of 1974 (known as the Buckley Amendment), institutions of higher education have undoubtedly been subjected to increased cost in connection with the management of records and the release of information.

Emancipation of Youth. In recent decades, a veritable revolution has occurred in the degree of freedom of young people with respect to manners, mores, dress, general mode of life, and personal life decisions. Along with this has come a rejection of paternalism both within the family and within educational institutions. The chief legal manifestation of this social change has been the constitutional amendment lowering the age of majority to eighteen.

Higher education has been deeply influenced by the emancipation of youth. Institutions have largely abandoned the concept of *in loco parentis* and now treat their students as adults. They have greatly reduced specific curricular requirements and social rules and narrowed their responsibilities for supervision and guidance. The percentage (though not the absolute number) of students living in institutional residences has declined. Also, the increased informality of collegial life-style and manners has reduced the traditional emphasis on gracious surroundings, served meals, formal parties, and receptions. These changes may have resulted in somewhat lower costs. These savings may have been offset, however, by changing conditions in the job market which have led to expanding services in vocational guidance and placement and to the introduction of new vocational curriculums; by new sexual mores which have led to new demands for medical services; by the increasing use of cars, television sets, stereos, and the like, which have increased utility and parking costs; and by new behavior patterns which have increased the need for campus security. On balance, though the emancipation of students itself may have reduced costs, other factors have probably been offsetting.

Perhaps the most important effect of the emancipation of youth has been on student financial aid. In the past, a student's financial aid was largely determined by the financial circumstances of his or her family—the family defined to include the student, his parents, and other contributing members. But if a student becomes emancipated from his family, as increasing numbers do, the parental family is no longer relevant to student aid allotments. The "family" of a single student then becomes simply the student himself and the family of a married student becomes the student, a spouse, and children if any. Thus the amount of financial need of an emancipated student may be more than that of one who is still part of a parental family. This situation is aggravated by the increasing average age of students in college.

Emancipation also affects in-state and out-of-state tuitions in public colleges and universities. Historically, the residence of a student has been deemed to be the residence of his or her parents. But in many states emancipated students, and others as well, may establish residence where they go to college (regardless of where their parents reside) and thus qualify for in-state tuition. The impact of emancipation upon expenditures for student aid and on income from tuitions has probably already been substantial. If the trend toward emancipation continues, the financial effect could be enormous.

Public Information. Colleges and universities have been required to supply increasing amounts of public information about their activities. The expenses of compliance include money, administrative time, and staff frustration. The requests for information primarily concern five areas: consumer protection, fund raising, enforcement of governmental programs, general statistical needs of society, and general public demands for accountability. The information is furnished mainly through special written reports, published documents, and site visits to the campus by public representatives, foundation officials, accreditation teams, and others.

Although consumer protection has a long history in American society, it has been gathering steam in recent decades. Its purpose has been to protect health and safety and to prevent deception and exploitation of consumers. In the case of higher education, the concern has been mainly to avoid deception and exploitation of students. The traditional agency in this regard has been voluntary accreditation through regional associations of colleges and universities. Over recent decades, however, increasing numbers of specialized professional associations have become active in accreditation with respect to particular professional fields. In some states, departments of education, statewide coordinating agencies, departments of finance, and even legislative committees have become involved in accreditation. The federal government also has been involved marginally. In addition, various educational associations, journalists, and private entrepreneurs have gathered information from institutions and published their findings, evaluations, or rankings. Recently, abuses in the proprietary sector, the proliferation of degree mills, and a general concern for the accountability of colleges and universities have led to further demands for consumer protection.

Over the years, both federal and state governments have demanded increasing amounts of information during their review of institutional appropriations and applications for grants or contracts. These demands are due, in part, to the rapidly growing appropriations, which encourage greater scrutiny, and to the increasing use of categorical grants and contracts that require special review of each project. Similarly, as institutions receive increasing amounts of money from private foundations, corporations, and individuals, the demands for information multiply. Institutions must supply information in applications for appropriations and grants, in interim reports during the period of the grants, and in retrospective reports after the grants expire.

Government agencies also request information during the auditing of programs such as student aid or affirmative action, and the enforcement of regulations about worker safety and health, building codes, radiation safety, and protection of human and animal subjects used in research and teaching. As these programs proliferate, requests for information multiply apace. Moreover, as colleges and universities collectively occupy a more influential role in society and become a larger part of the total economy, the demand for general statistical information about higher education increases.

Finally, occasions of adverse public attitudes and increased political attention directed toward colleges and universities has led to the "accountability" movement involving new demands for statistical information, self-studies, special reports, justification of fund requests, inspections, investigations, new layers of accreditation, and so on. Most of this activity originates from the state governments and most—but not all—has been directed toward public institutions. Vast amounts of detailed information have been requested, often on short notice, by legislative committees, governors, state finance officers, state personnel offices, coordinating boards, and other agencies. Finally, institutions have had to answer frequent attacks upon higher education by political candidates and public officials.

These developments not only have produced additional demands for information, they also have impaired institutional autonomy as decision making has moved from the campus to the central offices of multicampus institutions, super-boards, legislative committees, and state finance offices. The intensified monitoring of higher education by federal and state government increases the institutions' need for information about existing and proposed laws, regulations, and programs. It also requires increased attention to formulating positions on proposed legislation or regulation and to advocacy of these positions. As a result, colleges and universities must hire an increasing number of lawyers and public policy analysts.

There can be no doubt that colleges and universities—along with companies and private individuals—have been faced with increasing government demands for information. Some of the demands have been seemingly useless, or ambiguous, or redundant. Most agencies request that data be supplied on special forms and be compiled in certain ways. The time, effort, and frustration involved in answering each specific form have been substantial, although the agencies' rationale for requesting information may be unimpeachable. Indeed, colleges and universities cannot justly object to the load of questionnaires and reports they must file because, as research organizations, they are among the leading perpetrators of requests for data. Many graduate students and professors conduct their research by gathering responses to questionnaires and in personal interviews, and much of the data collected by government is of greater use to academic researchers than to any other group. In the request for information, colleges and universities clearly place a heavier burden on society than society places on higher education. Nevertheless, compliance with government in the supply of data does impose significant costs on higher education.

Environment. A major feature of recent decades has been a growing social concern for the environment. In evaluating the cost to education, one must consider both the effects of higher education on the environment and the effects of the environment on higher education.

The effects of colleges and universities on the environment tend to be benign. However, they do sometimes emit pollutants from their power plants, or discharge liquid wastes into streams, or inadequately dispose of solid wastes. They sometimes create neighborhood nuisances related to traffic, parking, and student behavior; they sometimes use (or wish to use) land in ways contrary to overall city plans; and they sometimes engage in research that may conceivably endanger the environment, for example, research involving radiation or recombinant DNA. Responding to informal social pressures and government mandates, many institutions have incurred substantial costs to correct these problems. The overall costs related to environmental issues probably have been modest in relation to institutions' total budgets.

The impact of neighborhood environments on institutions of higher education may have generated more significant costs, especially in urban institutions. In recent decades there has been a visible increase in urban decay, crime, vandalism, and militant protest in many of the communities where higher education operates. These social changes have increased the costs of higher education. Neighborhood deterioration has required increased provision for security, higher insurance premiums, losses from theft and vandalism, and unwelcome changes in mode of operation. Some institutions have found it expedient to expend large sums to acquire property, and to renovate and improve neighborhoods adjacent to their campuses.

Shared Costs in Federal Grants and Contracts. In connection with governmental grants and contracts to support research and training in academic institutions, provision for indirect or overhead costs is a major issue because the federal government treats universities less generously than private business in allowances for such costs. The theory underlying this discriminatory treatment is in two parts: (1) because one of the established functions of colleges and universities is to conduct research, their regular funding sources should share in the costs of governmentally sponsored research, and (2) because colleges and universities are going research enterprises, the overhead costs related to governmentally sponsored research do not increase in proportion to the expanded volume of research undertaken and reimbursement of marginal rather than average overhead costs is adequate. This theory, as well as specific cost reimbursement formulas, have been a perennial subject of debate. Many educators argue that institutional costs are increased by reasons of federal research grants and contracts and that what is euphemistically called "cost sharing" probably places a considerable burden on higher educational institutions. However, billions of dollars worth of grants and contracts have been accepted voluntarily by higher educational institutions on terms that do not begin to cover full overhead cost. Indeed, much of the cost sharing merely involves charging overhead costs to research rather than to other activities. The question of what is a fair distribution of overhead cost remains unresolved, and the extent of the burden on the institutions is unknown.

Special Costs of Teaching Hospitals and Clinics. Government has imposed many requirements affecting teaching hospitals and clinics that tend to add cost or reduce income. These requirements govern the time and effort involved in health planning procedures, patient care review, accreditation and licensure, accounting requirements, drug and blood regulations, radiation protection, use of human and animal subjects for research, liaison with the Veterans Administration,

and many other activities. Government also controls the reimbursement of hospitals and clinics for medical services performed for
Medicare, Medicaid, and patients in other programs whose bills are
paid partly or wholly by public agencies. The issue here is similar to
that of overhead cost reimbursement in the case of research contracts
and grants. The socially imposed costs are substantial.

Tax Reform. In recent years, a slow erosion of the traditional tax-
exempt privileges of higher education has occurred. In some respects,
this has tended to raise costs and in others to lower income. The
federal government has modified taxes in ways that may inhibit
philanthropy and constantly threatens more drastic action. The Internal Revenue Service has carefully scrutinized the operations of
nonprofit organizations—partly to discover taxable income and partly to enforce affirmative action. Such audits place significant new
demands on the time and effort of college and university administrative staffs. In many areas of the nation, local and state governments
have become less lenient in exempting nonprofit institutions from
property and sales taxes. Colleges and universities have often been
persuaded—in some cases pressured by threats of adverse rulings on
zoning—to make contributions in lieu of property taxes. Other
local and state governments have stiffened their policies on taxation
of property not directly used for educational purposes, taxation of
"unrelated" income, and tax treatment of charitable contributions.

Aggregate Expenditures for Socially Imposed Costs

In this section I shall consider the aggregate dollar impact of socially
imposed costs over the twenty-year period 1959–60 to 1979–80. Because of lack of relevant data, and serious conceptual problems as
well, estimates of cost are bound to be no more than guesses, and so I
shall not dwell at length on the estimation procedure. In general, I
reviewed increases in administrative expenditures, increases in fringe
benefits, several studies of socially imposed costs (especially Van
Alstyne and Coldren, 1976), and a great deal of anecdotal information
on the effects of socially imposed costs on particular institutions
(especially University of Iowa, 1976).[1] My guess is that the addition to

[1]The following sources were consulted in estimating the aggregate sum of socially
imposed costs: Andringa (1973, 1976), "Another Campus Revolt . . ." (1976), Bender

the annual expenditures of higher educational institutions resulting from socially imposed costs over the period from 1959–60 to 1974–75 was in the neighborhood of $2 to $2.5 billion. These costs have continued to mount since 1974–75. New pressures and demands have been imposed, though I suspect at a slower rate than during the late 1960s and early 1970s. Also these costs, like many others, have been affected by inflation. I would guess that the increase in annual expenditures for socially imposed costs, over the twenty-year period 1959–60 to 1979–80, might be $3.5 to $4.0 billion (in 1979–80 dollars), or roughly 7 to 8 percent of total current expenditures. These figures apply to the total activities of higher education including research, public service, and auxiliary enterprises. The amount allocated to the education of students (as distinct from research, public service, and auxiliary enterprises) would be about $2.3 to $2.7 billion, or about 7 to 8 percent of total educational expenditures.

Estimates of socially imposed costs are unreliable not only because needed data are unavailable but also because the category of socially imposed costs is somewhat elastic. My estimates include the following costs: payroll taxes and other fringe benefits; cost of collective bargaining, minimum wage and overtime legislation; expenditures for equal opportunity, affirmative action, and other programs for minorities and women; shared costs in government grants and contracts; costs of general compliance, statistical reports, and other paperwork; and costs for mandatory changes in buildings required by new building codes, fire marshalls' directives, OSHA, access for the handicapped, new needs for security precautions, and the like (conceptually, I have considered modifications of physical plant to be amortized over a period of fifty years). However, if one calculated the cost of increased student financial aid, new adult education pro-

(1977), Birnbaum (1976), Bok (1976), Bork (1977), W. G. Bowen (1968), Brewster (1975), Brown and Stone (1977), Chambers (1977), Cheit (1975, 1977), Commission on Federal Paperwork (1977), "Do Unionized Faculty . . . ?" (1976), Enarson (1976, 1977), Finn (1975–1976), Heyns (1977), Interagency Task Force on Higher Education Burden Reduction (1976), Lilley and Miller (1977), McGill (1977), Mezvinsky (1976), Oaks (1977), O'Neil (1972), Saunders (1975, 1976), Scott (1978), Seabury (1979), Southern Association of Colleges and Schools (1976), Spriestersbach and Farrell (1977), U.S. Office of Civil Rights (1972), University of Iowa (1976), University of Wisconsin (n.d.), Van Alystyne and Coldren (1976).

grams, and new public service programs, the percentage of expenditures for socially imposed costs would be much larger.

We have no way of knowing to what extent institutions have financed these socially imposed costs by decreasing other expenditures (for example, salaries) or by increasing revenues (for example, increased appropriations, gifts, and tuitions from government, donors, and students, respectively). In the recent and present psychological and financial climate, it is likely that some part of these costs have been financed by retrenchment of programs, impairment of educational quality, or reduction in operating efficiency.

We can only speculate that had colleges and universities not had to meet certain socially imposed costs, they might have increased expenditures for salaries, improvement of programs, or maintenance of facilities; but we cannot be certain. Indeed, some policy makers argue that socially imposed costs represent more judicious investments than some expenditures that educators would make if the decisions were left wholly to them. Similarly, demands on faculty and administrators to fill out forms, read government regulations, negotiate with public officials, lobby in Washington or in state capitols, and mollify pressure groups may have impaired their effectiveness as educational leaders. Yet, one may argue that educators should be brought into the processes of democratic government rather than to remain isolated in their autonomous ivory towers. Such issues allow for honest differences of opinion. However, because of the limited financial resources of higher education in the past decade, the costs of recent social demands may have impaired, or at least threatened, educational excellence and academic freedom. The public interest would seem best served by a pause in the imposition of new social costs that would allow the financial system and the administrative structure of higher education to assimilate the costs of recent social changes.

Conclusions

Most higher educational costs are socially imposed in the sense that most are in response to the needs or demands of society. The question of which ones are to be selected out and labeled "socially imposed" or "governmentally mandated" is wholly arbitrary. It is asking only: What does society expect higher education to do today that it was not doing last year, ten years ago, or twenty-five years ago? Or what is higher education doing voluntarily in the public interest (at least as it is perceived by educators), that it was not doing before? With this all-inclusive definition of socially imposed cost, the dollar amount over a given period of time could be computed merely by comparing total expenditures at the beginning of the selected period with those at the end of the period. Even the rising costs due to inflation could be said to be socially imposed. Thus, efforts to calculate the amount of expenditures associated with socially imposed costs is not a hugely rewarding activity. The basic issues relating to socially imposed costs are philosophical or political. Four general questions about public policy and the public interest should be considered.

First, are some of the socially imposed programs or activities directed toward improper objectives? Is higher education being asked to engage in socially harmful or socially useless activities? My reading of the literature suggests that there is little complaint among educators about the objectives of most of the socially imposed activities. Hardly anyone opposes efforts to improve personal security, equality of opportunity and access, environmental conditions, and the like.

Second, are the procedures by which government programs are administered adequate and efficient? Among educators one hears much criticism of clumsy administration, lack of understanding of the academic community, arbitrariness, tactlessness, redundancy, and inefficiency. Educators also complain about the large number of new programs being imposed over so short a period of time that they cannot be readily assimilated.

Third, who should finance the cost of new social demands? Educators often argue that the government should finance the additional costs it foists upon higher education. Their argument, however, is simply part of the ongoing debate over the question of how much money higher education should receive. If society (represented by legislative bodies and donors) believes that higher education gets more money than it needs, then the imposition of new costs does not necessarily call for increased appropriations and gifts, but only for rearranged priorities within given levels of expenditures. However, if it is believed that higher education is impoverished, then the new costs will call for comparable increases in revenues. The question of financing socially imposed costs is thus simply a corollary of public policy regarding the proper level of financing for higher education and of the distribution of the burden among the federal government, state and local governments, donors, and students.

Fourth, do new government regulations and programs threaten academic freedom? Many educators believe that the proliferation of socially imposed activities and governmentally mandated programs represents a threat to the kind of institutional autonomy which is the foundation of academic freedom. This view leads to the recommendation that desirable ends sought by the society should be achieved through means that would bear down less heavily on institutional autonomy.

In summary, the objectives of new social demands on higher education are, on the whole, laudable. The execution is often clumsy and wasteful. More new demands are being piled on the higher education community in a short span of time than can be readily assimilated; in the financing of higher education, inadequate attention is being given to financial needs created by socially imposed costs; and, Cheit (1975, p. 33) points out, educational leadership may be losing a sense of "the larger vision" because of its preoccupation with immediate social and governmental demands. Even more important, the proliferation of new socially imposed programs and governmental laws and regulations poses a serious threat to academic freedom because it increases the number of points at which social and governmental influences can be exerted on the academic community —the number of regulations that must be observed, the number of penalties that can be inflicted, and the number of agencies that have a part in campus decisions. These often bear tangentially on the questions of who can attend, who can teach, what can be taught, and what methods of instruction can be adopted. Perhaps the greatest need in connection with socially imposed costs is to explore carefully the question of how the legitimate needs of society for such benefits as security, equality, and environmental improvement may be reconciled with the needs of the academy for intellectual freedom.

5

Costs of Asset Maintenance and Prices of Purchased Goods and Services

Before concluding the investigation of long-term trends in the educational costs of American higher education, two additional factors affecting these trends should be considered, namely, deferred maintenance of assets and the prices of purchased goods and services.

Asset Maintenance

The costs of colleges and universities are mainly in the form of cash expenditures, which are visible and easily recognized. They can readily be compared with cash revenues to reveal the condition of the budget. These cash expenditures, however, sometimes fail to cover completely one important type of cost, namely, the deterioration of assets when insufficient provision is made for their maintenance. Thus, when cash budgets are in balance, it does not follow automatically that total costs, including the costs of maintaining assets, have been fully recognized. What may be a balanced cash budget may prove to be seriously out of kilter. The cash budget of an institution reflects total costs only when enough money is being spent on maintenance or set aside as reserves to offset the deterioration of assets. Such deterioration often is not readily visible and is almost always difficult to evaluate. Nevertheless, a proper accounting for cost must give adequate recognition to asset deterioration (Jenny, 1979).

The assets of colleges and universities include such tangible items as land, buildings, equipment, and inventories. These are the assets usually thought of in connection with inadequate maintenance. But institutions also have intangible assets of vastly greater significance than their physical property. The intangible assets in combination largely determine the degree to which colleges and universities are capable of producing excellent educational services. These intangible assets include:

- The ability to recruit and retain qualified faculty and staff
- The capacity to recruit and retain qualified students
- Ties to sources of appropriations, grants, and gifts
- The ongoing internal organization including division of labor, definition of roles, communication systems, rules, customs, traditions, and morale

Clark (1973) refers to the "moral capital" of colleges and universities meaning the ability to weather crises without abandoning basic missions or educational principles. These intangibles are the stuff of which strong colleges and universities are made.

If an institution is successful in bettering its position with respect to these intangibles it is in effect augmenting its most precious assets. If its position is deteriorating and these assets are declining then costs are correspondingly mounting—regardless of what the accounting statements may show about the flow of cash. The importance of these intangibles is suggested by a hypothetical question. Suppose a successful college or university were to be forced to divest itself of either its physical assets or its intangible assets, which would it choose? It would almost surely decide to keep its ability to recruit and hold staff and students, its ties to sources of financing, and its internal organization in preference to its physical assets. With the intangibles, it could soon replace the physical assets, but with the physical assets alone, the recreation of a successful institution would be a long and costly process. The importance of intangible assets is illustrated on a national scale by the quick recovery of Japan and Germany after the physical devastation of World War II or by the prosperity of countries like Norway and Switzerland with their limited physical resources. It is also illustrated in the acquisition of business firms by the remote relationship between the prices paid and the value of physical assets alone (Bowen, 1978c, pp. 123–126).

Just as it is possible for colleges and universities to fail to maintain physical assets they also may fail to maintain intangible assets. In fact both kinds of undermaintenance frequently occur within the higher educational system. Undermaintenance is especially common in periods of financial stringency. For example, in the effort to balance dollar budgets, institutions often allow physical plant to deteriorate or fail to raise salaries sufficiently to maintain the faculty and staff at a satisfactory level of quality. In so doing, the decline in asset value becomes an unrecognized cost. In the remainder of this section, various types of undermaintenance will be considered.

Depreciation of Physical Assets. Physical assets used in higher education such as buildings, furniture and fixtures, scientific apparatus, pianos, and lawn mowers deteriorate over time or become obsolete even before they wear out physically. Each year, a fraction of each such asset is used up. The amount of that depreciation or obsolescence is rightfully a part of the cost of conducting higher education in that year. Yet, under the conventions of accounting for colleges and universities, that cost is seldom included in the total operating expenses.

This understatement could be corrected in either of two ways. One way would be for an institution to count actual capital expenditures in each year as an ordinary expense to be included in operating costs. This method would work well if capital expenditures were made in about equal annual amounts so that each year's expenditures would approximately offset each year's depreciation and obsolescence. But in fact, capital assets tend to come in big lumps and expenditures for them tend to be quite irregular from year to year. Yet depreciation and obsolescence of existing buildings and equipment goes on steadily year after year and is not closely related to the amount of spending for new capital assets. There is another way to account for asset costs, a way that overcomes the problem of irregularity and assigns to each year its proper share of depreciation and obsolescence. Institutions could estimate the amount of depreciation and obsolescence that takes place each year and contribute that amount to a reserve for depreciation that would be expected to grow over time to an amount sufficient to replace capital assets as they wear out or become obsolete. The contributions to this reserve then would be regarded as a current expense. Thus, each year's operation would be assigned its proper share of the cost of the capital assets employed. Private business firms ordinarily use the reserve method and thus include capital costs among their operating expenses. But as things now stand, most colleges and universities ignore capital costs in their accounting for current expenditures.

The underlying problem of depreciation and obsolescence of plant is not merely that the conventional accounting records do not reflect depreciation and obsolescence. Indeed, the usual accounting formulas for the recognition of depreciation are far from satisfactory especially in turbulent times of inflation, deflation, and rapid technological change. The underlying problem is that governing boards and administrators of colleges and universities are not made aware of these unacknowledged costs when they are appraising the condition of their institutions. A so-called balanced budget that may be a source of considerable satisfaction may not be balanced at all when capital costs are considered.

The faith that justifies omitting depreciation as a current cost is that when capital assets wear out or become obsolete special appropriations or gifts will be available to replace them. This is a valid theory if, as depreciation is going on, institutions are in fact developing sources of the funds needed for replacement. In that case there is no deterioration of assets because the growth of an intangible asset (ability to raise funds) offsets the depreciation of a tangible asset (physical plant).

Plant Maintenance. Virtually all physical plant requires regular maintenance and repair. Buildings and equipment need constant care to keep them in working condition and to retard the rate at which they depreciate. A regular part of the operating budget of every college or university is assigned to building and equipment maintenance. If each year's budget for the purpose is adequate to the task—if money is provided as needed to tuck-point the masonry, paint the window frames, fix leaky roofs, or keep the electrical system working—then the expenditures necessary for adequate maintenance are being made and the full cost of maintenance is being recognized in the accounts. But if for any reason—the usual reason being short-age of funds—the expenditures for plant maintenance are insufficient to keep pace with the total need, then maintenance is being "deferred" to the future and a cost in the form of plant deterioration is not being recognized in the accounts. Moreover, deferral of plant maintenance tends to shorten the life of buildings and equipment and thus increase the annual cost of depreciation.

A special case of deferred maintenance is the failure in any given year to replace capital items purchased with operating funds; library books and other library materials are the most important example. Library acquisitions are usually treated as a current expense rather than as a capital outlay. The presumption is that each year's acquisitions will at least renew the collection and offset the steady wear and tear, losses, and obsolescence of the books acquired in past years. Some books, to be sure, do not wear out very rapidly and some never become obsolete. Some even gain in value over time. But most academic library collections deteriorate without sufficient annual acquisitions. If the acquisitions fall short, then deferred maintenance—unrecognized in the accounting system—will have set in.

The same principle applies to other durable items purchased with operating funds, for example, filing cabinets or typewriters. If current purchases of these items are sufficient to offset depreciation and thus to maintain the stock of these items, their costs are being fully recognized. But if current purchases fall behind the rate of depreciation, then deferred maintenance has occurred and some costs have gone unrecognized.

Deferred Maintenance of Intangible Assets. Just as institutions may undermaintain their physical assets, they may also fail to maintain their incomparably more important intangible assets. One of the most common reasons for undermaintenance of physical plant is to divert resources to the support of the intangible assets that are accorded higher priority. Nevertheless, undermaintenance of intangible assets is not uncommon—especially so because in the short run it does not show as obviously as broken window panes, leaky roofs, and untended trees.

Undermaintenance of faculty and staff resulting in quality deterioration not infrequently occurs in times of financial stress. To maintain a faculty of a given size and level of competence, each institution must provide salaries, fringe benefits, and working conditions comparable to those offered in other similar institutions. And the higher educational system as a whole must offer compensation and working conditions comparable to those provided by business, government, hospitals, independent professions, and other employments for workers of similar qualifications. If faculty and staff compensation and working conditions fall below the competitive level, ' either for individual colleges and universities or for the higher educational system as a whole, there will be a slow attrition of quality. Some of the more competent faculty and staff will be lured away and there will be difficulty in attracting capable new people and in maintaining a diversified age distribution. Gradually, the overall quality of the faculty and staff, the most important asset of any college, will decline.

The same kind of deterioration can happen to an institution's relationships to sources of funding, to its capacity to recruit students, and to its internal organization. These, together with faculty and staff, are the most vital assets of a college or university. Such deterioration is insidious because it comes on gradually and may at first not be noticed. But after a time it will become as obvious as the broken sidewalks, the utility failures, the flaked paint, and the dead trees of an undermaintained campus.

Financial Deterioration. Another set of unrecognized costs are related to the financial operations of colleges and universities. First among these is a decline in the value of many endowment or quasi-endowment funds. For example, during the 1970s, because of reverses in the stock market and erosion of security values through inflation, many portfolios declined in value. The losses were mostly unrealized paper losses that may be recovered. Nevertheless, many institutions have been unable to reap the real income they expected from their investments, and have sustained losses that may be permanent.

Colleges and universities have become lenders, mainly in connection with student loans, and are therefore subject to bad debts. Many businesses and other organizations establish reserves for bad debts. As these reserves are accumulated year by year, they have the effect of recognizing this cost over the duration of the loans, not merely when uncollectable loans are written off. But higher educational institutions usually do not establish such reserves and hence these costs tend to be unrecognized until actual defaults occur.

Colleges and universities are sometimes borrowers as well as lenders. Some of their obligations take the form of long-term loans for the construction of buildings with repayment of principal amortized so that the cost is spread over the duration of the loans and is recognized year by year. But some institutions borrow, usually through renewable short-term loans, without provisions for amortization of principal. Sometimes substantial debt is carried over long periods without any provision for repayment and without any recognition in the annual operating budgets of the eventual cost of repaying the principal.

Still another area of cost that is often unrecognized is provision for contingencies. Colleges and universities are vulnerable to various misfortunes: sudden declines in enrollment, catastrophic residence hall fires, unanticipated demands to remodel buildings for seismic safety, cancellation of research grants, and so on. When subject to unpredictable misfortunes, businesses and other organizations often build up financial reserves for contingencies and thus spread the costs over long periods of time. Some colleges and universities also accumulate reserves usually in the form of quasi-endowment—invested funds serving as endowment but available for other uses as directed by the governing board. But many institutions are unprepared even for minor contingencies. In such institutions the costs of contingencies are not recognized until the year in which they happen—when they become disasters.

Concluding Comments. Failure to maintain assets in the present spells trouble in the future. Eventually, if institutions are to survive and prosper, they will be forced into cash expenditures to make up for past undermaintenance. At some point, buildings and equipment will have to be repaired or replaced; faculty and staff will have to be restored in numbers and quality; neglected library collections will have to be renewed; depleted inventories will have to be rebuilt; bad debts will have to be written off; unamortized loans will have to be paid; contingencies as they occur will have to be surmounted.

The insidious aspect of these deferred costs is that they accumulate over time. If, say, $3 billion a year of deferred cost is incurred by the American higher educational system year after year during a spell of financial stringency like the 1970s, the total costs facing the institutions can become equal to a fourth or even a half of a whole year's budget. To cope with amounts of this magnitude is indeed difficult.

Why, it may be asked, would colleges and universities put off maintaining their various assets? Financial stringency is only a partial answer. When institutions are hard-pressed financially, postponing maintenance in all its forms is the least unpalatable expedient. Therefore, the amount of hidden cost tends to be greater in hard times than in good times. There is a cyclical pattern of undermaintenance in lean periods and of partial catching up in good years. However, the priorities and politics of colleges and universities are such that even in good times, it is tempting to strengthen instruction, student services, and research and to launch "exciting new programs" rather than to carry out the drab and unspectacular tasks of maintaining plant and equipment. Such maintenance can always be postponed "for just one more year." If one examines most campuses carefully, one will find considerable deferred maintenance of plant even at the best of times. Things are never so good that a complete catching up is possible. In a period of inflation, the problem is intensified. Each postponement increases the eventual cost.

Another part of the answer to the question of why colleges and universities dare to postpone maintenance is that they can appeal to sources of financial support—legislatures or donors—for special funds to catch up on maintenance or to replace worn-out assets. Or in case there is quasi-endowment, it is possible to appeal to boards for permission to draw upon these funds. When a steam plant finally issues its last wisp, when residence hall conditions become intolerable, when a structure is declared dangerous, when the library collection becomes outmoded, when faculty salaries become impossibly noncompetitive, special appropriations, gifts, or quasi-endowment often provide bail-out money.

If there were not such financial backing, institutions managed in the style of colleges and universities would soon expire. Their capital simply would give out and they would have no place to replenish it. Colleges and universities capable of surviving must constantly build up deferred assets in the form of potential appropriations, gifts, and tuitions to defray deferred costs. Much of the work of financing colleges and universities consists in cultivating these deferred assets to match the deferred liabilities. Many of the transactions involved are reported in the capital accounts and never appear in the current operating accounts. That is why a true accounting for higher educational institutions should include capital as well as operating funds.

The secret to the survival of American higher education has been its ability to cultivate deferred assets in the form of potential sources of funds that will offset deferred maintenance of its various assets. The undoubted progress of American higher education has been due to the fact that, on balance, the deferred assets always have ultimately exceeded deferred maintenance. In the process, a great many roofs have leaked, numerous plumbing systems have broken down, many libraries have gone through periods of undermaintenance, there have been times of serious deterioration in quality and morale of staff, and many crises have occurred. But in the end, the higher educational system has been maintained because it has had generous and concerned financial backing. But American higher education has been through long periods of asset deterioration of a kind that does not show in the financial records. It probably has been in such a period during the 1970s and the depressed condition may continue into the 1980s. At this writing, there is no guarantee that financial backing to offset the asset deterioration is poised ready to launch a rescue operation.

To estimate with any precision the present dollar amount of deferred maintenance in all its forms would be difficult if not impossible. Even if the data were available, any estimate would have to be based on standards against which deficiencies could be measured. And standards, even about building maintenance, not to mention faculty size and quality, are notoriously controversial. One approach to estimating deferred maintenance would be to select a past year at the end of a period when higher education was relatively prosperous, say 1969–70, and try to estimate the cost in 1979–80 of restoring that standard. The results of such an effort will be presented in Chapter Ten.

Prices of Purchased Goods and Services

About a quarter of the educational expenditures of colleges and universities go to buy goods and services from outside vendors (see Table 1). These purchases are partly for current goods and services such as library books, fuel, postage, legal counsel, and building materials; and they are partly for capital goods, for example, the acquisition of land, the construction of buildings, and the purchase of major pieces of equipment.

It is sometimes thought that the prices of the goods and services colleges and universities buy rise more rapidly than the general price level in the economy as a whole and that inflation therefore has an especially pernicious effect on higher education. The sole purpose of this section is to test this idea.

The prices paid by colleges and universities are, of course, no different from those charged private business firms or other organizations for identical goods and services. A gallon of fuel oil, a particular book, a long-distance call, or a new building of given specifications are likely to carry the same price tag for higher educational institutions as for other comparable organizations. The difference lies in the proportions in which various kinds of goods and services are purchased. Steel mills buy a lot of coal, banks spend a great deal for computers and computer services, colleges and universities buy many books and periodicals. The trend of costs for any of these organizations will be affected by the price behavior of the particular "market basket" of goods and services it buys. If its assortment includes many items with rapidly rising prices, its costs will go up more rapidly than those of an organization which buys many items with stable or falling prices. The question then, is whether the purchases of colleges and universities are distributed in such a way that their costs tend to rise more or less rapidly than the prevailing general price level. This question may be approached—at least for the past—by comparing price indexes for higher education with relevant indexes for the general economy. Price indexes for the "market basket" of current goods and services purchased by higher education have been carefully devised by Halstead (1975) of the National Institute of Higher Education. When one compares the Halstead index with the Producer Price Index (formerly called the Wholesale Price Index) of the U.S. Bureau of Labor Statistics, one finds that the two indexes move closely together. Between 1966–67 and 1979–80, the Halstead index rose from 100 to 255 while the Producer Price Index rose from 100 to 249, a difference of 2.5 percent. When the same comparison is made between 1969–70 and 1979–80, the increase in the two indexes is found to be almost exactly the same. Though the two indexes vary slightly from each other from time to time, there is little support for the theory that the prices of goods and services purchased by higher education rise more rapidly than the general price level.

What is true about goods and services purchased by colleges and universities is that the amount of such purchases makes up a larger percentage of the budget in well-to-do institutions than in impoverished ones. This matter is considered in some detail in Chapter Seven.

Data are not available for comparing the capital goods prices paid by colleges and universities with the prices paid by other industries. In general, the inflation of capital goods prices has been steeper than that of current goods and services. Thus, industries that are heavy buyers of capital goods, relative to their purchases of current goods, would on the whole have a steeper upward trend of prices than industries that purchase relatively fewer capital goods. Higher education is not an exceptionally heavy buyer of capital goods. In higher education, gross additions to capital plant have ranged from 12 to 20 percent of total expenditures over the past twenty years; for the economy as a whole, private domestic investment has ranged from 14 to 20 percent of gross national product. Particularly during the financially lean years of the 1970s, purchases of capital goods by higher education have slowed up considerably. Thus, it is not likely that capital expenditures would tend to raise the prices of goods and services purchased by higher education relative to the prices paid by other industries.

This chapter concludes Part One, a longitudinal study of costs. The four chapters of Part One have traced long-term trends in the costs of higher education and have considered several critical factors influencing these trends, among them, faculty and staff compensation, student-faculty ratios, socially imposed costs, asset maintenance, and purchased goods and services. These matters will be reviewed in the final section of the book (Chapter Ten) where the question of what higher education *should* cost is under consideration. We turn now to Part Two, which is a cross-sectional study of costs based mainly on data from a sample of 268 institutions.

Part Two

Costs of
Individual Institutions

The preceding chapters have been concerned with long-term trends in the costs of the American system of higher education. The approach has been that of macroanalysis of the entire system and little attention has been given to individual institutions. In the next four chapters, the perspective shifts to microanalysis of higher educational institutions viewed as separate entities. Chapter Six is focused on the amazing differences in cost per unit among institutions. Chapter Seven explores the relationship between institutional affluence and expenditure patterns in order to learn what affluence enables rich institutions to buy or what poverty condemns poor institutions to do without. Chapter Eight carries the analysis of cost differences further by relating them to institutional outcomes. Because outcomes are difficult to identify and measure, it would be rash to promise definitive conclusions on the relationship between affluence and outcomes. But some interesting data will be presented and some tentative conclusions will be drawn. Finally, Chapter Nine is a study of the much-discussed relationship between institutional size and cost per student.

6

Cost Differences Among Institutions

Diversity among institutions is a conspicuous and on the whole a desirable trait of American higher education. The word *diversity*, however, can be used to condone shoddiness, to cover up narrow provincialism, to excuse shockingly inadequate financial support. But in the best sense, diversity enhances the ability of higher education to serve persons of different backgrounds, abilities, and interests. It encourages institutions to invent and try out new programs and methods. It disposes them to tap varied sources of support. In no respect are colleges and universities more diverse than in their unit costs, that is, in the amount they spend per student. The range of differences in cost per student is astonishing. Some of the variation may be explained by differences in mission. For example, colleges or universities heavily involved in graduate and professional study are likely to have higher costs per student than those concentrating on the instruction of freshmen and sophomores. And those emphasizing the natural sciences, technology, or medicine may have higher costs per student than those concentrating on the humanities and social studies. Cost differences also may be explained to a minor extent by location in urban or rural settings, by location in different sections of the country, and by size of institution. But differences in expenditure remain even when only educational costs are considered and when the institutions being compared seem to have similar missions, location, and size and to be rendering services of similar quality. The extent of these cost differences will be explored in this chapter.

The Concept of Educational Cost per Student Unit

At the risk of repetition, it may be useful to clarify exactly what is being measured when the costs of different institutions are being compared. For a more complete description, see Appendix C.

Educational cost refers to current expenditures after excluding outlays for organized research and public service, a *prorated* share of overhead cost attributable to research and public service, and outlays for the operation of auxiliary enterprises such as residence halls, dining facilities, student unions, and teaching hospitals. What remains after these exclusions is current expenditures for the education of students. These include outlays for instruction and departmental research, student services, student financial aid paid from institutional funds, and a *prorated* portion of expenditures for academic support facilities such as libraries, computers, administration, and plant operation and maintenance. This remainder is called *educational cost*.

A student is the unit of service to which educational cost is to be related. Students are, however, a mixed lot. Some are part-time and others full-time; some are beginners and others are candidates for advanced degrees. To achieve a standardized unit of service, students are counted as full-time equivalents and weights are assigned to them according to academic level as follows: freshmen and sophomores 1.0; juniors and seniors 1.5; first-year graduate students 2.1; advanced professional students 2.5; and advanced graduate students 3.0. (For information on the source of the weights, see Appendix C.) These weights were based on estimates of the relative average costs of educating various categories of students. The result of these adjustments is a standardized *student unit* expressed in terms of one full-time lower division (freshman or sophomore) student. Thus, each upper division and each advanced professional or graduate student is counted as an appropriate multiple of one lower division student. For example, a Ph.D. candidate counts as three student units.

The basic data for reviewing institutional cost differences were derived from a sample of 268 representative institutions. The source was the Higher Educational General Information Survey (HEGIS) of the National Center for Education Statistics. The institutions represented were selected as a random sample stratified by type according to the classifications of the Carnegie Council on Policy Studies in

Higher Education (1976), and stratified also by size and geographic region. For a description of the sample see Appendix C.

Dispersion of Unit Costs Among 268 Representative Institutions

Table 12 presents data on educational costs per student unit for the 268 institutions in the sample. As shown in the table, unit costs differed widely among institutions. The maximum unit cost for various types of institutions ranged from three to eight times the minimum unit cost. For all institutions combined, the maximum was nearly ten times the minimum. And the unit cost for third-quartile institutions was 1.5 to 2.0 times that for first-quartile institutions. Though the median unit costs for various types of institutions tended to converge, the variance of unit costs among individual institutions remained astonishingly great.

The cost dispersions shown in Table 12 are corroborated by many surveys made over the past two decades. For example, the National Federation of College and University Business Officers Association (1960), in a report known as *The Sixty College Study*, collected comparable financial data for a nationwide sample of sixty-six well-known liberal arts colleges. The results reveal wide differences in total Educational and General Expenditures per student for institutions of comparable size and mission. Similarly, the Carnegie Commission on Higher Education (1971) assembled data on Educational and General Expenditures per FTE student for colleges and universities of various types. These figures again reveal striking differences among institutions. Jenny and Wynn (1972, p. 81) gathered financial statistics on forty-eight leading private liberal arts colleges for the year 1970–71. They too found wide cost disparities. The range in Educational and General Expenditures per student (FTE) varied from $1,552 to $5,135. Comparable findings were reported by Columbia Research Associates (1971) in a study prepared for the U.S. Office of Education on colleges and small universities and by McKinsey and Company (1972) in a study of twelve well-known liberal arts colleges in Pennsylvania. Heller and his associates described two "prestige colleges" of roughly the same enrollments with costs of $4,380 and $2,740 per student (Carnegie Commission, 1972, p. 40) and Brinkman (1980) computed differences in instructional costs per full-time-

Table 12. Dispersion of educational expenditures per student unit, 268 representative colleges and universities, by type of institution, 1976–77

	Number of institutions reporting	Minimum	First (lower) quartile	Median	Third (higher) quartile	Maximum
Research and doctorate-granting universities						
Public	35	$1,076	$1,758	$2,020	$3,120	$4,786
Private	35	1,517	2,262	3,341	4,528	8,039
Total	70	1,076	1,915	2,677	3,844	8,039
Comprehensive universities and colleges						
Public	32	1,177	1,761	2,025	2,538	3,721
Private	52	1,134	1,893	2,242	2,640	4,249
Total	84	1,134	1,827	2,147	2,615	4,249
Liberal arts colleges, private	65	824	2,546	3,183	3,920	6,492
Two-year colleges						
Public	26	1,102	1,636	1,959	2,859	4,150
Private	23	1,597	1,959	2,736	3,016	6,748
Total	49	1,102	1,791	2,175	2,907	6,748
All institutions (unweighted)						
Public	93	1,076	1,727	2,020	2,848	4,786
Private	175	824	2,149	2,813	3,458	8,039
Total	268	824	1,938	2,545	3,286	8,039

Source: Special tabulation of data from Higher Education General Information Survey, U.S. Department of Health, Education, and Welfare. See Appendix C for detailed description of the data.

equivalent student among fifty leading universities ranging from $1,619 to $12,171.

Cost Comparisons Among Similar Institutions

The degree of cost dispersion shown in Table 12 conceivably could be due to heterogeneity of the various categories of institutions being compared. To explore this possibility, I made an effort to compare costs among small groups of selected institutions that appear to be closely similar. The criteria for selection were: total enrollment; relative commitment to research and public service and to instruction; educational programs; distribution of students among undergraduate, graduate, and professional programs; size of city where located; and Carnegie classification (see Radner and Miller, 1975, p. 158). Also, my own judgment as to comparability had some influence on the selection. The results are shown in Table 13. In each group of institutions chosen for close comparability, substantial differences in cost remained.

Similar comparisons were made by Meeth (1974, pp. 74–98). He selected at random three pairs of liberal arts colleges for which cost data had been provided in *The Sixty College Study* (National Federation of College and University Business Officers Association, 1960). Having found substantial cost differences between the institutions of each pair, he then gathered data reflecting the "quality" of the academic environment achieved by each pair of institutions. Such qualitative differences as he discovered tended to be in favor of the low-cost institutions.

In another pertinent study (Bowen and Douglass, 1971, pp. 95–103), an effort was made to simulate costs of instruction in a typical selective liberal arts college assuming different modes of instruction. The estimated cost per student course enrollment was about $240 (1970 dollars) when instruction was conducted in a conventional fashion. The authors found that this cost might vary from $134 to $334 by altering the mode of instruction. These changes in cost would come about through moderate changes in such variables as course proliferation, average faculty teaching load, building utilization, and instructional methods. The authors concluded that cost might easily vary in the range of $200 to $300 per course enrollment

**Table 13. Arrays of educational expenditures per student unit in
selected closely comparable institutions, 1976–77**

Six major public universities	*Six major private universities*	*Six state colleges (all located in small cities)*
Located in large cities or suburbs	Located in large cities or suburbs	
$2,665	$2,214	$1,194
3,060	3,341	1,762
3,636	4,517	1,936
	4,533	2,067
Located in small cities	Located in small cities	2,133
1,920	4,029	3,430
2,020	5,242	
2,676		

Six selective liberal arts colleges, , located in large cities	*Seven selective liberal arts colleges located in small cities*
Enrollment: 1,000–1,500	*Enrollment: 1,000–1,500*
$3,183	$3,137
3,525	3,686
	4,154
	5,223
Enrollment: 1,500–2,000	*Enrollment: 1,500–2,000*
$2,881	$4,062
3,281	4,079
3,450	4,972
4,228	

Note: These institutions are comparable with respect to total enrollment, relative commitment to research and public service, and instruction, educational programs offered, and mix of students among undergraduate, graduate, and professional levels.

Source: Special tabulation of data from Higher Education General Information Survey. See Appendix C for detailed description of data.

without noticeable differences in educational outcomes. The important conclusion was that substantial differences in cost do not necessarily connote significant differences in outcomes. That is why the costs for institutions of similar missions and similar levels of quality may differ, and it is why institutions of similar cost may have different outcomes.

Cost Comparisons Among the States

Another indication of differences in institutional costs is found in comparative figures on average cost per student in the public institutions of the various states. Table 14 presents the data for 1976–77. These figures are adjusted for comparability with those presented in Table 12. That is to say, the expenditure figures relate only to the costs of educating students and the enrollment figures are expressed in full-time-equivalent student units weighted for academic level of students. The data also are adjusted for differences in consumer prices among the states.

The five leaders in expenditures per student unit were: Montana ($2,956), District of Columbia ($2,820), Iowa ($2,426), Pennsylvania ($2,325), and Vermont ($2,310). (Alaska might possibly belong in this list. However, although it is known that the cost of living is far higher in Alaska than elsewhere in the United States, no index was available for adjusting the figure for that state.) The bottom five were: Connecticut ($1,266), Massachusetts ($1,344), West Virginia ($1,480), New Jersey ($1,544), and Oklahoma ($1,563). Unit costs ranged from $1,266 in Connecticut to $2,956 in Montana, a ratio of 1 to 2.3.

Differences in cost per student would be expected to vary among the states according to the makeup of the several public higher educational systems. For example, states with a large proportion of their students in major universities (New Mexico) might have different costs per student from those with most students in two-year colleges (California). Therefore, I tried to group states with similar proportions of their students in research and doctorate-granting universities, comprehensive colleges and universities, and two-year colleges. It was not easy to find large groups of such states because there is great diversity in the composition of statewide systems of higher education. Nevertheless, in most groups, substantial variations in cost per student occur even among similar statewide systems of higher education. To cite one extreme case, the unit costs were $1,344 in Massachusetts, $1,544 in New Jersey, and $2,130 in New York.

Even if one could select tiny groups of comparable institutions so homogeneous as to eliminate all cost differences, one would not change the reality that the cost of carrying out essentially the same services varies widely among American colleges and universities. The dispersion of costs is astonishingly great—so great that one may rea-

**Table 14. Educational expenditures per student unit,
all public institutions, by states, 1975–76**

Alabama	$2,035	Missouri	$1,754
Alaska	—	Montana	2,956
Arizona	1,580	Nebraska	1,908
Arkansas	1,892	Nevada	1,734
California	1,663	New Hampshire	1,663
Colorado	1,761	New Jersey	1,544
Connecticut	1,266	New Mexico	1,573
Delaware	1,930	New York	2,130
District of Columbia	2,820	North Carolina	2,191
Florida	1,935	North Dakota	2,012
Georgia	1,794	Ohio	1,832
Hawaii	—	Oklahoma	1,563
Idaho	2,179	Oregon	1,837
Illinois	1,746	Pennsylvania	2,325
Indiana	2,063	Rhode Island	1,998
Iowa	2,426	South Carolina	2,007
Kansas	1,896	South Dakota	1,725
Kentucky	1,785	Tennessee	1,988
Louisiana	1,697	Texas	1,981
Maine	1,918	Utah	2,083
Maryland	1,803	Vermont	2,310
Massachusetts	1,344	Virginia	1,605
Michigan	1,969	Washington	1,592
Minnesota	1,837	West Virginia	1,480
Mississippi	2,040	Wisconsin	2,207
		Wyoming	2,116
		U.S. all states combined	2,003

Source: National Center for Education Statistics, *Financial Statistics of Institutions of Higher Education, Fiscal Year 1977, State Data;* and *Fall Enrollment in Higher Education 1976.* The index for adjusting the data for differences among the states in cost of living is that of McMahon and Melton (1978, p. 331).

sonably question the rationality or equity in the allocation of resources among higher educational institutions. This state of affairs may be tolerated because so little is known about the relationships between the amount of resources and educational outcomes. The depth of this ignorance is indicated by the almost universal tendency to judge institutional results or quality in terms of inputs rather than outputs and to assume without evidence that more inputs somehow will inevitably produce commensurately greater or better results.

Institutional Differences in the
Internal Allocation of Expenditures

Not only do colleges and universities differ widely in their total expenditures per student, they also show great variety in the way they deploy these expenditures among various programs and functions. Certainly there is no one best allocation toward which most institutions tend to converge. Rather, there are numerous and widely divergent patterns of expenditure, even among seemingly comparable institutions. As shown in Table 15, the maximum percentages spent on any function are from 2 to 10 times the minimum percentages and the percentages for third-quartile institutions generally range from 1.5 to 2.0 times the percentages for the first-quartile institutions. These differences might be ascribed to heterogeneity of the institutions being observed. Table 16 shows the distribution of expenditures for a few closely similar institutions as shown in Table 16. Despite the homogeneity of the institutions, substantial differences in the percentages remained. For example, for six major public universities expenditures for teaching varied from 59 to 72 percent; for six state colleges from 39 to 68 percent; and for thirteen liberal arts colleges from 25 to 51 percent. Similarly, the percentage spent for student services varied from 4 to 7 percent for major private universities and from 7 to 13 percent for liberal arts colleges.

Comparable disparities have been obtained in cost studies of the past, for example, those of the National Federation of College and University Business Officers Association (1960), McKinsey and Company (1972), Jenny and Wynn (1972), and Columbia Research Associates (1971, 1972, 1975). An especially interesting study by Swords and Walwer (1974) shows remarkable differences in the cost per student for legal education. They show that in 1970 the cost per student among the 115 accredited American law schools ranged from $250 to $2,350 with the first quartile at $650, the median at $850, and the third quartile at $1,150. Similarly, Lupton and Moses (1978) show substantial disparities among small liberal arts colleges in cost per matriculant for recruitment and admissions of students.

Concluding Comments

Wide differences among institutions in cost per student have been observed in every study of comparative costs. These differences have

Table 15. Dispersion among institutions in the percentage distribution of educational expenditures among various programs and functions, 1976–77

	Minimum	First quartile	Median	Third quartile	Maximum
Research and doctorate-granting universities, public					
Teaching	41%	53%	59%	63%	72%
Student services	3	4	6	8	11
Scholarships and fellowships	0	5	7	8	11
Academic support	4	6	9	11	15
Institutional support	2	6	8	11	25
Plant operation and maintenance	5	7	9	10	15
Research and doctorate-granting universities, private					
Teaching	36	48	55	60	69
Student services	2	4	5	6	11
Scholarships and fellowships	2	8	10	16	19
Academic support	2	6	7	9	18
Institutional support	5	8	10	13	27
Plant operation and maintenance	5	7	8	10	14
Comprehensive universities and colleges, public					
Teaching	35	43	54	61	68
Student services	2	4	5	6	9
Scholarships and fellowships	0	1	3	5	25
Academic support	3	6	8	11	16
Institutional support	4	9	12	16	27
Plant operation and maintenance	6	11	12	14	20
Comprehensive universities and colleges, private					
Teaching	31	39	44	50	61
Student services	2	6	8	9	18
Scholarships and fellowships	5	9	11	14	30
Academic support	2	4	6	7	15
Institutional support	2	13	17	19	27
Plant operation and maintenance	3	8	9	12	18
Liberal arts colleges, private					
Teaching	22	32	38	41	58
Student services	2	7	9	11	18
Scholarships and fellowships	0	10	12	15	45
Academic support	2	5	7	8	27
Institutional support	5	15	17	23	33
Plant operation and maintenance	5	9	11	13	25

Table 15 (continued)

	Minimum	First quartile	Median	Third quartile	Maximum
Two-year colleges, public					
Teaching	29%	49%	56%	60%	79%
Student services	2	5	7	8	12
Scholarships and fellowships	0	0	2	4	5
Academic support	2	4	6	8	16
Institutional support	6	10	17	19	37
Plant operation and maintenance	5	7	10	15	19
All institutions, public					
Teaching	29	49	57	62	79
Student services	2	4	6	7	12
Scholarships and fellowships	0	1	4	7	25
Academic support	2	5	8	11	16
Institutional support	2	8	11	16	37
Plant operation and maintenance	5	8	10	13	20
All institutions, private					
Teaching	22	36	41	49	69
Student services	2	5	8	10	21
Scholarships and fellowships	0	8	11	13	45
Academic support	2	4	7	8	29
Institutional support	2	12	16	21	41
Plant operation and maintenance	3	8	10	17	29
All institutions, total					
Teaching	22	38	47	55	79
Student services	2	5	7	9	21
Scholarships and fellowships	0	4	9	13	45
Academic support	2	5	7	9	29
Instituitional support	2	10	15	20	41
Plant operation and maintenance	3	8	10	12	29

Note: Educational expenditures are those related to the education of students; they exclude expenditures for auxiliary enterprises, research, and public service.

Source: Special tabulation of data from Higher Education General Information Survey. See Appendix C for a detailed description of data.

Table 16. Dispersion among selected closely comparable institutions in the percentage distribution of educational expenditures among various programs and functions, 1976–77

	Teaching	Student services	Scholarships and fellowships	Academic support	Institutional support	Plant operation and maintenance	Other
Six major public universities Located in large cities or suburbs							
A	68%	4%	5%	9%	8%	7%	—
B	59	9	11	8	7	7	—
C	59	7	8	15	7	5	—
Located in small cities							
D	72	4	2	11	5	7	—
E	63	4	8	12	6	8	—
F	63	6	8	9	4	10	—
Five major private universities Located in large cities or suburbs							
G	60	4	15	7	7	7	1
H	49	6	17	13	7	8	—
I	56	7	18	7	7	5	—
Located in small cities							
J	56	5	17	8	5	9	—
K	49	7	17	9	9	10	—
Six state colleges (all located in small cities)							
L	61	2	2	5	11	10	9
M	68	4	3	8	5	13	—
N	65	7	1	8	10	10	—
O	49	6	5	15	8	17	—
P	39	5	3	4	27	10	13
Q	42	9	1	7	13	15	14

Table 16 (continued)

	Teaching	Student services	Scholarships and fellowships	Academic support	Institutional support	Plant operation and maintenance	Other
Thirteen distinguished liberal arts colleges							
R	51%	11%	6%	7%	12%	12%	—
S	50	8	15	9	10	8	1
T	41	13	12	5	14	13	1
U	47	12	11	18	12	10	—
V	48	7	14	6	10	15	1
W	43	10	9	8	20	10	—
X	40	7	11	16	13	13	1
Y	45	9	12	6	12	16	1
Z	42	11	13	8	14	11	1
AA	25	10	13	9	26	17	—
BB	41	8	10	6	21	14	1
CC	44	8	11	18	7	12	1
DD	32	8	12	7	16	25	—

Source: Special tabulation of data from Higher Education General Information Survey. See Appendix C for a detailed description of data.

been found to persist even when great care has been taken to compare closely-similar institutions, to adjust for geographical differences in price levels, and to adjust and refine the cost data so as to exclude expenditures for research, public service, and auxiliary enterprises and to standardize student units. What do these differences signify?

One possible answer is that the institutions being compared are actually less homogeneous with respect to the educational programs offered than they seem. This may be especially so at the two extremes: in the case of the major research universities each of which has a considerable claim to uniqueness in the range and characteristics of educational programs, and in the case of community colleges which vary especially in their relative emphasis on expensive vocational programs and less costly academic programs. But for the many institutions that lie between these extremes, the program differences are likely to be far fewer. In the case of selective liberal arts colleges, they are likely to be minuscule. Be that as it may, there is a serious logical problem in declaring that cost differences are due to differences in program. It is by no means clear whether expensive programs are a result or a cause of high costs. An institution which succeeds in raising ample funds can afford to offer expensive programs. It can offer and even require science, fine arts, or classics, whereas a less affluent institution will tend to steer away from these subjects toward less costly sociology and education. Similarly, a rich institution may have highly developed psychological counseling, art museums, and expensive athletic facilities, whereas a less affluent institution may have to streamline its student services and cultural offerings. High-cost institutions cannot maintain that their high costs are due solely to the character of their offerings; the historical facts may be the exact opposite. If, however, the high-cost programs have been mandated by a public agency or an accrediting body, or if it can be proven that they are essential to education of high quality, then the claim can properly be made that costs are high because of programs offered. Although the dispersion of costs among institutions would be narrowed (though not eliminated) if comparisons were restricted to institutions having similar assortments of programs, such a procedure would beg the question because cause and effect cannot be clearly sorted out. (For an interesting and opposing discussion of this issue, see Czajkowski, 1979.)

The wide differences in cost per student are sometimes justified by citing significant though subtle differences in institutional quality. This argument comes in four forms all relating to the benefits of diversity.

First, it is sometimes argued that the higher educational system, since it is called upon to serve widely varied clienteles, must be diverse. Substantial cost differences are therefore held to be legitimate and even necessary. The widely acknowledged need for diversity does not, however, explain why institutions serving the same or very similar clienteles—for example, selective liberal arts colleges or large state colleges—should exhibit such disparate costs per student. And it does not explain why average costs should be lower in some states than in others even when the states being compared distribute their students among similar assortments of institutions.

Second, it is argued that diversity among institutions is beneficial as it fosters innovation in higher education. The acknowledged benefits from innovation do not, however, explain the substantial cost differences among institutions that are similar not only in size and mission but also in their traditionalism.

Third, it is argued that rich institutions lead the way for the less affluent institutions in showing how to make good use of increasing resources as the funds for all of higher education grow. This argument may go into reverse in a period of declining real resources. In that case, the less-affluent institutions may be able to instruct their rich neighbors in how to cope with poverty.

Fourth, it is argued that diversity leading to cost differences among colleges and universities is essential to intellectual and cultural excellence. It is held that there is not enough money or talent to produce such excellence in every institution and that if all institutions were to subsist at the same level of cost per student, the result would be widely diffused mediocrity. The only feasible alternative, it is said, is to concentrate exceptionally talented students and faculty and abundant resources in a few institutions and thus to achieve a few peaks of excellence even at the cost of financial and educational poverty elsewhere. But even accepting the importance of special peaks of excellence there is no explanation of the fact that institutions that could be said to have reached the highest peaks of excellence operate at widely different costs per student.

Another approach to the puzzle of cost differences relates to academic freedom. It may be argued that academic freedom, which everyone admits is essential on non-economic grounds, will almost inevitably result in cost differences which appear to reflect uneconomical allocations of resources. According to this argument, since each institution is a semi-independent entity free to gather funds from all available sources and to exert some control over the use of these funds, costs per student unit will then be determined by the amount of money an institution is able to raise and by the number of student units it chooses (or is required) to serve. If this argument is accepted, cost differences among institutions will tend to be great, and indeed will exhibit a quality of randomness. It is as though the unit costs in the 3,000 American colleges and universities were determined by a vast, complicated, and decentralized philanthropic lottery rather than by rational decisions based on the economic allocation of resources.

This apparent randomness is tolerated in part because of a sincere belief that colleges and universities should enjoy freedom of thought and inquiry and therefore should be semiautonomous entities. It is also tolerated because no one knows with any certainty the relationship between money spent and true educational outcomes and it is perhaps desirable not to have all the educational eggs in one basket. However, many taxpayers, legislators, and donors suspect that wide variance in costs does not necessarily produce correspondingly varying results. The current concern of legislators and donors for cost analysis and accountability is an indication of the uneasiness with which public leaders view this situation and suggests the need for educators to give close attention to evaluation of results.

The data presented in this chapter provide no obvious standards as to the financial needs for conducting higher education. They tell nothing about the relationship between cost and educational, intellectual, or cultural excellence. They give no clues as to whether high-cost institutions are over-financed or low-cost institutions under-financed, nor do they reveal whether the total funds allotted to higher education are excessive or deficient. They point to no single best way to allocate resources within institutions. The data presented raise questions about the financing of education; they do not answer them. We shall return to these matters in Chapter Eight. Meanwhile we shall compare the expenditure patterns of affluent institutions with those of institutions of more modest means.

7

Institutional Affluence and Patterns of Resource Allocation

More than a century ago, a German statistician, Ernst Engel (1821–1896), studied the relationship between the incomes of families and the allocation of their expenditures among various classes of consumer goods. He (and many consumer economists after him) discovered that as incomes increase, the proportion spent for various purposes changes in a systematic way. Most such studies show that the percentages of income spent for food and other necessities decline, that the percentages spent for clothing and housing remain about constant, and that the percentages spent for other less urgent items increase. These relationships are known as Engel's law (see Houthakker, 1957). In his influential theory of employment, Lord Keynes also drew upon Engel's law with his assumption that as family incomes grow, the percentage of incomes saved increases. The purpose of this chapter is to discover whether there is an Engel's law of higher education—whether the expenditure patterns of colleges and universities vary in some systematic relationship to income.

The preceding chapter established that there are glaring differences among institutions in the amounts they spend per student unit for the education of their students. It also revealed equally wide differences in the way institutions allocate their expenditures among various programs and functions. Substantial disparities were found even among institutions having ostensibly similar programs conducted at seemingly comparable levels of performance. The evidence cited strongly suggested, but did not prove, that the amount and allocation of expenditures are not closely proportioned to educational outcomes.

In this chapter, the analysis is carried a step further by investigating the relationship between the affluence of institutions and the allocation of their expenditures among various budgetary components. The questions to be addressed are: How do the educational budgets of more affluent colleges and universities differ from those of their poorer neighbors? What can the more affluent institutions afford that the less well-to-do must do without? Answers to these questions may be suggestive in judging the intrinsic educational significance of those incremental expenditures institutions can afford to make as they become more well-off. This line of inquiry may provide some insights concerning the basic question addressed in this book: What levels of expenditure may be needed, or justified, to operate the American system of higher education?

A word of caution must precede this discussion. The available data do not permit observation of institutional budgets in detail. They give us only broad and general information that is suggestive but hardly definitive. Moreover, there is great diversity—even randomness—in the way institutions allocate their funds, and the correlations between affluence and expenditure patterns are weak. Most of the coefficients are less than 0.3, and only a few are greater than 0.5, though the signs tend to be consistent. Despite these obstacles, some interesting and pertinent relationships do emerge.

The allocation of resources within a college or university may be viewed in several different ways. One way is to consider the allocation of current expenditures among various functions such as teaching, student services, academic support, and so on. I shall call this *functional allocation*. A second way is to view the allocation of the same current expenditures among (1) compensation (salaries and fringe benefits) paid to various categories of staff, (2) purchases of goods and services such as fuel, stationery, books, and chemicals from outside the institution, and (3) scholarships and fellowships, which are also included in the functional allocation. I shall call this *recipient allocation* because the focus is on the division of expenditures among various categories of staff, outside vendors, and students. A third approach is to consider the allocation of resources to capital items such as physical plant and endowment. This, I shall call *capital allocation*. This chapter explores the relationship between the affluence of institutions and the allocation of their resources with respect to functional allocation, recipient allocation, and capital allocation.

Institutional *affluence* is defined simply as educational expenditures (or cost) per student unit. The more money an institution spends on education per student unit, the greater its affluence. The task before us is to show the relationship between the affluence of institutions as so defined and the way they spend their money. The data used in this chapter were derived from a representative sample of 268 institutions of all types, sizes, and geographic locations. (For a description of the data and their sources, see Appendix C.) For each dependent variable—for example, the percentage of educational expenditures devoted to student services—the relationship of that variable to institutional affluence was established by computing a straight-line regression curve using the least-squares method. The comparison for any variable between less affluent and more affluent institutions was then made by comparing points on the relevant regression curve that represent the least affluent fifth of the institutions and the most affluent fifth of institutions.

Affluence and the Functional Allocation of Expenditures

The data relating affluence to the functional distribution of expenditures are shown in Tables 17 and 18. These tables show comparative expenditure patterns for the most affluent fifth of the sample institutions and for the least affluent fifth. They show how institutions allocate their educational expenditures among the major functions of teaching, student services, scholarships and fellowships, academic support, institutional support, operation and maintenance of plant, and mandatory transfers and other.

Tables 17 and 18 reveal immediately that public and private institutions differ considerably in their expenditure patterns— entirely aside from the effects of affluence. For example, as shown in Table 17, public institutions devote 54 to 56 percent of educational expenditures to teaching, whereas private institutions allocate only about 44 percent. Similarly, private institutions spend a correspond-

Table 17. Functional allocation of educational expenditures, 268 representative colleges and universities, by institutional affluence, 1976–77

	Least affluent fifth of institutions		Most affluent fifth of institutions	
	Percentages	Dollar amounts per student unit	Percentages	Dollar amounts per student unit
All institutions, public and private				
Teaching	49.2%	$ 794	44.6%	$2,051
Student services	7.4	119	8.0	368
Scholarships and fellowships	7.9	127	12.4	570
Academic support	7.7	124	7.6	349
Institutional support	15.3	247	15.8	727
Operation and maintenance of plant	11.1	178	10.3	474
Mandatory transfers and other	1.4	23	1.3	60
Total	100.0	1,612	100.0	4,599
All public institutions				
Teaching	56.4%	$ 835	54.3%	$2,096
Student services	6.1	90	6.4	247
Scholarships and fellowships	4.6	68	5.3	204
Academic support	8.6	127	7.7	297
Institutional support	12.0	177	14.3	551
Operation and maintenance of plant	11.5	170	9.5	367
Mandatory transfers and other	0.8	12	2.5	96
Total	100.0	1,479	100.0	3,858
All private institutions				
Teaching	43.9%	$ 748	44.3%	$2,185
Student services	8.4	146	8.1	400
Scholarships and fellowships	10.8	187	13.7	675
Academic support	7.5	122	7.7	380
Institutional support	17.2	302	15.0	740
Operation and maintenance of plant	10.7	186	10.6	523
Mandatory transfers and other	1.5	27	0.6	30
Total	100.0	1,718	100.0	4,933

Source: Special tabulation of data from Higher Education General Information Survey. See Appendix C for detailed description of data.

Table 18. Functional allocation of educational expenditures, 268 representative colleges and universities, by institutional affluence and by type of institution, 1976–77

	Public institutions		Private institutions	
	Least affluent fifth	Most affluent fifth	Least affluent fifth	Most affluent fifth
Research and doctorate-granting universities				
Teaching	61.5%	54.8%	53.7%	56.3%
Student services	5.8	7.2	5.8	6.1
Scholarships and fellowships	6.6	6.2	8.0	12.5
Academic support	8.7	9.0	8.0	7.7
Institutional support	7.4	11.0	13.8	8.7
Operational and maintenance of plant	9.3	8.7	9.3	8.1
Mandatory transfers and other	0.7	3.1	1.4	0.6
Total	100.0	100.0	100.0	100.0
Comprehensive universities and colleges				
Teaching	58.3%	45.0%	48.9%	42.8%
Student services	5.3	5.5	7.3	8.6
Scholarships and fellowships	3.5	5.0	11.0[a]	11.5[a]
Academic support	10.2	6.8	6.6	6.4
Institutional support	9.9	20.1	14.2	18.2
Operational and maintenance of plant	12.5	11.7	10.3	9.6
Mandatory transfers and other	0.3	5.9	1.7	2.9
Total	100.0	100.0	100.0	100.0
Liberal arts colleges				
Teaching	—	—	38.5%	36.5%
Student services	—	—	9.2	10.0
Scholarships and fellowships	—	—	13.2	12.5
Academic support	—	—	7.0	8.2
Institutional support	—	—	19.3	18.4
Operational and maintenance of plant	—	—	11.1	12.8
Mandatory transfers and other	—	—	1.7	1.6
Total			100.0	100.0
Two-year colleges				
Teaching	54.8%	55.2%	38.1%	30.0%
Student services	7.1	7.0	11.2	10.9
Scholarships and fellowships	1.5	3.9	6.3	11.0
Academic support	7.1[a]	6.8[a]	9.0	5.5
Institutional support	17.4	15.6	20.5	28.6
Operational and maintenance of plant	11.9	11.4	12.6	14.0
Mandatory transfers and other	0.2	0.1	2.3	0.0
Total	100.0	100.0	100.0	100.0

[a]Estimates based on incomplete data.

Source: Special tabulation of data from Higher Education General Information Survey. See Appendix C for detailed description of data.

ingly higher percentage on scholarships and fellowships and on institutional support than public institutions. These differences may be explained partly by the relatively small size and higher tuition of private institutions: their overhead and managerial costs are spread over a limited volume of "business." These differences may be explained also by the need of private colleges and universities for expensive programs of public relations and development related to fund raising, for elaborate admissions programs related to student recruitment and selection, and for student aid to assist low-income students to meet high tuitions. Public institutions are spared some of these costs because they receive public subsidies and can, thus, devote a comparatively high percentage of their total expenditures to teaching. These basic differences between public and private institutions suggest that expenditure patterns should be studied separately for public and private institutions.

Comparison of the expenditure patterns of the least affluent and the most affluent institutions, classified by type, shows remarkably small differences. Presumably, as institutions become richer they spread their additional money around so that almost all functions get a share. This behavior is consistent with the opinion of most educators that needs are almost unlimited and that almost every department or function could put additional funds to good use. It is also consistent with internal institutional politics, in which every sector of an institution presses constantly for more funds and demands a "fair share" when additional resources are available. Whatever the reason, it is astonishing that the most affluent fifth of the institutions and least affluent fifth allocate their spending among various functions and programs in roughly the same proportions. This finding is on the whole confirmed by separate data on expenditures for libraries as related to institutional affluence. Although library costs constitute only a tiny percentage of institutional budgets, they are considered important to academic quality and are often regarded as status symbols. Library costs also are subject to rapid inflation in the prices of books and periodicals. Thus, expenditures for libraries might be expected to command a larger percentage of the budget in rich colleges and universities than in poor institutions. But, in fact, the percentages of educational and general expenditures devoted to libraries are roughly similar in both. Public two-year colleges are the only significant exception to this generalization.

Closer scrutiny of the data in Tables 17 and 18, however, reveals certain tendencies worth noting. First, the percentage spent on teaching is somewhat smaller among richer institutions than among the poorer ones. However, two categories of institutions—private research and doctorate-granting universities and public two-year colleges—do not follow this pattern. Second, the percentage spent on operation and maintenance of plant is somewhat smaller for the most affluent fifth of institutions than for the least affluent fifth. Two categories of institutions—private liberal arts colleges and private two-year colleges—are exceptions in this area. Third, the percentage spent for student services generally is a little greater among well-to-do institutions than among poorer ones. Fourth, with two exceptions, the percentage spent for scholarships and fellowships is a bit larger among the most affluent than among the least affluent. Finally, the percentages spent for academic support, institutional support, and mandatory transfers show no clear relationship to affluence.[1]

These are far from dramatic conclusions. In view of the limited size of the sample on which they are based and the wide dispersion among institutions in expenditure patterns, the most reliable overall conclusion is that the expenditure patterns do not vary much in response to differences in affluence. As funds increase, they are rather evenly allocated to various programs and functions. In response to the question of what rich institutions can afford that poor institutions must do without, our answer is that rich ones can afford more of everything and in about the same proportions. On the whole, they spend a somewhat smaller percentage for teaching and physical plant operation and maintenance, and a somewhat larger percentage for student financial aid and student services. But

[1]These findings are based on cross-sectional data for 1976–77. One would expect the effects of institutional affluence to appear also in longitudinal data that show changing expenditure patterns in the entire higher educational system during the 1950s and 1960s, a period of increasing revenues. In fact, the percentages spent for teaching and for plant operations and maintenance declined from 67 percent to 61 percent over this period (National Center for Education Statistics, *Digest of Education Statistics, 1977–78,* 1978, p. 134).

they generally distribute their affluence widely among all functions and programs.

These findings suggest that the allocation of academic expenditures by functions is much less sensitive to differences in income than are the allocations of family expenditures; Engel's law does not seem applicable to the budgets of higher education. However, insofar as academic budgets do respond to income, teaching and plant operation and maintenance appear to be the "necessities" of higher education—analogous to food in family budgets. Once these necessities have been provided, institutions devote relatively more of their resources to "luxuries" such as student financial aid and student services.

Had I expected to find clear and pronounced regularities in the effect of affluence on the expenditure patterns, along the lines of Engel's law, I would have been disappointed by these sparse results. But my expectation was that there would be a kind of randomness in the internal allocation of resources and that relative affluence would bear a weak relationship to expenditure patterns. These expectations were based on two assumptions. First, since there is such pervasive ignorance about the effect of different allocations on educational outcomes and since colleges and universities are at least partly spared the discipline of profit-seeking and of the marketplace, there would be only the vaguest norms toward which expenditure patterns would tend to converge. Second, internal politics within each institution would tend to perpetuate whatever allocations had developed in the past as part of the unique historical development of each institution. The data presented are at least consistent with these expectations. But it would be prudent to reserve judgment on these matters until recipient allocation and capital allocation are considered.

Affluence and the Allocation of Expenditures to Recipients

Most of the current educational expenditures of colleges and universities are paid out as compensation—salaries and fringe benefits—to employees. These include faculty, administrators, other professional persons, and nonprofessional persons. The balance of the educational expenditures is paid out partly to outside vendors for the purchase of goods and services and partly to students for scholarships and fellowships. In this section, we shall explore the relationship between institutional affluence and the allocation of resources among these various recipient groups. The first task is to review data on the numbers of staff and on their average rates of compensation.

Staff numbers. Institutions of higher education differ greatly in their use of personnel. The effect of affluence on size of staff is by no means uniform or regular. By comparing the average staffing of the most affluent fifth of institutions with that of the least affluent fifth, however, some broad general relationships emerge. Tables 19 and 20 show such comparisons for all institutions combined and for various categories of institutions. In these tables, staff numbers are expressed as full-time-equivalent employees per 1,000 student units. The number of staff members is adjusted to include only those engaged in

Table 19. Number of full-time-equivalent staff per thousand student units, 268 representative colleges and universities, by institutional affluence and type of institution, 1976–77

	Least affluent fifth of institutions	Most affluent fifth of institutions	Ratio of most affluent to least affluent
All institutions, public and private			
Faculty	36	60	1.7
Administrators	5	11	2.2
Other	63	155	2.5
All staff combined	104	226	2.2
All public institutions			
Faculty	33	43	1.3
Administrators	4	6	1.5
Other	65	112	1.7
All staff combined	102	161	1.6
All private institutions			
Faculty	40	67	1.7
Administrators	7	14	2.0
Other	61	157	2.6
All staff combined	108	238	2.2

Note: Includes only the prorated portion of the staff allocated to educational services. Excludes the portion allocated to research, public service, auxiliary enterprises, and other activities.

Source: Special tabulation of data from Higher Education General Information Survey. See Appendix C for detailed description of data.

Table 20. Number of full-time-equivalent staff per thousand student units, 268 representative colleges and universities, by institutional affluence and type of institution, 1976–1977

	Public institutions			Private institutions		
	Least affluent fifth	Most affluent fifth	Ratio of most affluent to least affluent	Least affluent fifth	Most affluent fifth	Ratio of most affluent to least affluent
Research and doctorate-granting universities						
Faculty	27	47	1.7	30[a]	68	2.3
Other staff	75	208	2.8	81	191	2.4
Total	102	255	2.5	111	259	2.3
Comprehensive universities and colleges						
Faculty	46	63	1.4	42	57	1.4
Other staff	66	104	1.6	55	161	2.9
Total	112	167	1.5	97	218	2.3
Liberal arts colleges						
Faculty	—	—	—	60	80	1.3
Other staff	—	—	—	72	188	2.6
Total	—	—	—	132	268	2.0
Two-year colleges						
Faculty	30	34	1.1	—	—	—
Other staff	53	73	1.4	—	—	—
Total	83	107	1.3	—	—	—

[a] Estimate based on incomplete data.

Source: Special tabulation of data from Higher Education General Information Survey. See Appendix C for detailed description of data.

educational services (as distinguished from organized research, auxiliary enterprises, public service, and so on).

As would be expected, the tables show that the number of staff per 1,000 student units is far greater in the more well-to-do institutions than in the less prosperous ones. A pronounced effect of affluence is to expand staff of all kinds relative to the student body. Surprisingly, however, as institutions become more affluent the numbers of administrative and nonprofessional staff increase more than the numbers of faculty. The fruits of growing affluence lie more largely in additional administrative and nonprofessional staff than in additional faculty.

This finding is consistent with the results obtained by Strein and McMahon (1979, p. 1) who hypothesized that "administrative expense in a university system is a function of discretionary revenue. Discretionary revenue is defined as that part of the current operating budget over and above that required to maintain the minimum quantity and quality of activities acceptable to the governing agencies." They concluded "that there is a tradeoff between quality improvement and administrative expense" (p. 22). (See also Legislative Analyst, State of California, 1977.)

Two incidental findings on staffing are also of interest. Well-to-do colleges and universities tend to have a substantially higher proportion of their full-time faculties in the rank of professor than do less affluent institutions. Professors constitute 31 percent of the faculty in the most affluent fifth of institutions, and 20 percent in the least affluent fifth. With respect to faculty women, the situation is reversed. In the more affluent institutions 18 percent of the full-time faculty are women, and in the least affluent institutions 21 percent. These differences are consistent among all types of institutions, with the exceptions of public two-year institutions (for percentage of professors) and private liberal arts colleges (for percentage of women). One result of affluence is that institutions can afford relatively more senior professors; a result of poverty is that institutions employ relatively more faculty women—presumably because women's salaries are less costly.

Faculty Salaries. The more affluent colleges and universities pay higher faculty salaries on the average than their less well-to-do neighbors. The differences, however, are not very wide. Faculty salaries are determined largely in the competitive national market for qualified professional personnel. At least in the long run, all colleges and universities must offer salaries high enough to attract and retain minimally qualified people who might otherwise be employed in government, other nonprofit organizations, private business, or the independent professions; and they need pay no more than is necessary to attract and retain such persons. These conditions tend to restrict the range of average salaries. The more affluent institutions do, of course, attempt to lure the most capable talent and therefore tend to pay premium salaries. As shown in Table 21, this premium is about 8 percent for all institutions combined and is of the order of 5 to 25 percent within any category of institutions. If, however, one compares the average faculty salary in the most affluent group of research and doctorate-granting institutions with that in the least affluent

Table 21. Mean salary, full-time faculty all ranks, 268 representative colleges and universities, by institutional affluence and type of institution, 1975–76

	Least affluent fifth of institutions	Most affluent fifth of institutions	Ratio of most affluent to least affluent
Research and doctorate-granting universities			
Public	$13,200	$16,000	1.21
Private	13,810	17,425	1.26
Comprehensive universities and colleges			
Public	12,700	13,700	1.08
Private	11,395	12,569	1.10
Liberal arts colleges, private	11,283	12,921	1.15
Two-year colleges, public	11,200	11,800	1.05
All institutions			
Public	12,300	14,600	1.19
Private	11,894	13,885	1.17
Total	12,570	13,534	1.08

Note: These figures represent the unweighted means of the mean salaries of institutions. Because of the composition of the institutions in the sample, these figures are lower than the true means weighted by numbers of faculty members.
Source: Special tabulation of data from Higher Education General Information Survey. See Appendix C for detailed description of data.

two-year colleges, the premium is about 56 percent. The difference is far less than that for total educational expenditures per student unit, which runs two to three times as much in the more affluent institutions as in the less affluent ones.

Total Outlay for Faculty Salaries. One of the most significant cost figures relating to colleges and universities is *total outlay for faculty salaries*. This figure reflects the combination of average salary paid and number of faculty employed. When expressed in terms of student units, it is perhaps the best measure of an institution's direct commitment to instruction and possibly one of the better measures of the academic effort of institutions. Table 22 compares total faculty salary outlay (for full-time faculty only) per student unit for the least affluent and the most affluent institutions. Generally, the most affluent ones spend 1.4 to 2.2 times as much for faculty salaries as the least

Table 22. Total expenditures for faculty salaries per student unit, full-time faculty all ranks, 268 representative colleges and universities, by institutional affluence and by type of institution, 1975–76.

	Least affluent fifth of institutions	Most affluent fifth of institutions	Ratio of most affluent to least affluent
Research and doctorate-granting universities			
Public	$283	$589	2.1
Private	368	569	1.6
Comprehensive universities and colleges			
Public	421	621	1.5
Private	270	600	2.2
Liberal arts colleges, private	559	902	1.6
Two-year colleges, public	375	536	1.4
All institutions			
Public	365	515	1.4
Private	404	783	1.9
Total	375	702	1.8

Source: Special tabulation of data from Higher Education General Information Survey. See Appendix C for detailed description of data.

affluent ones. However total educational expenditures per student unit for all purposes in the most affluent institutions averages around 2.9 times that in the least affluent ones (Table 17). Thus, as total expenditures for all purposes increase, the proportion spent directly for teaching tends to decline.

Allocations to All Recipients. Unfortunately, inadequacy of data has prevented extending the analysis to the salaries of administrators and other staff, and the purchase of goods and services from outside vendors. Therefore, any effort to present the allocation of total expenditures by recipient groups must rely on rough estimates that show general orders of magnitude but not precise numbers. Table 23 presents the relevant figures, drawn from sources including detailed budgetary information from a small sample of institutions. Table 23 should be regarded as no more than a model or illustration and not as a compilation of accurate statistics.

The conclusions to be drawn from the data regarding recipient allocations, as illustrated and summarized in Table 23, are that as institutions become more affluent: they spend substantially more for everything—all categories of faculty and other staff, purchased goods and services, and scholarships and fellowships; they spend proportionately much less for faculty and moderately less for other staff; and they spend proportionately much more for scholarships and fellowships. These conclusions differ from those obtained from our analysis of the functional allocation of resources, earlier in this chapter. As institutions become more affluent, they allocate their funds among programs or functions in a fairly even way. But the analysis of the recipient allocations shows that funds are not appropriated evenly among the various groups. Affluent institutions spend a larger portion of their budget for purchased goods and services and a smaller portion for faculty than do less wealthy institutions.

There is no logical inconsistency between the two sets of results. Affluent institutions allocate their resources more or less equally among programs, and a larger percentage of their "luxury" spending consists of purchases from outside vendors, while a smaller percentage is reserved for staff compensation. Thus, the two sets of conclusions suggest what every economist knows: Successive increments of expenditure are devoted to successively less important objects. When

Table 23. Illustrative model of the recipient allocation of educational expenditures, 268 representative universities and colleges, by institutional affluence, 1975–76

	Least affluent fifth of institutions		Most affluent fifth of institutions	
	Dollar amount per student unit	Percentage	Dollar amount per student unit	Percentage
Employee compensation				
Faculty	$ 823	51%	$1,640	36%
Other staff	452	28	1,508	33
Subtotal	1,275	79	3,148	69
Purchased goods and services	210	13	872	19
Scholarships and fellowships	127	8	570	12
Total	1,612	100	4,590	100

Note: The assumptions used in calculating these estimates are as follows: fringe benefits are 15 percent of salaries; average administrative salaries are 130 percent of average faculty salaries; average salaries of special support staff are 75 percent of faculty salaries; average nonprofessional salaries are 66 percent of faculty salaries. These estimates are based in part on Bowen (1978a). Expenditures for scholarships and fellowships are taken from Table 17. Expenditures for purchased goods and services were estimated as a residual after all other items had been estimated.

expenditures are viewed as they are allocated among programs, affluent institutions support all programs more richly, without much discrimination among them. When allocation among various recipient groups is considered, it is clear that affluent institutions allot a much smaller share for faculty, a slightly smaller share for nonacademic personnel, and a much greater share for purchased goods and services than poorer institutions. Using the analogy supplied by Engel's law, we may describe institutional budgets by noting that the faculty is the necessity of higher education, comparable to food and housing for families; that the services rendered by nonacademic staff are the intermediate goods, comparable to clothing and transportation; and that the goods and services purchased from outside are the luxuries, comparable to recreation and savings.

Affluence and Capital Assets

Colleges and universities acquire capital assets such as land and buildings, durable equipment, and income-earning investments, just as families do, by saving. Saving is the act of refraining from spending some or all of the money received. Higher educational institutions seldom save substantial amounts from their ordinary current receipts, derived from appropriations, tuitions, and unrestricted gifts. Their savings are more likely to be in the form of public appropriations designated for physical plant or private gifts designated either for physical plant or endowment. However, some institutions set aside reserves from current receipts, and some institutions acquire physical plant and endowment by following a rule that sizable gifts, even if unrestricted, should be used for these purposes. This section is concerned with physical plant and endowment as they are related to institutional affluence.

Physical Plant. Table 24 compares the actual square feet of building space per student unit in the least affluent and the most affluent institutions. As would be expected, the richer institutions acquire and use substantially more physical plant per student unit than their poorer counterparts.[2] Generally, however, as affluence increases, the

---

[2]This is true whether one uses data on book value of physical plant assets, square footage of building space for educational and general purposes, or square footage of building space devoted directly to the instruction program (as distinct from research, public service, administration, and the like).

Table 24. Total building space and expenditures for additions to physical plant, 268 representative colleges and universities, by institutional affluence and type of institution, 1975–76

	Square footage of total building space per student unit[a]		Expenditures for additions to physical plant as percentages of total educational and general expenditures[b]	
	Least affluent fifth	Most affluent fifth	Least affluent fifth	Most affluent fifth
Research and doctorate-granting universities				
Public	97	109	18%	12%
Private	70	170	15	8
Comprehensive universities and colleges				
Public	69	118	25	7
Private	64	167	13	12
Liberal arts colleges, private	163	207	14	11
Two-year colleges, public	60	90	13	8
All institutions (unweighted)				
Public	84	100	19	10
Private	77	218	14	11
Total	80	180	16	10

[a] Includes space for research and public service but excludes hospitals and residential facilities.

[b] Includes land, buildings, and major equipment. Since physical plant is used for research and public service as well as teaching, expenditures for additions to physical plant are related to educational and general expenditures rather than to educational expenditures only.

Source: Special tabulation of data from Higher Education General Information Survey. See Appendix C for detailed description of data.

amount of building space per student increases less than proportionately. Whereas total educational expenditures per student are nearly three times as great in the most affluent fifth of institutions as in the least affluent fifth, building space per student is on the average only a little more than twice as great. This relationship, however, varies for different types of institutions.

Table 24 also presents data on expenditures for additions to physical plant. For purposes of comparison, these expenditures are expressed as a percentage of educational and general expenditures. As the table shows, expenditures of the most affluent institutions for new physical plant are smaller relative to educational and general expenditures than the plant expenditures of the least affluent institutions.

Table 25 provides information on building space assigned directly to instruction. The percentage of building space assigned to classrooms is smaller in the more affluent colleges and universities than in the less affluent institutions. Yet, as shown in the same table, the percentage of building space assigned to instruction in all its aspects is greater in the more affluent institutions. More affluent institutions have a variety of instructional facilities other than barebone classrooms: laboratories, studios, study areas, faculty offices, and the like. Their instructional facilities are more varied and ample and possibly more luxurious.

Endowment. Size of endowment is also related to institutional affluence. Endowments are derived primarily from private gifts and are found in substantial amounts mostly in private colleges. Public institutions occasionally acquire endowments from earnings on patents and royalties, from private gifts, and historically from land grants. However, according to the Council for Financial Aid to Education (1979) only 17 of the 1,300 public institutions in the United States have endowments whose market value in 1977–78 was in excess of $20 million (an amount that might yield an average annual income of $1 million or more). Neither are substantial endowments the general rule in the private sector. Only about 100 of the 1,400 private institutions have endowments in excess of $20 million. For all of American higher education combined, endowments provide only about 2 percent of the aggregate revenues, though of course they provide much more for a minority of fortunate institutions.

Table 25. Building space for instruction, 268 representative universities and colleges, by institutional affluence and type of institution, 1975–76

	Square footage of building space for instruction per student unit		Classrooms as percentage of building space	
	Least affluent fifth of institutions	Most affluent fifth of institutions	Least affluent fifth of institutions	Most affluent fifth of institutions
Research and doctorate-granting universities				
Public	41	47	9%	6%
Private	30	63	13	8
Comprehensive universities and colleges				
Public	36	56	13	10
Private	29	77	17	13
Liberal arts colleges, private	74	84	14	11
Two-year colleges, public	34	52	18	15
All institutions (unweighted)				
Public	39	45	12	9
Private	42	90	15	10
Total	40	73	14	10

Note: Building space for instruction excludes health care and residential facilities.

Source: Special tabulation of data from Higher Education General Information Survey. See Appendix C for detailed description of data.

As shown in Table 26, the most affluent fifth of the institutions have many times the endowment of the least affluent fifth. This is true for two reasons. First, endowment generates an income that helps institutions to become affluent, that is, to spend relatively large amounts per student unit. To build endowment, however, an institution must already be relatively affluent in the sense that it regularly receives a surplus of funds (usually in the form of gifts and grants) that is not desperately needed to finance current operations or capital expenditures and that can be set aside as savings. Therefore, endowment per student unit tends to be greater among the more affluent institutions than among the less affluent ones, and it tends to be proportionately greater in relation to the degree of affluence. Whereas the top fifth of institutions of various types spend per student unit about three times the amount spent by the bottom fifth, the top fifth hold six to twenty-eight times the amount of endowment per student unit.

Table 26. Average endowment at market value and average endowment per student unit, representative sample of 154 private four-year institutions, by institutional affluence and by type of institution, 1977–78

	Least affluent fifth of institutions	Most affluent fifth of institutions
Average total endowment per institution		
Research and doctorate-granting universities	$22,181,000	$258,630,000
Comprehensive universities and colleges	7,399,000	20,703,000
Liberal arts colleges	2,636,000	29,028,000
Average endowment per student unit		
Research and doctorate-granting universities	$1,550	$25,520
Comprehensive universities and colleges	1,040	6,490
Liberal arts colleges	666	19,025

Note: These 154 institutions are included in the basic sample of 268 institutions used throughout this chapter.
Source: Council for Financial Aid to Education, 1979, pp. 13–62.

Concluding Comments

My findings on the relationship between institutional affluence and budgetary allocations are essentially very simple. Well-to-do institutions have more of everything than poor institutions. They spend more on their various programs such as teaching, student services, or administration; they employ more staff members of all kinds; they pay higher compensation; they have more senior faculty and fewer women; they buy more goods and services from outside vendors; they enjoy a more opulent physical plant; and they accumulate more endowment. The more well-to-do institutions do not, however, spend for everything in proportion to their affluence. They are in some respects selective—allocating relatively more or less along some lines of expenditure than others. In allocating expenditures among various functions, more affluent institutions as compared with less affluent ones:

- devote a smaller percentage of their current expenditures to educational purposes
- devote a smaller percentage of their outlays to physical plant
- devote a somewhat larger percentage of their expenditures to student services and student financial aid
- employ a much larger nonacademic staff, including administrators, specialist support staff, and nonprofessional persons
- purchase a much larger amount of goods and services from outside vendors
- accumulate relatively more endowment

The most significant finding is that as institutions become more affluent they spend a smaller portion of their budget for instructional functions and more on nonacademic staff and purchases of goods and services from outside. This condition is well illustrated by the following statistics: the least affluent fifth of the institutions employ twenty-two faculty members for each $1 million of educational expenditures; whereas, the most affluent fifth employ thirteen faculty members for each $1 million spent. As institutions become increasingly affluent, they seem to create overlays of administrators, secretaries, clerks, assistants, counselors, office equipment, travel, stationery, supplies, in relation to the amount of resources devoted directly to education, which takes place primarily when faculty members are in the presence of students and when faculty and students are quietly studying. It is not surprising that more affluent institutions apply their incremental expenditures to successively less important purposes. Families, and to some extent profit-seeking businesses, behave in the same way. This pattern of allocation may be related to institutional lifestyle more than to educational quality or performance and may explain why some low-budget institutions are able to achieve educational results that appear to be about as good as those of high-budget institutions. Indeed, the proportion of the budget or of the payroll that is allocated directly to teaching if it reaches a very high level may be an indication of poverty, but within reasonable limits it may also be an indication of efficiency.

In discussions of higher educational efficiency, the spotlight often is focused on faculty because they along with their students are at the front-line of the educational process. Enormous emphasis is given to the "faculty-student ratio," and there are many suggestions to the effect that higher education could and should reduce the size of the faculty in relation to the number of students. When it is understood that faculty members represent only about a third of the entire personnel employed in higher education (Table 19) and only about half the payroll, and when it is realized that direct expenditures for teaching have been a declining percentage of total expenditures over a long period, a strong case can be made that economies should be sought in the nonacademic part of institutional budgets rather than in the academic part. The focus should be on the ratio of nonacademic staff to students rather than on the ratio of faculty to students.

The tendency as institutions become richer to devote a smaller proportion of their resources to teaching suggests, but does not prove, that educational outcomes or quality do not necessarily increase in proportion to total resources. At least, in this matter, the burden of proof may be on the more affluent institutions.

8

Effect of Institutional Affluence on Educational Outcomes

One of the most lamentable blind spots in the study of higher education is the lack of reliable information on the relationship between the educational expenditures of colleges and universities and their educational results. There is no shortage of claims that more funds will produce commensurately greater educational returns. And there is no shortage of estimates of institutional "quality" based on the amount of money spent. Indeed, institutions are commonly ranked on the basis of their faculty salaries, faculty-student ratios, number of books in the library, and student scores on entrance examination, all of which are resource inputs. Institutions are seldom judged on the basis of actual educational performance as measured by the personal growth of students that reasonably can be attributed to their educational experience.

As O'Neill (1971, pp. 43-44) observed:

> We are now faced with the issue of whether or not differences in inputs per credit hour among the different schools can be taken to reflect quality differences. Under the conditions of a perfect market with a working price system, one could say yes with some confidence. But in the education industry there are grounds for doubt. The different kinds of schools are financed in different ways. This prob-

ably results in differing degrees of insulation from the
market. Unfortunately, the effects of public control on
efficiency, or of philanthropic support in non-profit institutions, have received so little study by economists that no
answer can be given. Casual speculation suggests that the
quality differences implied by these estimates of inputs per
credit hour are probably in the right direction, though the
magnitudes of the true differences may be more or less.

In a previous study, I explored the relationship between various
characteristics of colleges and universities and their educational outcomes (Bowen, 1977). Among the characteristics considered were size
of institutions, faculty salaries, curricular emphasis, method of instruction, religious emphasis, extracurricular activities, residential
arrangements, and student-faculty relationships. The outcomes were
defined in terms of "value added," that is, desirable change in students from the way they were as entering freshmen to the way they
were as graduating seniors. Though available data were sparse and
not wholly consistent, several tentative conclusions emerged. First, it
was found that on the average the graduating seniors from various
institutions differed widely on outcomes such as academic achievement, religious interest, and esthetic sensibility. Also it was found
that at most colleges, regardless of specific characteristics, considerable value added occurred as students were transformed from
freshmen to seniors. But the surprising conclusion was that differences among institutions in value added were slight. Small,
parochial, low-cost institutions were bringing about changes comparable in magnitude to those occurring in large, cosmopolitan, and
expensive institutions. The differences among institutions' graduating seniors, which were substantial, could be explained largely by
differences among the same students when they were entering freshmen, which was also substantial. Those institutions that recruited the
ablest students produced the ablest graduates; those admitting students with strong religious interest produced religiously interested
graduates, and so on. The general conclusion was elaborated as
follows "On the whole, the evidence supports the hypothesis that the
differences in impact are relatively small—when impact is defined as
"value added" in the form of change in students during the college

years. But this conclusion hardly comes as a surprise, for the benefits from college education are so widely available, and the overlap among colleges in the environmental features they offer is so great, that striking differences in outcomes are unlikely" (1977, p. 257).

This conclusion was, however, offered with some reservations. A few studies had shown modest institutional differences in value added. Also, several studies of economists had indicated that the returns to higher education as measured by lifetime earnings of alumni were higher for persons who had attended high-cost institutions than for those who had attended less affluent institutions. And in any event, much of the data pertinent to the question of outcome differences were fragmentary and inconclusive. In particular, most of the data did not deal directly with the basic issue of concern in this chapter, namely, the relationship, if any, between the affluence of particular institutions and the value added in the form of educational outcomes they are able to generate.

We have seen (Chapter Six) that there are wide differences among institutions in affluence as measured by costs per student unit, and that substantial cost differences are found even among institutions that share the same mission and *seemingly* achieve that mission to about the same degree. Here we shall be exploring in greater depth the relationship between costs per student unit and various indicators of educational outcomes.

In preparing this chapter, the assistance of C. Robert Pace and his colleague, Oscar Porter, both of the University of California at Los Angeles, was invaluable. Full responsibility for the results and for their interpretation, however, rests with the author.

Affluence and Educational Benefits

In one series of studies, Pace (1974) measured the educational outcomes of higher education by asking large samples of students about the benefits they had received. He collected data from a random sample of juniors and seniors in sixty-seven public and private institutions. The students were presented with a list of educational benefits and were asked: "In thinking over your experience in college up to now, to what extent do you feel that you have made progress or been benefited in each of the following respects?" Students were to respond by choosing "very little," "some," "quite a bit," and "very much."

The student responses were assigned weights from 100 ("very little") to 400 ("very much"), and a mean score between 100 and 400 was computed for each institution with respect to each benefit.

The list of benefits included (pp. 51–52):

1. Benefits related to knowledge, understanding, and intellectual skills:

    Critical thinking—logic, inference, nature and limitations of knowledge

    Background and specialization for further education in some professional, scientific, or scholarly field

    Broadened literary acquaintance and appreciation

    Understanding and appreciation of science and technology

    Awareness of different philosophies, cultures, and ways of life

    Aesthetic sensitivity—appreciation and enjoyment of art, music, drama

    Vocabulary, terminology, and facts in various fields of knowledge

    Writing and speaking—clear, correct, effective communication

2. Benefits related to personal development and interpersonal relationships:

    Social development—experience and skills in relating to other people

    Personal development—understanding one's abilities and limitations, interests, and standards of behavior

    Appreciation of individuality and independence of thought and action

    Development of friendships and loyalties of lasting value

    Tolerance and understanding of other people and their values

3. Benefits related to preparation for practical life:

    Vocational training—skills and techniques directly applicable to a job

    Citizenship—understanding and interest in the style and quality of civic and political life

    Appreciation of religion—moral and ethical standards

    Bases for improved social and economic status

Table 27 shows the correlations between these scores for each institution in Pace's study and the costs per student derived from the Higher Education General Information Survey. Although Pace's data were gathered in 1968–69, the cost data for that year were not available and cost data for 1972–73 were used. Because the relative expenditures of institutions change slowly, the lapse of time between the two sets of data is probably not significant.

Table 27 and the illustrative scatter diagrams presented in Figure 4 show rather substantial correlations between benefits and costs with respect to more than two thirds of the several educational benefits. The inference is that most benefits, as perceived by advanced undergraduates, bear some relationship to institutional expenditures for instruction. Of course, the benefits students believe they are receiving may not correspond with the true outcomes. Yet these correlations cannot be dismissed lightly. Students may well be the best judges of what is happening to them during their college years. And one must ask: What better source is presently available?

In Table 27, a high positive correlation for any particular benefit indicates that affluent institutions yield a greater return, as reported by juniors and seniors, than low-expenditure institutions; a high negative correlation indicates that affluent institutions produce a smaller benefit than financially poor institutions; a correlation of under .20—either positive or negative—indicates that the benefit is not significantly related to expenditures per student. The four negative correlations between benefits and institutional affluence seem quite plausible. The negative correlation for vocational training means that, on the whole, more affluent institutions devote less attention to vocational programs than do less affluent institutions. The negative correlation for social and economic status probably indicates that low-expenditure institutions draw more upwardly mobile persons from low-income and low-status families than do affluent institutions. The negative correlation for religion probably indicates that the well-known tendency for students' formal religious interest and observance to decline during the college years is more pronounced in well-to-do than in low-budget institutions. The low positive correlations for vocabulary, friendships and loyalties, and citizenship probably reflect the ability of all institutions, regardless of relative affluence, to produce results with respect to these benefits.

Table 27. Relationships between educational expenditures per student and mean scores of educational benefits, sixty-seven colleges and universities, 1968–69

	Coefficient of correlation[a]	Increase in mean scores associated with a doubling of expenditures per student from $1,000 to $2,000	
		Percentage increase in mean scores[b]	Increase in mean score as a percentage of standard deviation
Knowledge, understanding, and intellectual skills			
Critical thinking	.41	4%	92%
Background for further study	.30	3	65
Broadened literary acquaintance	.55	9	125
Science and technology	.06	2	—
Awareness of different philosophies and cultures	.49	8	113
Aesthetic sensitivity	.33	6	77
Vocabulary, terminology, and facts	.16	1	—
Writing and speaking	-.19	-3	—
Personal development and interpersonal relationships			
Social development	.28	3	62
Personal development	.38	4	86
Individuality and independence	.55	9	127
Friendships and loyalties	.04	1	—
Tolerance and understanding	.47	7	51
Practical affairs			
Vocational training	-.55	-20	—
Citizenship	.07	1	—
Social and economic status	-.44	-7	—
Religion	-.45	-21	—

Note: Expenditures are those for instruction and departmental research in 1972–73. Mean scores are weighted on the following scale: very little = 100; some = 200; quite a bit = 300; very much = 400 (Pace, 1974).

[a] Coefficients of less than .20 are not significant and are assumed to imply little or no relationship.

[b] Computed from straight-line regression coefficient.

Figure 4. Scatter diagrams and regression curves showing relationships between educational expenditures per student and mean scores of educational benefits

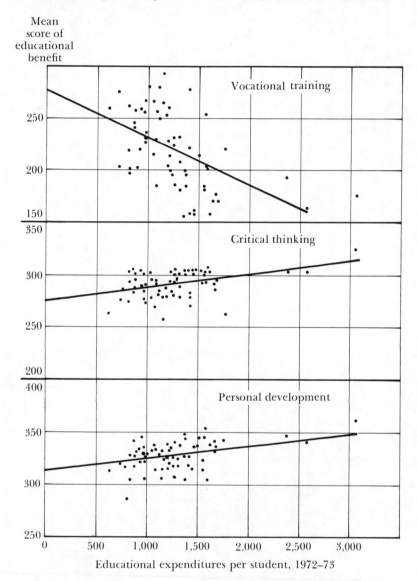

Mean score of educational benefit

Educational expenditures per student, 1972–73

The only surprises are low correlations for writing and speaking and science and technology. One would have expected these to loom relatively large in the more affluent institutions. One possible explanation is that few faculty members in any institutions, rich or poor, are willing to assume the difficult tasks of teaching communication skills and supervising undergraduate science laboratories. For the remaining benefits, the presumption is that increased educational expenditures per student lead to greater outcomes.

Table 27 also presents data derived from straight-line regression curves which indicate for each type of benefit the amount of change associated, on the average, with a doubling of institutional expenditure per student from $1,000 to $2,000. This measurement allows us to estimate the relationship between increases in expenditures and changes in benefits. The results are at first sight less than spectacular. For the most part, changes in the mean scores reflecting benefits are tiny compared with the assumed doubling of expenditures. In only three cases are they as much as 9 percent; the median is 4 percent for those benefits for which the sign of the index is positive and 1 percent for all seventeen benefits. It is, of course, difficult to interpret changes in mean scores based on student reports that are couched in terms of "very little," "some," "quite a bit," and "very much." It is possible, for example, that a 4 percent shift in the mean score from 250 (halfway between "some" and "quite a bit") to 260 (three-fifths of the way between "some" and "quite a bit") would be a major change well worth a doubling of cost. The difficulty here is that the index of benefit provides only ordinal information, expressing more or less, not cardinal information indicating amounts of change. So it is not really clear from the data how much change is represented by the median gain of 4 percent associated with a doubling of expenditure. In any case, the important comparison to make is not between the percentage increase in expenditure and the percentage increase in benefit, but rather the increase in expenditure and the improvement in the lives of students. If a doubling of educational expenditures from $1,000 to $2,000 a year improved the lives of students by 4 percent along many dimensions, the cost over four years of college would be only $4,000. But the benefit to a student over a lifetime of sixty years would be 4 percent of the value of a whole human life and would surely exceed $4,000. In short, it is not necessary to achieve huge increases in benefits to justify investments in educational excellence.

In interpreting the data in Table 27, it is useful also to consider the changes in mean scores relative to the standard deviations. The third column of the table shows the increases in scores (associated with a doubling of the expenditures for student) as percentages of the standard deviations. As these figures indicate, the change associated with a doubling of cost ranges from a half to more than a whole standard deviation, suggesting that the effect of additional money on outcomes may be considerable.

The comparison of institutional affluence and student's perceptions of benefits yields correlations that are substantial but not overwhelming. Affluence has some effect on outcomes, yet the data leave considerable uncertainty as to the degree and strength of this effect.

Parenthetically note that the data presented in this section were derived from a merged sample of public and private institutions. The data also were analyzed separately for public and private institutions. The results were on the whole similar for the two groups. With respect to fourteen of the seventeen educational benefits, however, the correlations were higher for private than for public institutions. The exceptions were social and economic status, tolerance and understanding, and science and technology. The correlations for the private group were substantially higher for personal development, critical thinking, writing and speaking, broadened literary acquaintance, awareness of different philosophies and cultures, social development, and individuality and independence.

Affluence and Academic Environment

In another study, using data for 1968–69, Pace (1972) gathered information from upperclassmen about various features of the academic environments of a sample of 265 institutions. He developed the College and University Environment Scales (CUES) to measure the following features: campus morale, quality of teaching, and the institution's degree of emphasis on practicality, scholarship, community, awareness (of self, of society, and of aesthetic stimuli), and propriety. These environmental features, though not directly reflecting educational outcomes, would seem to be related to outcomes, thus it is of interest to correlate educational expenditures per student with the CUES scores.

Pace derived the scores by presenting to sophomores, juniors, and seniors a list of over 100 statements regarding institutional characteristics. The following are examples of such statements:

- The professors really push the students' capacities to the limit.
- Concerts and arts exhibits always draw big crowds of students.
- Many students here develop a strong sense of responsibility about their role in contemporary social and political life.
- Many upperclassmen play an active role in helping new students adjust to campus life.
- Students are conscientious about taking good care of school property.
- The college offers many really practical courses such as typing, report writing, and so on.

Students were asked to indicate whether each statement was true or false. Those statements on which at least two thirds of the respondents agreed were considered "characteristics" of the institution. An institution's score for each environmental feature was simply the number of statements that were reported as characteristic (Pace, 1972, p. 18).

The coefficients of correlation between the CUES scores and expenditures for instruction and departmental research (in 1972-73) for 265 institutions are:

Campus morale	.08
Quality of teaching	.24
Practicality	-.45
Scholarship	.30
Community	-.02
Awareness	.32
Propriety	-.20

Expenditures per student are positively related to quality of teaching, scholarship, and awareness, negatively related to emphasis on practicality and propriety, and unrelated to campus morale and community. These relationships are about what would be expected. Affluent institutions are likely to emphasize teaching, scholarship, and awareness in the political, social, and aesthetic realms. They tend to play down practicality and propriety. (Surprisingly, however, their morale appears to be little higher than in less affluent institutions.) On the whole, the relatively modest correlations suggest that money does not automatically create effective educational environments.

Affluence and Educational Performance

One of the more penetrating studies of the outcomes of higher education is that by Clark and others (1972), a detailed longitudinal study of changes in the characteristics of students in eight diverse institutions during their four years of college, conducted between 1958–59 and 1963–64. The study did not produce any single index of student change or value added for each of the eight institutions, but it did provide a wealth of comparative data. From these data I attempted to draw conclusions as to how the eight institutions ranked in value added and to compare that ranking with the ranking in cost per student unit:

Institution	Estimated ranking in value added	Ranking in expenditures per student unit
A	1	1
B	2	2
C	3	6
D	4	3
E	5	4
F	6	5
G	7	8
H	8	7

Clearly, there is a high, but not perfect, correlation between performance and expenditure per student. However, institution A, the most expensive institution, spent almost three times as much as

G, the least costly institution, and nearly twice as much as B, which ranked second in performance. These results hint that the range of costs greatly exceeds the range of performance.

A Study of Organizational Effectiveness. Cameron's studies (1977, 1978) of forty-one public and private institutions in the northeastern United States provide another set of data on institutional performance. Cameron's data on institutional effectiveness are based on questionnaires answered by fifty administrators (including department chairmen) at each institution and on supplemental factual information obtained from the records of the institutions and from published sources. The institutions were scored on a scale from 1 (low effectiveness) to 7 (high effectiveness) on the following dimensions:

- Student educational satisfaction
- Student academic development
- Student career development
- Student personal development
- Faculty and administrator employment satisfaction
- Professional development and quality of faculty
- System openness and community interaction
- Ability to acquire resources
- Organizational health

Table 28 shows the relationships between institutional affluence, as measured by educational expenditures per student unit, and mean scores on various dimensions of Cameron's survey of institutional effectiveness. The coefficients of correlation are on the whole quite high, with most between .40 and .80. One can only conclude that institutional expenditures are related to most of the variables that Cameron believed to be indicative of institutional effectiveness. Table 28 also shows the results of a regression analysis that estimates the effects of a doubling of expenditures per student unit from $1,500 to $3,000. This doubling yields increases in scores on effectiveness of 1 to 21 percent, the median increase being 12 percent. As noted earlier, the significance of such increases in educational performance cannot be specified, yet the data do suggest that increased expenditures might well be worth the cost. However, one must keep in mind

Table 28. Relationship between educational expenditures per student unit and mean scores on various aspects of institutional effectiveness, forty-one colleges and universities, 1977–78

	Public	Private	All institutions
Coefficients of correlation			
1. Student educational satisfaction	.47	.62	.64
2. Student academic development	.15	.82	.79
3. Student career development	.13	.34	.27
4. Student personal development	.49	.31	.46
Dimensions 1, 2, and 4 combined	.44	.85	.79
5. Faculty-administrator employment satisfaction	.47	.39	.45
6. Professional development and quality of faculty	.05	.79	.76
Dimensions 5 and 6 combined	.36	.80	.78
7. Systems openness and community interaction	.03	.14	.12
Percentage increase in mean scores associated with a doubling of educational expenditure per student unit from $1,500 to $3,000			
1. Student educational satisfaction	18%	11%	13%
2. Student academic development	4	17	21
3. Student career development	4	5	4
4. Student personal development	11	3	6
Dimensions 1,2, and 4 combined	11	10	12
5. Faculty-administrator employment satisfaction	16	3	6
6. Professional development and quality of faculty	-2	22	18
Dimensions 5 and 6 combined	8	11	12
7. Systems openness and community interaction	1	1	1

that the data on institutional effectiveness are appropriate only for ordinal comparisons, and so one cannot be sure whether increases in effectiveness are, or are not, commensurate with the increases in expenditures.

Gains on Test Scores During the College Years. In recent years the American College Testing Program has instituted the College Outcomes Measure Project (COMP). This project seeks to develop instruments and procedures for evaluating knowledge and skills acquired in undergraduate general education—knowledge and skills necessary for successful functioning in adult society. The particular knowledge and skills are: communicating, solving problems, clarifying values, functioning within social institutions, using science and technology, and using the arts. The procedures include a composite examination involving simulation of adult activities, an objective test, and an activity inventory.

At thirteen institutions, the instruments have been administered to freshmen and seniors thus providing information on gains over four years of college. When these gains were correlated with educational expenditures per student unit, the coefficient of correlation was about .49. This is an impressive number. However, the samples of both institutions and students were small and the comparisons of freshmen and seniors were cross-sectional rather than longitudinal. Therefore, the relatively impressive correlation, though an important bit of evidence, should not be regarded as definitive.

Another source was data from the Gourman Report (1978). This publication provides ratings of major institutions with respect to undergraduate education. The report does not reveal how the ratings are determined (see "The Gourman Report. . . ," 1978). However, Gourman's data are sometimes used in studies of factors bearing upon educational quality, and it is of interest to relate data on expenditure to them. Though the correlation between Gourman's ratings and cost per student unit are far from striking, there was a clear positive correlation. The average unit cost for the institutions grouped as quartiles is shown at the top of the following page. These figures may not be of much significance, however, since expenditure per student probably was, directly or indirectly, a factor in Gourman's determination of institutional ratings.

First (highest) quartile	$5,115
Second quartile	3,986
Third quartile	4,085
Fourth (lowest) quartile	2,781

Concluding Comments

The conclusions from the several attempts to correlate institutional expenditures with educational performance are highly tentative. This is so for several reasons. The data on educational performance are in most cases subjective. They are partly based on resource inputs rather than on true outcomes. Moreover, most studies do not include all of the many benefits that may be derived from education, particularly the consumer benefits received by students and the broad benefits that flow to society from higher education. Most outcomes are in an ordinal form which permits a ranking of institutions by educational performance but does not allow estimates of the *amount* of difference in performance between more and less affluent institutions. Finally, the data on cost per student unit may contain possible errors in cost allocations to education as distinct from research and public service. Thus, the data and analysis assembled in this chapter are by no means a final word on the relationship between institutional affluence and outcomes. Nevertheless, some modest inferences are sufficiently plausible to put the burden of proof on those who would dispute them.

First, institutional affluence is probably correlated with educational outcomes in the sense that, with many exceptions, affluent institutions appear to generate greater outcomes than impecunious institutions. Second, the coefficients of correlation between unit cost and outcomes are not very impressive. The variance among institutions is substantial. Clearly some institutions of lower cost perform as well as or better than other institutions of higher cost, and these cost differences are in many cases substantial. Third, it seems likely (though not proven) that increases in expenditures per student unit are cost-effective, though seemingly small, when the benefits are considered as accruing over the lifetime of the students. Small percentage increases in benefits may well justify substantial expenditures.

These conclusions, even though tentative, are of the utmost significance. They imply that many affluent institutions could perform as well, or nearly as well, with less money or that many institutions could achieve greater results with the same money. They imply also that increases in affluence do not automatically result in improvements in performance, as is so often claimed. Yet, they do suggest that on the average, but with many exceptions, money does make a difference. As the Carnegie Commission concluded (1972, pp. 40–41): "To suggest that differences in expenditures per student are largely explained by variations in the relative capacities of colleges and universities to attract income is not to deny that relatively high expenditures for students are likely to be associated with comparatively high quality. . . But this does not necessarily mean that cost differences among institutions—or among particular programs within institutions—invariably reflect differences in quality."

Consumer Benefits

The results reported in this chapter are related mainly to the effect of differences in unit cost on educational benefits or on institutional characteristics believed to be productive of educational benefits. No effort was made, or could be made with available data, to consider the relationship between unit costs and the "consumer benefits" students receive from higher education. By "consumer benefits" I refer to the immediate pleasures and satisfactions students receive from their education without regard for the desirable changes in students that are usually held to be the main purpose of education. The time spent by students in higher education is a substantial slice of their lives. One of the benefits of higher education is simply the satisfaction students derive from the experience of going to college and this satisfaction derives not only from extracurricular life, pleasant surroundings, and agreeable associations but also from experiences such as learning from outstanding teachers, having access to ample libraries, reading great books, attending chapel, appreciating and taking part in the social and recreational life of the campus. Had these benefits been counted among the outcomes, the correlations between costs and outcomes would have been considerably higher. Some of the expenditures of high-cost institutions are almost surely designed more largely for the students' satisfaction than for their educational growth. Indeed, in evaluating unit cost, we should not ignore the returns in students' satisfaction. The costs of higher education are strongly affected by the prevailing standard of living in the society, and one source of increasing costs in higher education is the rising standard of living in American society. When students expect central heating and air conditioning, when they come to college with cars and stereo sets, and when they demand psychiatric counseling and career guidance, the costs of operating colleges and universities rise. It is probable, moreover, that high-cost institutions cater more generously to the rising standard of living than do low-cost institutions.

There may well be other more subtle benefits that are not fully recognized in the data on outcomes presented in this chapter. For example, affluent institutions may effect barely perceptible but desirable and important changes in student's attitudes and values, outlook on life, aspirations, and perspective. At the same time, high-cost institutions may confer outcomes with negative connotations, outcomes such as prestige, sense of social superiority, and arrogance that accentuates class differences to the disadvantage of those attending less costly institutions.

Assessing Institutional Outcomes

This chapter illustrates vividly the urgent need for educational leaders to explore their institutional outcomes.[1] Knowledge of costs, or even of costs per student unit, gives precious little information that is relevant to either accountability or administration unless accompanied by knowledge of outcomes. There is no way for higher education to become properly accountable without knowledge of the overall results from institutional efforts. And there is no way that higher education can be administered rationally without knowledge of the differences in results that flow from different ways of operating. Both accountability and management are concepts closely linked with the idea of *efficiency*. As Chapter Eleven indicates, efficiency is measured or judged as a ratio between outcomes and resources employed—that is, between benefits and costs, or less elegantly, between outputs and inputs. Accountability implies an obligation to produce outcomes that are commensurate with the costs. Likewise, management implies that different technologies (or methods or procedures) will produce

---

[1]This section is based in part on Bowen, 1978d. For an excellent discussion of the history and possibilities of outcomes measurement, see Pace, 1979.

different outcomes and that it is the task of management to select those technologies which will produce the best outcomes in relation to the amount of resources employed. In either case, the assessment of outcomes need not always be precise. To make either of the concepts meaningful, however, there must be some notion of outcomes expressed in terms of more or less. All decisions about staff, curriculums, teaching methods, facilities, institutional organization, governance, and even finance can be arrived at rationally and deliberately only if there is some knowledge of effects on outcomes.

At present, institutions know very little about their results and next to nothing about the effects of changes in their procedures and methods on the results. There have been sporadic one-time studies of outcomes in particular institutions and also a number of one-time studies of small samples of institutions but few systematic ongoing efforts to assess outcomes and certainly few cases where the study of outcomes has been linked with either accountability or management. Such studies are urgently needed if institutions are to have better information for accountability and management, and if the profession is to learn more about the consequences of alternative procedures and methods. Without such knowledge, institutions are destined merely to follow tradition, or to do what is expedient in the light of prevailing pressures of the market and of politics, or to be vulnerable to every fad that sweeps through the educational community, or to manage by intuition, or to do some of all four. One may respect tradition because it is the result of a kind of natural selection achieved through many trials and errors; one may understand the need for adjusting to political pressures; one may believe that institutions should be open to the new; and one may respect intuition especially when it is practiced by experienced and sensitive persons. Yet, decision making need not be based solely on tradition, political pressure, fad, and intuition and these can be supplemented by knowledge. If the nature of our task is such that we often must fly blind, it would be good to have radar to give at least a general sense of direction if not a detailed picture of the whole landscape.

In the remainder of this chapter, I shall suggest some basic principles that might be followed in the identification and evaluation of the outcomes of particular colleges or universities. I shall confine my comments to the outcomes of education, but of course a complete assessment of higher educational outcomes would embrace the important outputs in the form of research and scholarship and public service.

First, the study of outcomes should avoid the common confusion of inputs and outputs. Most evaluation of institutions is conducted in terms of such variables as faculty-student ratios, proportion of Ph.D.s in the faculty, size of endowment, current expenditures per student, College Board scores, number of library books, range of facilities and equipment, value of physical plant, extracurricular programs, and so on. These are all inputs and it is by no means established that there is any systematic positive correlation between these inputs and the true outcomes defined in terms of the personal development of students in either cognitive or affective realms. Indeed, in view of the wide differences in expenditures per student among seemingly comparable institutions, the burden of proof is upon the high-cost institutions to demonstrate that their generous expenditures actually yield commensurate outcomes. It is not even appropriate to define outcomes in terms of the experiences of students in connection with their college education. Such measures as attendance in the libraries and laboratories, number and type of courses taken, attendance at public events, and the like are technologies, not results. Even such variables as absenteeism or dropout rates are not conclusive indicators of outcomes. It is possible that some students are doing the right thing, in terms of their personal development, by staying away from formal programs, or by changing institutions, or by dropping out of college altogether. The critical tests of educational outcomes are: What happens in the development of persons? How do persons change and grow as a result of their college experiences?

Second, the assessment should be linked to all the major goals of education, and not confined to particular aspects of human development, for example, those that can be measured easily or that are related to economic success. In general, five kinds of goals will be of interest to most institutions:

1. Cognitive development of students with respect to such qualities as verbal and quantitative skills, substantive knowledge, rationality, critical thinking, intellectual tolerance, lifelong learning.

2. Aesthetic sensibility.
3. Emotional and moral development in such areas as personal self-discovery, human understanding, religious interest, psychological well-being.
4. Practical competence relating to citizenship, economic productivity, family life, consumption, leisure, and health.
5. Direct satisfactions and enjoyment from college education during the college years and in later life.

The goals of an institution are its intended outcomes, and hence institutions are prone to confuse their outcomes with their intentions and hopes. But they should be on the lookout also for unintended outcomes. Some of these may by serendipity be positive. But college also may generate discouragement, boredom, suppression of creativeness, acquisition of bad habits, needless failure, and even suicide. These negative outcomes should be taken into account.

Third, educational outcomes should relate to the development of whole persons. Most evaluation of students employs instruments that measure only particular aspects of students' personalities. Such instruments measure, for example, verbal skills, religious interest, aesthetic sensibility, general knowledge, or life goals. Each of these kinds of instruments tells us something about groups of students with respect to a particular dimension of their personalities but tells us very little about what happens to individual students considered as whole persons. Indeed, the average changes on these various personality dimensions are usually small and lead the unwary to the conclusion that college really does not matter very much. Actually, college may exert a major impact on its students, considered as whole human beings, even when there is little or no change in average scores on particular characteristics. The explanation of this paradox is that there can be enormous dispersion among individuals with respect to particular characteristics while the averages change little or not at all. Every tabulation of scores on specialized test instruments shows wide differences in what happens to individuals as they are affected by college. On any given dimension some students will gain ground, some will lose ground, and some will not change at all. Aggregates and averages reflect the central tendency of all these wide variations and conceal the substantial differences experienced by different individuals. For example, Feldman and Newcomb (1969, p. 9) cite a study in which a group of freshmen achieved an average score on religious value of 41.75 and the identical students as seniors scored 41.57. But the individual students making up the group showed changes as follows: -19, -16, -14, -12, -2, +1, +3, +7, +11, +12, +16. A comparison of the two averages would lead to the conclusion that no change had occurred; yet the individual scores revealed enormous variability.

The purpose of higher education is not necessarily to produce positive changes for all its students along every dimension of personality development. This clearly would be impossible and undesirable. Colleges accept individual differences among their students and encourage their students to develop individually along lines consistent with their unique interests and talents. For any individual, such development inevitably means substantial progress along some lines, no change along others, and regression along still others. Regression along some lines is not necessarily a sign of failure. For example, a student who in high school had devoted much time to music may discover interests in science. As a result, he or she may regress during college on aestheticism and progress on intellectuality. Or, to take another example, a student may come to college with highly developed mathematical skills. He or she may discover new interests in social issues that result in a regression in mathematical skills but a progression in political awareness. These regressions are not necessarily negative outcomes; they may represent constructive changes in personality configuration as a result of exposure to new opportunities.

No student is likely to progress simultaneously along all possible lines of development. One reason is that people differ in the distribution of their talents. Some individuals have highly specialized talents and interests, others more diversified ones. But few if any are so well-rounded that they can be expected to make equal progress across all possible lines of personality development. Another reason is that the cultivation of any one interest takes time and energy. To pursue every interest equally would be at the sacrifice of significant achievement in any one area. The totally well-rounded individual who pursued every conceivable interest surely would be a bland, innocuous, mediocre, and exhausted person. Excellence of personality involves choices based on a weighing of values in relation to interests and talents, not the equal pursuit of every value that can be conceived of. There may be some values that should have high priority for all, for example, personal honor or consideration for others. But among the wide range of values that life presents, there are tradeoffs involving choices based on the unique characteristics of each individual. Each individual does and should make use of the opportunities available in the college environment for the development of his unique personality. In the process every individual may change, but the averages for each personality characteristic may change relatively little.

To study the true outcomes of higher education in all their variability, then, calls for the study of individual students in some depth. One must ask not what was the average gain in verbal skills of a college's entire student body but rather what happened in the total personality and in the life experience of individual students as a result of their college careers when those students are seen as whole human beings. The few studies that focus on whole persons yield results that come closer to the changes that educators observe in their students during and after college than typical studies based on average changes in particular dimensions of personality.

A fourth principle is that outcomes assessment should be based upon the study of alumni as well as of students in courses. The study of alumni raises questions that barely have been touched in educational research. For example, there is almost total ignorance of carryover to adult life of substantive learning. The residue of a college education—after the initial forgetting of detail—is a virtual mystery. But we should be interested also in the effects of college experience on the values and attitudes of alumni, their interests, their citizenship, their family life, and their careers.

Fifth, outcomes assessment should be concerned with *change* in students as a result of their college experiences, not merely with their absolute level of performance during and after college. By far the most important factor determining the performance of students during and after college is their background and ability at the time of admission to college. If an institution admits mainly bright young people from affluent families, the performance of its students in their studies and in their later careers will almost certainly be superior to those of students of an institution which admits students of limited backgrounds and abilities. For the more selective colleges and universities to take credit for the achievements of their alumni, as they often do, is naive. There is evidence to indicate that many nonselective institutions bring about greater changes in their students than some selective ones, and it is *change*, not absolute performance, that is the criterion of true educational outcomes. The change may be measured relative to change achieved by those who do not attend college or relative to change achieved by students of other institutions, or relative to change achieved by the subject institution in past years.

Sixth, the evaluation scheme must be practicable. This means that it should not be impossibly expensive. It should concentrate on major goals and avoid trivial detail. To save money and to allow some depth, it should be based on small samples of students and alumni and not try to cover the entire population. The test of practicability means also that the results must be understandable to students, faculty, the public and their representatives. The results must carry conviction. Otherwise, outcomes assessment will be worse than useless in achieving accountability. Practicability implies also that the study of outcomes should be linked with serious educational decision making and not be merely a public relations gimmick. In short, practicability calls for simplicity, low cost, and integrity.

Seventh, there is the technical problem of controlling for extraneous variables. How does one know whether what happens to students in college is due to native ability, family background, mass media, or to the normal maturation process? I think this problem can be finessed in two ways. One way is to record change over time in the results obtained by any particular institution under study. For example, if over time one observes that gains between the freshmen and senior years are increasing or decreasing, that becomes evidence that the institution is progressing or retrogressing. Thus, an evaluation program carried on year after year establishes its own norms and provides a way of measuring, or at least judging, institutional progress. Another way, which I find appealing, is for institutions to join with other comparable institutions in the evaluative process, so that each institution could compare its results with others.

Eighth, and finally, outcomes assessment should develop from the bottom up within colleges and universities rather than be imposed from the top down by federal or state government or by national accrediting bodies. A great deal of experimentation in concepts and methods is needed. Assessment should be related to the special missions or philosophies of particular institutions. It should not be restricted to procedures and instruments that can be used nationally. Institutions should not be put in the position of having to adjust their goals and programs to the requirements of standardized evaluation schemes or to measure their performance using uniform standards set by others. Clearly, there is a place for procedures and instruments that have wide applicability, but there is great danger that outcomes evaluation will be dominated by conventional academic testing, and this, in my opinion, would be a grave mistake. The true outcomes of education cannot be expressed—except in small part—through techniques that produce neat and tidy numerical scores. They call for serious exploration of what happens in the lives of people as a result of their college experiences. Sound assessment of outcomes will focus on students as persons and will provide a vehicle by which institutions can become acquainted with their students as living persons rather than as numbers in a computer or grades on a transcript.

No one can pretend that outcomes assessment would be easy. Yet it is urgent that educators try to learn more about their outcomes. Through such efforts carried on independently in many institutions, educators might through trial and error gradually develop sound methods that would supplement their intuitive judgments and serve as a corrective for the wishful thinking and the unsubstantiated rhetoric in which they sometimes indulge. Over time, the assessment process might contribute to efficiency and might demonstrate the value of higher education in ways that would strengthen public confidence in it.

9

Economies and Diseconomies of Scale

One of the most settled principles of economics is that the size or scale at which a business or other organization operates is likely to affect its unit cost of production. This principle applies to organizations that produce physical goods and to those that render services to private business firms, nonprofit organizations, and governmental agencies. In some respects, increases in organizational size tend to lower unit cost and thus yield *economies of scale;* in other respects, increases in size tend to raise unit cost and thus lead to *diseconomies of scale.* This chapter explores the implications of institutional size on unit cost and allocation of resources within higher education.

A typical relationship of organizational size to cost is illustrated in Figure 5. As an organization's size increases, the forces tending to decrease unit cost tend to predominate until a point is reached at which the forces raising cost predominate. The result is a U-shaped curve whose minimal point represents the lowest attainable unit cost—given the basic technology and the prices of materials, labor, and other resources. In practice, this minimum cost position may not be a precise point but may be a considerable range over which the forces that keep costs down and those that push costs up are more or less in balance.

Private profit-making firms are under considerable compulsion to attain a scale of operation roughly consistent with the least cost per unit. Any firm that fails to do so will probably sacrifice profits and will also be vulnerable to competition (though some firms may be so

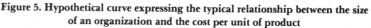

**Figure 5. Hypothetical curve expressing the typical relationship between the size
of an organization and the cost per unit of product**

Cost
per
unit

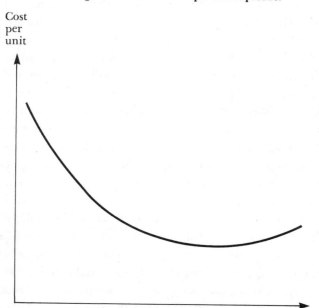

Size of organization (measured in number of units produced)

insulated from competition that they need not seek the lowest possible cost). Among not-for-profit organizations, on the other hand, the
compulsion to seek and achieve minimum cost is less rigorous. They
do not seek profit, and as we have seen, the unit costs of colleges and
universities can expand to whatever amount of money they are
able to raise relative to the number of student units they serve
because the institutions' finances are not wholly determined by a
market in which they sell their product. Furthermore, to the extent
that they are dependent on a market, many institutions enjoy a local
monopoly or they produce a service so distinctive as to shield them
from intense competition. Thus, they are permitted the luxury of
considerable latitude in scale of operation. Indeed, some institutions
deliberately choose to be smaller or larger than the size that would
yield the point of minimum cost on a production curve such as that
shown in Figure 5. They may be justified in doing so because size
affects educational quality as well as cost per student unit.

The principal force that pushes unit costs of any organization downward as scale of operation increases is the "lumpiness" of many of the resources it uses. In the case of higher education, if a college is to operate at all, beyond the pattern of "Mark Hopkins on one end of a log and the boy on the other," it must have some faculty, a few administrative officers, some minimal buildings and grounds, and some books and equipment whether it enrolls 500 students or 3,000 students. By simple arithmetic, the cost per student unit of these minimal overhead items decreases as the number of students grows until the initial staff and facilities are fully employed. As the college's enrollment expands further, there would still be further opportunities for the spreading of "lumpy" resources over more student units. For example, the institution might acquire a computer, an electron microscope, a pipe organ, an art studio, a swimming pool, a chapel, an auditorium, specialized administrative officials such as a dean of students or a controller, or a new department of Far Eastern Studies. Each of these acquisitions requires a large initial cost, but as enrollment grows, the cost is spread over more students, and unit costs tend to fall. Large enrollments also increase the average size of classes by raising the number of students in the less populated courses. This creates further economies as the instructors' salaries remain the same, while revenues increase. Institutions may also economize by sharing facilities with other institutions, employing part-time staff, acquiring small models of equipment, or modifying educational programs to avoid disciplines that require large capital investments.

In general, the larger the institution, the greater its ability to use expensive acquisitions to capacity and thus to reap the economies of scale. However, some institutions deliberately remain small because of their ability to raise enough money to operate on a small scale and their belief in the educational virtues of smallness. Institutions also may remain small simply because they are unable to attract the resources and students necessary to grow. Other colleges or universities may deliberately seek to grow beyond the optimum size, not necessarily because there are advantages of cost or of educational excellence in such growth, but because increased size may make the institutions more important and more visible and thus increase their ability to attract money, students, and faculty.

At the same time that "lumpiness" of resources gives rise to economies of scale, several other influences tend to push costs up as size increases. One of these is the rising cost of institutional coordination and the increasing cost of failures of coordination as colleges and universities become larger. Another is the possible deterioration of educational quality as institutions grow. A reduction in quality is tantamount to an increase in unit cost because the value of the service produced by each unit of cost diminishes. A third diseconomy of scale occurs because growth of colleges or universities usually involves recruiting an increasing proportion of the relevant population cohorts from the given market area or requires expansion of the market area. In either case the costs of student recruitment and student financial aid and the costs connected with student attrition are likely to increase. Also, when the market area expands, the transportation costs of students rise. While these costs usually are not paid for by the institutions, they nevertheless are part of the social cost of higher education. The forces leading to increasing unit cost will be considered in greater detail later in this chapter.

A curve showing the cost function tends to have the shape of a lop-sided cup (as shown in Figure 5). The impact of the "lumpiness" of resources tends to be especially pronounced among small institutions and accounts for the sharply downward slope in the left portion of the curve. The problems of coordination, quality, and transportation tend to become operative in large institutions and account for the moderately upward slope at the right. Between the two extremes is a considerable zone where the effect of size on unit cost may be quite small or even negligible.

There is no reason to believe, however, that institutions are bound to this curve. For quite sufficient reasons—educational or other—they may decide to give up some economies of scale and operate at below the theoretically optimal size, or to face some of the disadvantages of bloated size and operate at beyond the optimal level. The relationship between size and cost is too vague to apply the cost function rigidly to predicting or guiding institutional behavior and public policy.

With this brief excursion into the theory of the cost function, let us proceed to examine some data relating to actual institutions.

Overall Unit Costs

In the real world, the relationship between institutional size and cost per student unit is anything but close. As has been indicated repeatedly, the unit cost of any institution is determined more largely by its ability to raise funds than by its size, and any savings through economies of scale tend to be diverted to such purposes as higher salaries, new programs, and better equipment rather than to cost reduction. The enormous dispersion in the size-cost relationships was amply demonstrated by the Carnegie Commission on Higher Education (1971). They presented a series of scatter diagrams showing the relationship between size and cost for large numbers of institutions, each diagram relating to a particular type of institution. For these diagrams, the word "scatter" was highly appropriate. The dispersion was amazing and hardly any relationship between size and cost could be discerned. However, when the Carnegie Commission (1972) analyzed their data on cost by *detailed* size classifications, they found that costs tend to be excessive among very small institutions. They found that as liberal arts colleges and two-year colleges, both public and private, become larger, costs decline quite sharply until enrollments reach 600 to 800 and then level off. Among comprehensive institutions they found cost-reduction proceeding to a breaking point at around 1,000 to 1,300 students and among private research and doctoral-granting universities they found a breaking point at roughly 5,000 to 5,500 students.[1] The implication is clear. Though some institutions deliberately remain small and thus in a sense choose to be costly, many small institutions operate at a high cost simply because they have not been able to attain a scale of operation that allows them to spread their fixed overhead over enough students to bring costs down. The Commission's research suggests that liberal arts and community colleges with enrollments below 600 to 800 students and comprehensive institutions with fewer than 1,300 students are likely

[1]Using a different method, Maynard (1971, p. 123) found that the breaking point for four-year public colleges was around 5,000 students. Dickmeyer and Hughes (1979) found educational and general costs per full-time-equivalent student to be substantially higher in community colleges with fewer than 5,000 students than in larger institutions. Kress (1977) found "economies of scale" for the smaller community colleges of California.

Table 29. Institutional cost per student unit, 268 representative institutions, by size and by type of institution, 1976-77

	Smallest fifth of institutions	Second fifth	Middle fifth	Fourth fifth	Largest fifth of institutions
Research and doctorate-granting universities					
Public	$2,472	$2,255	$2,668	$2,328	$2,566
Private	4,545	3,010	3,138	4,159	3,524
Comprehensive universities and colleges					
Public	2,241	2,317	2,433	1,996	2,076
Private	2,388	2,511	2,354	2,429	1,900
Liberal arts colleges, private	3,523	3,221	3,470	2,997	3,426
Two-year colleges					
Public	3,243	3,244	1,479	2,474	2,116
Private	2,751	3,203	1,955	3,053	2,523
All institutions					
Public	2,522	2,364	1,954	2,345	2,386
Private	3,074	3,055	2,770	2,902	3,129
Total	3,163	2,774	2,752	2,475	2,835

Note: Institutional size is measured by number of student units, that is, enrollment adjusted for academic level of students.

Source: Special tabulation of data from Higher Education General Information Survey.

to be uneconomical. However, many individual institutions are living exceptions to these generalizations.

Another approach to the relationship between size and cost is
presented in Table 29. The sample of 268 representative institutions
is grouped into fifths by size (as measured in student units), and
educational cost per student unit is shown for each group. Diligent
and imaginative pondering of these figures yields a vague relationship between size and cost. For example, among six of seven types of
institutions, the average cost for the largest fifth of institutions is
lower than that for the smallest fifth; in the case of the public two-year
colleges, cost generally declines as size increases. Clearly, however,
the relationship between size and unit cost is problematic, although
common sense—if not the economists' theory of production—tells us
that size and cost are indeed related to the operation of institutions of
all sizes. This relationship will become clearer as we now examine the
effect of size on the institutions' internal allocation of resources.

Internal Allocations by Functions

Table 30 shows the percentage distribution of educational expenditures among major functions in small and large institutions of various types. The findings from this table are clear:

1. Large institutions spend a substantially smaller percentage of
   their educational expenditures for institutional support (administration) and student services than do comparable small institutions.
2. Most groups of large institutions spend relatively less for plant
   operation and maintenance than do comparable small institutions.
3. Large institutions spend a greater percentage of their resources
   for teaching than do the comparable small institutions.
4. Size appears to have no consistent effect on the percentages spent
   for scholarships and fellowships and academic support. However,
   as shown in Table 31, most groups of large institutions spend relatively less on one important category of academic support, namely,
   libraries, than do small institutions.

The economies of scale appear to be most pronounced for
institutional support, student services, and plant operation and

Table 30. Functional allocation of educational expenditures, 268 representative colleges and universities, by size and type of institution, 1976–77

	Public institutions		Private institutions	
	Smallest fifth	Largest fifth	Smallest fifth	Largest fifth
Research and doctorate-granting universities				
Teaching	56.8%	61.1%	53.0%	56.6%
Student services	6.8	5.6	6.0	4.2
Scholarships and fellowships	6.0	7.2	10.5	12.9
Academic support	7.5	10.5	8.9	7.0
Institutional support	10.6	7.3	12.0	11.4
Operation and maintenance of plant	9.7	8.3	9.1	7.9
Other (includes mandatory transfers)	2.6	—	0.5	—
Comprehensive universities and colleges				
Teaching	48.6	60.2	42.0	50.6
Student services	4.7	3.7	8.8	6.5
Scholarships and fellowships	5.7	2.5	12.7	12.2
Academic support	9.7	7.9	6.3	6.5
Institutional support	15.5	11.0	17.7	12.9
Operation and maintenance of plant	13.1	10.9	10.0	10.7
Other (includes mandatory transfers)	2.7	3.8	2.5	0.6
Liberal arts colleges				
Teaching	—	—	34.7	43.4
Student services	—	—	8.5[a]	8.2[a]
Scholarships and fellowships	—	—	14.8	12.2
Academic support	—	—	7.5	7.3
Institutional support	—	—	20.3	15.5
Operation and maintenance of plant	—	—	12.5	11.7
Other (includes mandatory transfers)	—	—	1.7	1.7

Table 30 (continued)

	Public institutions		Private institutions	
	Smallest fifth	*Largest fifth*	*Smallest fifth*	*Largest fifth*
Two-year colleges				
Teaching	54.6%	58.1%	33.7%	38.1%
Student services	6.5[a]	7.7[a]	11.4	9.2
Scholarships and fellowships	2.9	3.1	8.7	7.2
Academic support	7.2	6.0	7.7	9.9
Institutional support	17.8	12.7	23.5	20.7
Operation and maintenance of plant	10.8	12.2	13.8[a]	13.8[a]
Other (includes mandatory transfers)	0.2	0.2	1.2	1.1
All institutions				
Teaching	53.3	61.1	39.3	52.4
Student services	6.3	6.0	9.4	5.8
Scholarships and fellowships	3.9	6.4	13.9[a]	13.0[a]
Academic support	7.7	9.4	7.4	7.4
Institutional support	15.7	7.7	18.6	12.3
Operation and maintenance of plant	11.9	8.9	11.4	9.1
Other (includes mandatory transfers)	1.2	0.5	—	—

Public and private institutions combined

	Smallest fifth	Largest fifth
All institutions		
Teaching	43.0	57.9
Student services	8.4	5.7
Scholarships and fellowships	10.4	7.8
Academic suport	7.4	8.5
Institutional support	17.8	10.0
Operation and maintenance of plant	11.5	9.3
Other (includes mandatory transfers)	1.5	0.8

Note: Institutional size is measured by number of student units, that is, enrollment adjusted for academic level of students.

[a] Estimated from incomplete data.

Source: Special tabulation of data from Higher Education General Information Survey

Table 31. Libraries: operating expenditures as percentages of total educational
and general expenditures, by size and type of institution, 1975–76

	Smallest fifth of institutions	Largest fifth of institutions
Research and doctorate-granting universities		
Public	3.9%	3.5%
Private	4.3	3.6
Comprehensive universities and colleges		
Public	4.8	4.2
Private	3.8	4.6
Liberal arts colleges, private	4.0	4.6
Two-year colleges, public	4.7	2.9
All institutions		
Public	4.5	3.5
Private	4.2	4.0
Total	4.3	3.8

Note: Because libraries are used for research and public service as well as teaching,
library expenditures are compared to educational and general expenditures rather than
to educational expenditures alone.

Source: Special tabulation of data from Higher Education General Information
Survey.

maintenance. By reaping economies in these areas, large institutions
are able to devote relatively more of their resources to teaching. Most
observers would regard the ability to concentrate resources in the
academic heartland of teaching as a welcome and significant outcome
of large institutional scale. Even though the savings do not show up
conspicuously as reductions in overall unit cost, they count because
they get reassigned internally to the central function of teaching.

Internal Allocations by Types of Employees

Table 32 compares small and large institutions with respect to their
allocation of employment among faculty, administrators, and other
staff. The figures are expressed as number of staff per thousand
student units. The data show that in large institutions of all types the
number of faculty and administrators relative to enrollment is sub-

Table 32. Number of full-time-equivalent staff per thousand student units, 268 representative colleges and universities, by size and type of institution, 1976–77

	Public institutions		Private institutions	
	Smallest fifth	Largest fifth	Smallest fifth	Largest fifth
Research and doctorate-granting universities				
Faculty	32	31	—	—
Administrators	2.9	2.5	—	—
Other professional and nonprofessional personnel	84	115	—	—
Total	119	149	149	133
Comprehensive universities and colleges				
Faculty	44	38	54	38
Administrators	5.5	4.5	8.1	7.6
Other professional and nonprofessional personnel	68	99	75	43
Total	118	142	137	89
Liberal arts colleges				
Faculty	—	—	70	61
Administrators	—	—	—	—
Other professional and nonprofessional personnel	—	—	100[a]	119[a]
Total	—	—	170	180
Two-year colleges				
Faculty	36	26	—	—
Administrators	6	4	—	—
Other professional and nonprofessional personnel	61	46	—	—
Total	103	76	—	—
All institutions				
Faculty	39	33	68	27
Administrators	5	3	12	6
Other professional and nonprofessional personnel	61	107	61	91
Total	105	143	141	124

	Public and private institutions combined	
	Smallest fifth	Largest fifth
Faculty	54	30
Administrators	9	4
Other professional and nonprofessional personnel	65	94
Total	128	128

Note: Institutional size is measured by number of student units, that is, enrollment adjusted for academic level of students.

stantially less than in comparable small institutions. Thus it would appear that there are economies of scale in the employment of faculty and administrators. However, for three types of institutions (public research universities, public comprehensive institutions, and private liberal arts colleges), this economy of scale is more than offset by the tendency of large institutions to employ additional staff—professionals other than faculty and administrators and nonprofessional employees. Indeed, this tendency is so strong that in these three types of institutions total employment is substantially greater per thousand students in large institutions than in small ones. In these instances, the economies of scale are reaped as an expansion of support staff rather than as a reduction of total staff.

The situation is quite different for the other groups of institutions (private research universities, private comprehensive institutions, and public two-year colleges). Among these groups, the large institutions not only achieve economies of scale in the employment of faculty and administrators, but also in the employment of support staff. As a result, total employment per thousand students in the large institutions is substantially less than in the small ones.

Interestingly, the data for all institutions combined show that the number of faculty and administrators per thousand students is much smaller in large institutions than small ones, that the number of support staff is much greater, and that total employment per thousand students is the same. It appears that large institutions shift their resources from faculty and administrative personnel to support staff.

Caution is indicated in interpreting these results. Comparisons between large and small institutions may be misleading because large institutions of any given classification may be engaged in quite different activities from small ones and these activities may call on different numbers of support staff such as clerks, secretaries, laboratory workers, farm workers, or security guards. Some small institutions of any given type may employ relatively more faculty and administrators by deliberate choice, recognizing that their decision entails extra costs. They may wish to provide small classes, personalized instruction, rich programs of student services, and the like. Moreover, institutional affluence is not always positively correlated with size. For some categories of institutions, especially in the private sector, smaller institutions may be more affluent than larger ones. One may not legitimately infer from the statistics that there is a strict relationship between size of institutions and number of personnel per thousand students. Some large institutions are operated with staff-student ratios like those characteristic of small institutions; and some small institutions are operated with staff-student ratios like those common to large institutions. Yet the data do leave a strong impression that there are important economies of scale in higher education that tend to be realized through the internal allocation of resources, but which *could* be realized in the form of lower overall unit costs.

Faculty Salaries and Salary Outlays

Large institutions pay on the average higher faculty salaries than do small institutions (see Table 33). This appears to hold true for all institutional groups except liberal arts colleges. But as was shown in Table 32, large institutions employ fewer faculty per thousand students than small ones. When salary rates and numbers of faculty are combined to give total salary outlay per student unit (Table 34), it turns out that large institutions on the whole spend substantially less on faculty salaries per student unit than do small institutions. Thus, by economizing on numbers of faculty, large institutions are able to pay salaries substantially higher than those in small institutions and still save money on total faculty salary outlays.

Building Space

As shown in Table 35, large institutions have less building space per student unit than small ones. The difference is striking. They also have slightly less building space per student unit devoted to instruction. The implication of these two findings is that small institutions have much more space per student devoted to noninstructional purposes than do the large institutions. Apparently, there are important economies of scale connected with buildings. What is true of buildings would doubtless be true also of heavy equipment.

Economies of Scale: Summary

The data presented in this chapter yield a few simple generalizations about the allocation of resources within large and small institutions. The findings may be summarized as follows:

Table 33. Mean salary, full-time faculty all ranks, 268 representative
colleges and universities, by size and type of institution, 1976–77

	Smallest fifth of institutions	Largest fifth of institutions
Research and doctorate-granting universities		
Public	$14,148	$15,287
Private	14,780	16,431
Comprehensive universities and colleges		
Public	12,711	14,139
Private	11,606	12,876
Liberal arts colleges, private	13,498	12,166
Two-year colleges, public	10,612	13,782
All institutions		
Public	12,311	15,369
Private	12,512	14,944
Total	12,550	14,957

Source: Special tabulation of data from Higher Education General Information Survey.

1. In the allocation of expenditures among various major functions, large institutions spend relatively less for institutional support (administration), student services, and plant operation and maintenance than small institutions, and they spend relatively more on teaching.
2. In the allocation of employment among different categories of staff:

(a) Large institutions employ relatively fewer faculty and administrators (per thousand students) than small institutions.

(b) Among public research universities, public comprehensive institutions, and private liberal arts colleges, large institutions employ relatively more "other staff" (consisting of other professional and nonprofessional workers) and they employ substantially more staff in total than small institutions.

(c) Among private research universities, private comprehensive institutions, and public two-year colleges, large institutions employ relatively fewer "other staff" and total

Table 34. Total salary outlay per student unit, full-time faculty
all ranks, 268 representative colleges and universities, by size
and type of institution, 1975–76

	Smallest fifth of institutions	Largest fifth of institutions
Research and doctorate-granting *universities*		
Public	—	—
Private	$558	$258
Comprehensive universities and *colleges*		
Public	503	503
Private	526	326
Liberal arts colleges, private	629	529
Two-year colleges, public	464	364
All institutions		
Public	469	369
Private	616	416
Total	578	378

Source: Special tabulation of data from Higher Education General Information Survey.

employment is substantially less than in the small institutions.

(d) Overall, among all types of institutions combined, total employment per thousand students is about the same in large and in small institutions.

3. Large institutions pay higher faculty salaries on the average than small institutions. However, because they employ relatively fewer faculty members, their total salary outlay per student is less than that in small institutions.

4. Large institutions provide less building space per student unit than small institutions.

These results strongly suggest that institutional size has considerable impact upon unit costs of particular items in the budget even though it may not have much effect upon total unit cost. The reason that size exerts so little effect on total unit cost is that, as institutions

Table 35. Square footage of building space per student unit, 268 representative colleges and universities, by size and type of institution, 1975–76

	Square footage of total building space		Square footage of building space devoted to instructional program	
	Smallest fifth of institutions	Largest fifth of institutions	Smallest fifth of institutions	Largest fifth of institutions
Research and doctorate-granting institutions				
Public	110	97	49	39
Private	153	78	63	60
Comprehensive universities and colleges				
Public	103	58	55	53
Private	128	64	63	61
Liberal arts colleges, private	—	—	80	80
Two-year colleges, public	90	38	55	52
All institutions				
Public	—	—	48	38
Private	164	104	71	68
Total	142	89	63	61

Source: Special tabulation of data from Higher Education General Information Survey.

grow and achieve economies of scale, they shift any savings to new internal uses—to new equipment, higher salaries, or new programs. Seldom if ever are such savings passed back in the form of reductions in unit cost to those who finance higher education—to students, donors, and legislatures (Brinkman, 1980). But there can be little doubt that potential and significant economies of scale in higher education actually exist. They are especially evident in very small institutions having enrollments of less than 1,000 students. But "lumpy" resources abound in colleges and universities of all sizes, and almost any institution may find some gain, strictly from the standpoint of cost, in larger enrollment. This leads to a consideration of factors tending to increase cost as size increases.

Diseconomies of Scale

As indicated earlier in this chapter, growing organizations eventually become subject to three influences that tend to raise unit costs. Colleges and universities are not immune from these influences. As they grow, they become subject to: increasing costs of organizational coordination, possible deterioration of quality of product or service, and increasing costs of student recruitment and student transportation. This section considers each of these.

Coordination. As institutions grow, there can be no doubt that coordination gradually becomes more difficult and costly and that the costs associated with failures of coordination become steadily greater. These costs are clearly visible in a huge organization like the federal government with its swollen White House staff, its innumerable liaison officers, its thousands of boards, committees and interagency groups, and its constant need for reorganization. They are also visible in the widespread public dissatisfaction with the degree of coordination achieved. Colleges and universities, even the largest of them, are relatively small organizations, and the problems of coordination are less than horrendous. Nevertheless, the increasing costs of efforts to achieve coordination and of the failures to do so begin to appear in the larger institutions. They are clearly evident in the large multi-campus systems where in some cases central staffs of several hundred people are needed, or at least exist, for the ostensible purpose of coordination. Even individual campuses do not reach very large size before interdepartmental committees, formal newsletters, research coordinators, personnel officers, affirmative action specialists, and administrative lawyers make their appearance. Efforts to achieve coordination lead to formal regulations and these give rise to a bureaucratic mentality that no one intends or condones but which is an inevitable outcome of large organizations. On even the largest campus, however, actual costs of achieving coordination and the costs associated with failures to achieve it are probably not very high relative to the total budget. My guess is that these costs would in no case exceed two or five percent of the total budget. These costs do not cause overall cost per student unit to rise very much as institutional size increases (see Figure 5).

Quality. A possibly more important aspect of institutional size is its effect on the product, that is, on educational *quality*. (See Chickering, 1965; Rock, Centra, and Linn, 1969; Withey, 1971; Clark and others, 1972; Astin, 1972; Chickering, 1971; Feldman and Newcomb, 1969; Pace, 1974; Bayer, 1975; and Bowen, 1977.) So long as cost is reckoned merely in terms of student units, no allowance is made for differences in quality with changes in institutional size. But, if institutional growth should impair quality, this would be equivalent to increasing unit cost; and if institutional growth should enhance quality, this would be equivalent to decreasing unit cost.

The question of whether size significantly affects quality, other things equal, is often debated. Perhaps the most widely accepted opinion is in two parts. First, when institutions are very small—of the order of a few hundred students—quality improves with growth. This opinion is based on the theory that small institutions usually cannot afford adequate facilities or a diversified faculty or a cosmopolitan environment. It is assumed that growth up to at least 1,000 to 1,500 students enables institutions to give on the whole a better education. The second part of the conventional wisdom is that when institutions reach substantial size—some say the critical point is at 3,000, others at 25,000 students—they become rigid, bureaucratic, impersonal, lacking in collegiality. Others argue that there is no best size—rather that some students prosper best in small colleges, others in large institutions; and that what is needed is diversity rather than some theoretical size alleged to be optimal.

There is no doubt in my mind that excellent education without excessive cost could take place in diminutive settings. For example, aside from Mark Hopkins and the log, I can imagine excellent education occurring in a group of fifteen students with a single great teacher, with no facilities but a single room, a blackboard, a few hundred well-chosen books, the great out-of-doors, and the freely available resources of the community-at-large. In such a setting most of the institutional trappings would be absent. There would be no libraries, chapels, laboratories, football teams, faculty meetings, dormitories, student unions, trustees, and so on. There would be just students, a gifted professor, some books, and the imagination to use the abundant resources of nature and of the surrounding community. The problem with this model, of course, is that there are not enough skillful and dedicated teachers, and community resources would become overloaded if all higher education were conducted in this pattern.

At the other extreme, I can imagine a great university of 50,000 or even 100,000 students in which collegiality would thrive. Such an institution would be unified and yet so decentralized as to academic organization, living arrangements, and provisions for commuters that every student and every faculty member would achieve a sense of community within the small subdivisions and informal groupings out of which the whole university would be constructed. Indeed, one of the challenges before American higher education is to learn to convert the huge university—especially the institution that serves part-time commuters and large numbers of adults—into a place where individual students can achieve some of the valuable cultural and intellectual influences and inter-personal experiences that characterize the traditional residential college or university.[2] Many col-

[2]One of my critics commented on this passage as follows: "The idea of a 50,000 to 100,000 student university as a 'collegial' campus seems to me to be a worthy but unattainable hope. There are absolute limits on community size in which individuals can be known as individuals and can share in a community in the true sense, as opposed to being merely members of an organization. This is true of tribes and towns and states and, I suspect, of campuses as well. And I am quite sure that 50,000 is *far* beyond the limits—my guess is that 20,000 would be stretching it *very* hard. A *sense* of community is a matter of psychological identity. It is difficult to imagine any commuter student with outside family and job obligations ever shifting enough personal allegiance toward a place where he or she takes a few courses to become a true member of a campus community in the sense that a full-time residential student at a small college is a member of a community."

lege students, perhaps the majority, are not full-time students, do not reside in a campus community, do not have access to the cultural amenities of the campus, do not have the opportunity to fraternize with their fellow students, and do not even have access to libraries and laboratories or to fully qualified faculty. It is hard to believe that the educational experience of many students attending the huge multi-versities of our era is as influential on their lives as that obtained in the traditional and smaller residential institutions.

There is no reason why either smallness or bigness must be inefficient or stultifying. Yet within the context of the higher educational system as we know it today, educational quality probably is impaired when institutions are too small or too large (see Clark and others, 1972; Feldman and Newcomb, 1969). While these impairments may be overcome, institutions, especially large ones, are likely to incur costs in doing so. Thus the U-shaped curve depicted in Figure 5 appears to be plausible in its representation of increased costs at both ends of the size scale; loss of quality may result from both smallness and bigness.

Today, a tiny percentage of students attend institutions that may be regarded as too small. Only about 1 percent of the nation's students are in institutions having fewer than 500 students, and 4 percent are in institutions of fewer than 1,000 students; whereas, about half are in institutions with more than 10,000 students. (These estimates are based on data in Carnegie Council on Policy Studies in Higher Education, 1976.) Overly large institutions, thus, are of more concern than overly small ones. Most authorities who have investigated the matter of institutional size advise that it is prudent to restrict enrollments to the smallest size that is consistent with minimal cost. On this basis, for example, the Carnegie Commission (1971, p. 41) recommended that "state plans for the growth and development of public institutions of higher education should in general incorporate both minimum and maximum enrollment objectives" as follows:

	Minimum	*Maximum*
Doctoral-granting universities	5,000	20,000
Comprehensive colleges	5,000	10,000
Liberal arts colleges	1,000	2,500
Two-year colleges	2,000	5,000

In justifying these minimum and maximum limits, the commission suggested that enrollments either below or above these levels entail increased costs, impaired quality, or both. They recommended that state policy be designed to restrict or reduce the size of state institutions that have become too large, and increase the size of those that are too small. Events have partially passed by the commission's recommendations on maximum size, and the problem now is to learn to live more gracefully and productively with very large institutions. In doing so, institutions may well encounter increased unit costs.

Student Recruitment and Student Transportation. Many institutions grow by recruiting an increasing percentage of the population in their existing market area or by expanding the market area from which they draw students. In either case, unit costs for recruitment and student aid may increase. As institutions increase their enrollments they may also attract less capable or less motivated students, involving increased costs associated with instruction and student services, and higher rates of student attrition. Moreover, to the extent that growth involves an expansion of market area, the costs of transporting students may rise. While this cost is not borne by the institutions, it is a social cost that must be reckoned as part of the price of an expanded market.

More important than the costs of student recruitment and student transportation is the effect of large enrollments on students' access to higher education. A higher educational system with a few large institutions tends to present a barrier to students' access as compared with a system having many small institutions. As Anderson, Bowman, and Tinto (1972) and other scholars have reported, attendance at colleges and universities is strongly affected by the proximity of institutions. Thus in sparsely populated areas, economies of scale must be weighed against ease of access.

Institutional Motives

An inquiry into institutional size would be incomplete without a consideration of institutional power and the motivations related to it. As institutions grow they become increasingly visible. They loom large physically and they are seen and heard about by millions of people. They acquire prestige and notoriety. They figure in the news, especially on the sports pages. They have thousands of employees, alumni, students, and clients of many kinds. In all these ways they acquire influence or power which is useful in attracting appropriations, gifts, students, and faculty. The greater the institution's size, the greater its power. Under these conditions, the leadership of major institutions, and those associated with them—including faculty, staff, alumni, students, and others—are strongly motivated toward growth. The institutional advantages of growth, because of the power and resources it brings, tend to outweigh the educational advantages of more modest size.

Another even more potent motive for growth in public institutions is that state allocation of funds to these colleges and universities are usually based primarily on enrollment. As public institutions grow, they receive proportionately more money. Because their costs for salaries and capital expenditures do not grow in proportion to enrollment, these institutions can use the new revenues for new programs, higher salaries, new equipment, and other kinds of development. The hope of receiving this dividend encourages institutional leaders to promote growth.

These incentives toward institutional growth may influence institutions to exceed their optimal size. However, they also encourage colleges and universities to open their doors to more students. In a period when the nation is trying to extend opportunity, it may well be in the broad social interest for educators to be strongly motivated toward growth. Achieving the optimal size of institutions is not the only desideratum.

Concluding Comments

Perhaps the most important finding of this chapter is that institutional size and unit cost are not closely related in any rigid or mechanical fashion. It is possible to conduct higher education in many ways. Institutions of the same size operate at quite different unit costs, and institutions of quite different size operate at the same cost. The phenomenon of "lumpiness" of resources is real, yet institutions can adjust their resources to their size—in innumerable ways—by sharing facilities with other institutions, by leasing instead of owning, by employing part-time staff, by adjusting curricula to avoid fields with low enrollment like Chinese language or fields that require expensive equipment like high energy physics, or by deliberately trading off the cost advantages from larger size against the educational advantages of smaller size. As E. F. Schumacher told us in *Small is Beautiful* (1973), there is need to invent technologies suited to small scale operation. In the case of higher education, these technologies may be no more than such simple and ancient devices as programmed independent study, curricula geared to traditional basic subjects, or lecture courses given to large classes. In a study of the costs of undergraduate education, Gordon Douglass and I estimated the unit costs for different modes of instruction and we learned that with rather modest changes in the way instruction is conducted, costs per course enrollment could range from \$117 to \$334 (Bowen and Douglass, 1971, pp. 95–103). The possibilities for cost variation from adjusting the mode of operation greatly overshadow the effects of institutional size on cost. Similarly large institutions can invent methods to overcome the disadvantages of their bigness without losing the economic advantage of their size. All this is not to deny that there are forces causing particular unit costs to decline as size increases and other forces causing them to rise, and that in this sense institutional size is one factor among many in the determination of higher educational costs.

It is doubtful that much money would be saved either by consolidating higher education into large institutions or dispersing it to small institutions. Costs are still determined by the availability of funds. However, on grounds of educational quality, it may be desirable to err on the side of smallness. This tentative recommendation takes on special importance in the 1980s when enrollments may stop growing or even may decline. The American higher educational system might be improved qualitatively if public policy were to encourage a shifting of the weight of enrollments from very large institutions to the smaller and middle-sized ones. (See the Carnegie Commission, 1972, p. 41, for a similar recommendation.) Without such encouragement, it is possible that many smaller institutions will shrink or even disappear while large ones will eventually become even larger.

Part Three

What Should
Higher Education Cost?

This book is basically a study of costs and cost behavior in American higher education. It would be incomplete, however, without an attempt to distill from the data and argument some general conclusions and recommendations about future costs. A perennial question facing American society is: What should higher education cost? The purpose of this concluding part is to consider this question by drawing upon the previous chapters. The question will be considered not in detail and for particular institutions, but broadly for the entire American system of higher education.

To place the following three chapters in context, it may be useful to review the plan of the entire book. Part One, consisting of Chapters Two through Five, was a study of long-term trends in costs over nearly fifty years. Part Two, Chapters Six through Nine, was a cross-sectional study of the costs of a representative sample of 268 colleges and universities in a single year, 1976–77. Part Three, the next three chapters, deals with the implications of these findings as they bear upon the question of what higher education *should* cost.

10

Implications of the Study of National Trends

One way of judging the legitimate financial needs of American higher education is to review past trends in cost, and in factors affecting cost, and thus to gain insights about where higher education stands today and where it should be headed in the 1980s and beyond. Information from the past does not, of course, automatically answer a question as loaded with value as the one addressed in this chapter. But it does provide useful perspective in appraising the conditions of the present and the likely future.

This chapter traces the financial position of American higher education over the decade of the 1970s drawing on data in Part Two of this book. During the 1970s, America's colleges and universities probably lost ground both financially and educationally. The task before us is to assess the amount of this deterioration by estimating what it would have cost in 1979–80 to restore the higher educational system to the level of operation it had achieved in 1969–70.

The selection of 1969–70 as a base year does not imply that the level of operations in that year was a standard against which the future condition and progress of higher education should be judged. On the one hand, the financial squeeze in the years since 1969–70 may have introduced desirable economies that should be perpetuated. On the other hand, a mere restoration of unit cost to the 1969–70 level might not be sufficient to overcome all subsequent qualitative deterioration. The conditions since 1969–70 may have changed in ways that call for either decreased or increased real cost per student unit. Nevertheless, the year 1969–70 is a useful benchmark against which to measure recent cost trends. It was an important turning point in the history of higher education. It was the culmination of a long period of growing resources and rising costs and the beginning of the more austere and subdued 1970s. The precise turning point may be variously dated. Viewed as the end of a period of strongly enthusiastic public attitudes toward higher education, the turning point may have come as early as 1967 when student unrest was at its height. Viewed as a time when comparatively large increases in revenue per student ceased, it probably came around 1973. The year 1969–70 may thus be regarded as a kind of transitional year when public attitudes toward higher education were already becoming less enthusiastic but when unit costs had not yet peaked.

The era prior to 1969–70, often called the "golden years," may be interpreted in three ways. First, it was a time for correcting decades of neglect of higher education during the Great Depression, World War II, the Korean War, and recurrent periods of inflation. By the early 1950s, higher education was clearly under-financed. Salaries in constant dollars were lower than they had been twenty years earlier; the physical plant—symbolized by Quonset huts—was inadequate and obsolete; enrollments were down sharply following the departure of the GIs; and faculty and staff were dispirited if not demoralized. Second, the "golden years" represented a radical reevaluation of higher education on the part of society. Through the experience of World War II and its aftermath of rapid technological progress and Cold War, the American people gained a new appreciation of higher education as a base for economic development and national power. Third, because of libertarian and egalitarian stirrings in the society, higher education was seen, as never before, in terms of personal opportunity and human equality.

As higher education came to be appreciated and valued in a new light, the federal government, state legislatures, and private donors sought both to expand it and to improve it. They were willing to finance higher salaries and thus attract more capable talent, to provide better physical plant, and to support many training programs judged to be in the public interest. The result, of course, was higher unit costs which were deliberately planned and backed up by a strongly assenting public opinion. The momentum was sustained through the 1960s by the growing public concern with egalitarian values. The gradually changing emphasis from Cold War to egalitarian values was symbolized when the title of the National Defense Education Act was eventually changed to the National Direct Student Loan Program.

One may ask whether the enthusiasm of the late 1950s and 1960s had carried higher educational costs to unnecessary and unsustainable heights in 1969–70 from which the nation should have retreated at least part way. It is probable that the rapid escalation of revenues, and therefore of costs, did introduce some extravagance and waste into the higher educational system. And it should be no surprise that there would be a leveling off or even a decline from the position attained in 1969–70. But, in fact there was no hasty retreat from the 1969–70 unit cost, remarkably little public outcry against sustained support, and little public demand for drastic cutbacks. During the time of student unrest, politicians were tempted to attack higher education, but these attacks soon subsided and the general public mood became one of neither euphoric enthusiasm nor bitter attack but rather one of holding ground already gained. The level of financial support attained in the late 1960s had, and to a considerable degree still has, widespread public approval. The year 1969–70 therefore represents a useful base against which to compare costs ten years later. The immediate task before us, then, is to estimate how much money would be needed to carry on higher education in 1979–80 at the level of performance actually attained in 1969–70 (allowing for changes in the value of the dollar). This estimate would tell us how much higher education gained or lost financially during the 1970s, and might also provide some inkling of changes in quality.

Overall Unit Cost

Average cost per student unit for the enitre American higher educational system in the base year, 1969–70, was about $3,333. This figure refers to operating and capital expenditures for the education of students. It excludes costs for research, public service, and auxiliary enterprises, and is expressed in 1979–80 dollars.[1] The comparable

---

[1]The figure of $3,333 corresponds to $1,413 in Table 4 which is the same figure expressed in 1967 dollars.

figure for 1979–80 was about $3,215. The difference is only $118 per student unit or 3.5 percent of the unit cost in 1969–70. To bring unit costs in 1979–80 up to their 1969–70 level would involve a total expenditure of about $1.4 billion. (The number of student units in 1979–80 was about 12.2 million.)

These calculations suggest that the reduction in overall unit cost over the decade of the 1970s was quite modest. Superficially it might be interpreted as a minor correction, a trimming of fat, that was wholly appropriate at the end of a long and buoyant period of rising costs. This interpretation would, however, be incomplete. The higher educational system achieved this near stability of total cost per student unit only through substantial sacrifices that left the system weaker at the end of the 1970s than at the beginning. This near stability of unit cost was attained by holding increases in staff compensation below those prevailing in other industries, deferring the maintenance of assets, and making budget cuts to offset the effects of new socially imposed costs. Furthermore, partly because of these sacrifices and partly for other reasons, educational quality or performance probably deteriorated in some respects during the 1970s. The remainder of this chapter is devoted to estimating the amount of money needed to restore the higher education system to the 1969–70 level of performance. In so doing, it is by no means assumed that every reduction in funds is tantamount to a decline in educational quality or that money is all that would be required to catch up. In large measure, educational excellence is attained through intangibles such as dedication to learning, caring for people as individuals, strong sense of community, and valued traditions and these cannot all be bought with money.

Staff Compensation

As reported in Chapter Three, during most of the 1970s faculty and administrative compensation lagged behind the rising Consumer Price Index by only about 1 percentage point a year. This was something of an achievement because, in previous episodes of inflation in the twentieth century, faculty and administrative compensation suffered drastic cuts relative to the cost of living. However, in years of double-digit inflation, compensation in higher education fell behind even more. In any case, staying nearly abreast of inflation did not keep higher education competitive in the national labor market. In the 1970s faculty and administrative compensation slipped significantly relative to compensation paid in most other industries. The widening gap was 1 to 2 percentage points. This seemingly small differential, when cumulated over a decade, had a sizeable impact. If the gap should persist and widen for another decade or two, the calibre of talent attracted to higher education might be seriously diminished.

It is sometimes argued that it is not socially necessary or even desirable for the academic profession to attract a substantial share of the best talent—that it would be acceptable if more of this talent were drawn to business, government, and the independent professions. The work of academic people is not necessarily more significant than that of persons in comparable positions in business, government, and the professions. But the responsibilities of academic people do call for talent generally comparable to that in business, government, and the professions. The academic functions include teaching, advising young people, conducting basic research, engaging in philosophical and religious inquiry, providing social criticism and public policy analysis, cultivating literature and the fine arts, preserving the cultural heritage, and consulting with government and many other organizations and groups on particular issues and problems (Bowen, 1977, chap. 14). These functions require traits of intelligence, character, judgment, skills, and formal education at least equal to those for comparable work in other industries and in the long run require similar compensation.

It is also often assumed that academic people have no employment options and that it is not necessary to compensate them competitively. This is a dubious assumption. As pointed out in Chapter Three, faculty members as a class have substantial mobility. And this holds not only for those in professional fields but also for many in the natural sciences, economics, psychology, and other areas. The economic power of the faculty derives from its potential mobility. For that power to be exercised, it is not required that every faculty person decide to move; it is only necessary that a significant fraction at the margin be mobile. If the compensation gap continues to widen, increasing numbers will drift to other pursuits. Unfortunately, some of the most energetic, enterprising, and gifted people may be the first to go. The stereotype of the long-suffering faculty member who is incapable of mobility and who will supinely remain in academic work regardless of the financial sacrifices involved is a false image. Furthermore, at the entry level, already many of the ablest young people, comparable to those who came into the academic profession in the past three decades, are not planning to enter college teaching but are going into the independent professions and business. The nation probably is headed toward slow deterioration of the academic profession unless the pace of growth in compensation becomes closer to that in the outside world. The first sign of this deterioration, loss of morale, is already observable.

What is true of faculty is even more true of administrative and general service workers. These people are on the whole less specialized and less wedded to an academic way of life than are faculty members. It is not hard for managers, personnel directors, accountants, clerks, security guards, computer staff, mechanics, plumbers, cooks, and other nonfaculty workers to find employment beyond the campus. Unfortunately, little information is available about the earnings of general service workers in colleges and universities. Such data as can be found suggest that these workers are paid less than their counterparts in other industries.

To restore the competitive position that college and university faculty and staffs held in 1969-70 would cost about $2.3 billion in 1979-80. This figure is a rough estimate computed by calculating the amount of staff compensation in 1979-80 if annual increases over the previous decade had been 7.5 percent instead of 5.9 percent. It expresses the general size of the deficit that accumulated over the 1970s in the maintenance of higher education's most valuable asset, its people.

Staff Numbers

Changes in the number of staff persons relative to enrollments over the decade of the 1970s are mixed and trends are uncertain. This is so partly because of conceptual difficulties and partly because relevant data are inadequate.

The ratio of faculty to students expressed in simple full-time-equivalents has deteriorated since 1969-70. The ratio was about 1 to 13.3 in 1969-70 and 1 to 14.0 or 14.5 in 1979-80, a change of 6 to 9 percent (Table 5). These figures relate strictly to the change between

1969-70 and 1977-78. Fragmentary information suggests that little change in the ratio occurred between 1977-78 and 1979-80. But when faculty numbers are adjusted to exclude faculty time devoted to research and public service and when numbers of students are converted to student units adjusted for academic level of students, the result is different. Then, surprisingly, the ratio improved from about 1 to 28.6 in 1969-70 and to about 1 to about 26.4 in 1979-80. The rates improved because the relative amount of faculty time devoted to organized research and public service declined, leaving relatively more faculty time for teaching (see Appendix B). The growth in the number of graduate and professional students relative to undergraduate students slowed up, thus moderating the upward trend in the number of student units. For the educational functions of colleges and universities, more faculty time per student unit was available in 1979-80 than in 1969-70. The gain to institutions in resources available for instruction over the decade was perhaps the full-time-equivalent of 25,000 to 40,000 faculty members. At an average compensation of $24,159, the dollar amount of gain was of the order of $0.6 to $1 billion.

Unfortunately, little information is available on trends in the numbers of nonfaculty employees of colleges and universities. These include administrators, various categories of professional persons, office workers, physical plant employees, and others. Not only are data lacking, but there have been almost no studies of the ratios of nonfaculty employees to students. One relevant finding from Chapter Seven is that as institutions become more affluent they increase the number of nonfaculty workers (relative to students) more than they increase the number of faculty. One might infer from this finding that during the 1970s, when higher education became less affluent, the employment of nonfaculty workers would have decreased. This hypothesis is supported by data from annual surveys of 135 private institutions (Minter and Bowen, 1978, p. 29). These data show that between 1973-74 and 1977-78 the number of administrative staff increased by 10 percent, the number of other nonfaculty workers decreased by 4 to 5 percent, and employment of all nonfaculty workers combined decreased by 2 percent. During the same period enrollment of the 135 institutions grew by 7 percent. On the basis of these figures, one might surmise that the ratio of nonfaculty workers to student units declined over the decade. The number necessary to restore the ratio might be conservatively estimated at 25,000 to 30,000. Assuming average compensation at $15,000 the needed amount might be of the order of $0.4 to $0.5 billion.

Purchases of Current Goods and Services

Expenditures for goods and services purchased from outside vendors are affected by changes in both prices and quantities purchased. As indicated in Chapter Five, the prices of the particular assortment of goods and services purchased on current account by colleges and universities have risen over the years somewhat more rapidly than the Producer Price Index. However, over the particular decade 1969-70 to 1979-80, the period now under review, the rise in the Higher Education Price Index for purchased goods and services was exactly equal to the rise in the Producer Price Index for the economy as a whole. The presumption, then, is that the particular assortment of goods and services purchased by colleges and universities did not rise appreciably faster than the general level of prices for goods and services.

However, though data are scarce, it is almost certain that the quantity of goods and services purchased relative to enrollments, decreased somewhat over the decade of the 1970s. For example, library acquisitions declined absolutely despite a 39 percent increase in enrollment. From 1970-71 to 1975-76, the number of volumes acquired fell from 26.4 million to 22.9 million, and periodical titles acquired rose from 3.7 to 4.6 million, leaving a net decline from 30.1 million to 27.5 million (National Center for Education Statistics, *Digest of Education Statistics 1977-78,* p. 191). Similarly, strenuous efforts were made to slow the growth of energy use. Doubtless, financial stringency induced other savings in purchases of current goods and services. But higher education could not accommodate a growth in enrollment of 39 percent over the decade without substantial increases in the purchase of the myriad items used by colleges and universities. On the other hand, growth of enrollment may have introduced some economies in the use of purchased goods and services. The most that can be said, in view of the lack of data, is that the quantity of purchased goods and services probably increased proportionately less than the growth in enrollment. The quantity of goods and services purchased for educational purposes might have increased by 30 to 35 percent during the decade while enrollment increased 39 percent. On this assumption, to restore the 1969–70 level of expenditures per student unit might have cost $0.5 to $0.6 billion in 1979–80.

Replacement of Capital Goods

In considering the position of higher education with respect to the acquisition of capital goods—land, buildings, and equipment—it is useful to review the historical record. Table 36 presents estimates of the amounts of capital goods acquired and the stock of capital goods held by decades over the past half-century. Because the basic data, which are stated in terms of book value, are difficult to interpret and the adjustments lack precision, these data should be regarded as rough estimates. They do, however, probably reveal orders of magnitude and general trends.

As shown in Table 36, the additions to capital for educational purposes grew rapidly from $0.7 billion in the decade of the 1930s to $26 billion in the 1970s. When these figures are converted to constant (1979–80) dollars, the long-term growth appears less spectacular but was nevertheless substantial. The amount of capital acquired in the 1930s was $6.5 billion, a peak of $44.6 billion was reached in the 1960s, and then a modest decline occurred in the 1970s. As shown in the annual data, the decline during the 1970s persisted from year to year throughout the decade. The annual additions to capital fell exactly by half, from $5.6 billion in 1969–70 to $2.8 billion in 1979–80. This decline, however, was from the unprecedented levels achieved in the 1960s. Surprisingly, the amount of capital added in the 1970s was greater than in any other decade except the 1960s.

With the accumulation of new capital over the decades, the total stock of capital (in 1979–80 dollars) increased rapidly and steadily. Indeed, the stock of capital increased by a sizeable amount even during the 1970s, despite the decline in capital acquisitions during that decade. In 1969–70, the value of the capital stock (in 1979–80 dollars) was $91.9 billion; in 1979–80 it was $123.8 billion, an increase of 35 percent. Clearly, the addition of new plant in the 1970s was sufficient not only to maintain the capital stock of the higher educational system but also to achieve hefty growth.

	Estimated value of capital goods acquired during period			Estimated stock of capital goods held at end of period		
	Total (billions of current dollars)[a]	Total (billions of 1979–80 dollars)[b]	Per student unit (1979–80 dollars)[c]	Total (billions of current dollars)[d]	Total (billions of 1979–80 dollars)[e]	Per student unit (1979–80 dollars)[c]
By decades:						
1930s	$ 0.7	$ 6.5	$5,290	$ 2.3	$ 21.2	$13,500
1940s	1.5	10.2	5,890	3.0	28.3	9,840
1950s	4.6	17.8	6,280	6.6	42.7	11,370
1960s	14.7	44.6	8,210	23.2	91.9	10,420
1970s	26.0	40.9	3,890	47.7	123.8	10,124
By years:						
1969–70	2.4	5.6				
1970–71	2.4	5.3				
1971–72	2.4	4.9				
1972–73	2.2	4.3				
1973–74	2.5	4.4				
1974–75	2.8	4.5				
1975–76	2.7	4.2				
1976–77	2.7	3.8				
1977–78	2.7	3.6				
1978–79	2.8	3.1				
1979–80	2.8	2.8				

Note: Data reflect capital goods acquired for educational purposes only. Acquisitions for research, auxiliary enterprises, and other noneducational purposes are excluded.

[a] Amounts for educational purposes estimated on the basis of the educational and general expenditures allocated to education as a percentage of total current expenditures (see Appendix B, Table 39).

[b] Adjusted for price changes using index of construction and equipment prices (see Appendix B, Table 40 for data and sources). The index number for 1979–80 was estimated at 275.

[c] For enrollment data and sources, see Appendix B, Table 41.

[d] Assumes that $2.0 billion was carried over from investments made prior to 1929–30 and that investments made after 1929–30 depreciated at the rate of 20 percent a decade on a declining balance.

[e] Adjusted for price changes using index of construction and equipment prices (see Appendix B, Table 40). In making this adjustment, we converted the book value for each period to 1979–80 dollars.

Source: Tabulation of data from National Center for Education Statistics, *Digest of Education Statistics, 1977–78,* 1978, pp. 134–135; *Projections of Education Statistics to 1986–87,* 1978, p. 104.

When the figures on capital are related to enrollments, however, they present a less glowing picture. The number of students to be served by the buildings and equipment increased during the decade by about 39 percent. The acquisition of capital *per student unit*, therefore, was far less in the 1970s than in any decade of the last half-century. The figure for the 1970s was $3,890 per student unit, less than half the amount in the 1960s and even lower than acquisitions in the depressed 1930s and 1940s. As a result, the total stock of capital per student unit has been on a slow downward trend since the 1950s. Despite the sharp decline in annual capital accumulation during the 1970s, the stock of capital goods per student unit declined by only about 3 percent between 1969–70 and 1979–80. A decline in capital of this magnitude cannot be taken too seriously. The probable error in the data is such that one cannot be sure that there was in fact any decline.

The large growth of enrollment in the decade probably yielded some economies of scale in the use of physical plant. These savings could have offset any qualitative deterioration due to a modest decline in capital stock per student.

Maintenance of Capital Goods

It is one thing to maintain the capital stock of higher education through additions of new buildings and equipment—partly to replace outworn capital and partly to add facilities for new programs and functions—and quite another to maintain physically the existing plant that has been accumulated from past investments. New buildings and equipment are financed mostly by designated capital funds that are derived from special appropriations and gifts. The monies for plant maintenance, on the other hand, come mostly from current operating funds and so maintenance competes directly with faculty and staff salaries, purchases of goods and services, student financial aid and other pressing current items. Maintenance can be postponed, often until absolute breakdown occurs. The pressures on current budgets are always so intense that deferred maintenance is present in almost all institutions. The accumulated amounts at many campuses are substantial.

It is widely assumed that deferred maintenance was greater in 1979–80 than in 1969–70. The bases for this judgment are the reports of physical plant directors, a few surveys of the physical condition of campuses, budget data, and general impressions. The difficulty with these sources is that little comparable data are available for earlier periods. The problem of deferred maintenance is not new. A survey of campuses in 1969–70 or any other earlier year would have revealed substantial amounts of deferred maintenance. No one knows the extent to which the condition is getting worse or better. For example, my own impression is that the problem was more serious in 1950, after years of depression and war, than it was in 1979–80. My impression also is that the problem was worse in 1979–80 than in 1969–70, the base year for present review. But there are virtually no data to substantiate either impression—only a few shreds of evidence.

The elusive subject of deferred maintenance is also complicated by conceptual problems. Some deferred maintenance projects are intended only to keep buildings and equipment operable, to avoid costly breakdowns, and to prevent property from becoming prematurely useless. Other deferred maintenance is designed to improve property, for example, by making it more energy efficient, by bringing its safety up to government standards, or by making it accessible to handicapped persons.

A recent report on the subject states "that as much as $35 billion may now be needed nationwide to offset the cost of maintenance that colleges have put off since the campus building boom of the 1960s . . . . perhaps $15 billion of the total would be required just to cover the backlog of projects to bring facilities up to government standards and to take care of essential energy-related repairs" (Kaiser, 1979, p. 1; see also Editorial Projects for Education, 1980, pp. 1–2). This amount suggests that the annual accumulation of deferred maintenance may be of the order of $2 to $4 billion a year.

The same reports also cited local studies that cast some light on the matter. A 1970 study at the University of Syracuse identified $18 million of "backlogged work," and a 1976 study at the University of Nebraska revealed deferred maintenance of $21 million (Kaiser, 1979, p. 3). These two local studies confirm that the problem was present in the early 1970s. When these figures are related to the enrollments of the two institutions under study, deferred maintenance amounted to about $600 to $1,200 per student. If these amounts per student were representative of all institutions, the national total of deferred maintenance for a system of over 11 million students might be of the order of $7 to $15 billion—much less than the $35 billion previously cited. However, construction costs have escalated since the early 1970s. A 1980 University of Minnesota Study reports a need for $177 million for "energy, building maintenance, and bringing existing buildings up to code" (Educational Projects for the Future, 1980, p. 2). This amount is about $2,300 per student. If this figure were typical of all institutions, the national total of deferred maintenance would be about $25 billion.

Another approach to the matter of deferred maintenance is to trace the trend of expenditures for plant maintenance. Unfortunately, in the available statistics of higher education, these expenditures are combined with the outlays for plant operation including such items as fuel and utilities, labor for operating the power plant and other facilities, and housekeeping. So the trend of expenditures for maintenance alone tends to be obscured. The historical record of expenditures for plant operation and maintenance expressed as percentages of both current expenditures and plant value, as reported by the National Center of Education Statistics (*Digest of Education Statistics 1977–78*, 1978, pp. 134, 135, 139), is as follows: The figures indicate that over the decades prior to the 1970s plant operation and maintenance generally declined as a percentage of current expenditures. This decline could indicate improved efficiency of maintenance or relatively lower prices of fuel, utilities, and other purchases; or it could indicate deteriorating maintenance standards over a long period of

	Percentage of educational and general expenditures	Percentage of total current expenditures	Percentage of total value of plant
1929–30	16.1%	12.0%	3.0%
1939–40	13.4	10.4	2.5
1949–50	13.2	10.0	4.7
1959–60	10.4	8.4	3.5
1969–70	9.8	7.4	3.7
1971–72	10.0	7.5	3.8
1973–74	10.7	8.1	4.3
1974–75	10.1	8.0	4.5
1975–76	10.1	7.9	4.7
1976–77	9.5–10.5	—	—

time. However, plant operation and maintenance as a percentage of the value of plant rose slowly and unevenly over the same period.

If one focuses only on changes in the several percentages during the 1970s, the trend appears to have been somewhat uneven but generally upward. This rising trend undoubtedly reflects increases in relative prices of energy and wages more than greater attention to maintenance. No doubt if the data were available up to 1979–80, they would show unmistakably the effect of drastic increases in the price of energy. Moreover, because plant operation usually is charged to the same departmental budget as maintenance, there is undoubtedly a tendency to make up increased costs of energy with cuts in maintenance.

Another factor in interpreting a complex situation is that over time the average age of the plant has changed. In the years prior to 1950 the plant was much older than it was after the building boom of the 1960s and 1970s when the great bulk of the present plant was built. With new buildings and equipment, maintenance expenditures could be lower than with older plants. By 1979–80, however, the plant built in the boom years was aging and the amount of needed maintenance was increasing.

The conclusion from these many considerations is that in the 1970s maintenance did not obviously decline relative to other expenditures or relative to the value of the plant, and it may have increased moderately. It is not certain, however, that the standard of maintenance in the 1970s was sufficient to prevent a steady accumulation of deferred maintenance work. With the increasing average age of the plant and the financial stringency during the period, the amount of deferred maintenance probably did increase. To place a reliable dollar figure on the amount would be impossible, but it might well be equal to the entire maintenance budget (exclusive of plant operation) for two years, or perhaps $10 or $15 billion. This would not overcome all deferred maintenance, it would only bring the plant up to the standard of 1969–70 when there also was a substantial amount of deferred maintenance. If the cost of catching up on this deficiency were spread over five years, the annual budget for plant operation in the early 1980s would have to be increased by $2 to $3 billion.

Socially Imposed Costs

Chapter Four presented an extended discussion of costs imposed on colleges and universities through informal social pressure or governmental mandate. These costs relate mostly to personal security of workers, work standards, equality of opportunity, broad participation in decisions, demands for public information and accountability, and environmental protection. The great surge of new socially imposed costs occurred between 1959-60 and 1974-75; however, additional costs of this kind, for example, successive increases in social security taxes, continued to be imposed after 1974-75. The conclusion regarding these costs was that over the 15 years from 1959-60 to 1974-75 they amounted to $2.0 to $2.5 billion per annum. Over the period now under review, 1969-70 to 1979-80, allowing for inflation and for some slowing down in the imposition of new costs and including only costs related to education, the annual amount of increase was probably of the order of $1.5 to $2 billion.

Intangible Assets

Of critical importance to higher education are its intangible assets. These include favorable public attitudes that affect the ability to recruit and retain qualified students and faculty and to maintain ties to sources of funds. Above all, the intangible assets include the ability to deliver excellent educational services. Any review of the progress of higher education over the decade of the 1970s would be incomplete without considering progress with respect to these intangibles.

Public Attitudes. Throughout American history, public attitudes toward higher education have been ambivalent. On the one hand, education has been seen as the foundation of a democratic society, as essential preparation for specialized vocations in an advancing technology, as a way of facilitating the intellectual and moral growth of human beings, and as a means of achieving the good life. On the other hand, suspicion of education and of educated people always has been present in American society. The relative strength of these two attitudes has fluctuated over time, in a sort of manic-depressive cycle, and the fortunes of higher education have varied accordingly.

Following World War II the nation entered a manic phase which lasted through most of the 1960s. During that time, colleges and universities attained a wholly new level of financial support and expanded to a previously unheard of scale of operation. But beginning in the late 1960s, the nation entered the depressive phase of the cycle. People began to sense that higher education had not quite achieved all that had been hoped for it and that it certainly had not brought on the millennium. They were upset about the student unrest of the 1960s. They become concerned as to whether the colleges and universities were trying to educate more students than were qualified for college work. They questioned whether the labor market could supply enough jobs for all college graduates. And they worried about the ever-increasing cost of the higher educational establishment. There can be no doubt that public attitudes toward higher education were less enthusiastic in the 1970s than in the 1950s and 1960s. But to say that they were strongly negative would simply not be true. Study after study during the 1970s showed that both students and alumni were appreciative of their college experience. Similarly, most members of the general public expressed favorable attitudes toward higher education. Parents in particular indicated overwhelmingly that they hoped and expected that their sons and daughters would attend college (Bowen, 1977).

More convincing than what people said is what they did. The number of persons attending college increased from about 8 million in 1969–70 to about 12 million in 1979–80, or by 50 percent. The corresponding figures in full-time-equivalents were 6.3 million in 1969–70 and 8.7 million in 1979–80, an increase of 39 percent (National Center for Education Statistics, *Projections of Education Statistics, 1986–87,* 1979, pp. 20, 26). During no year in the decade did enrollment decline although the composition of the enrollment changed. At the end of the decade there was a lower percentage of men and a higher percentage of women than previously; a lower percentage of full-time students and a higher percentage of part-time students; and a lower percentage of younger students of conventional college age and a higher percentage of older students. But the overall participation of the American people both in absolute numbers and in percentages increased over the 1970s.

American higher education also fared reasonably well in the 1970s in its capacity to maintain financial support. Current revenues and expenditures for educational purposes per student unit (in constant 1979–80 dollars) held almost steady. The figures were $3,333 in 1969–70 and $3,239 in 1977–78 (computed from Table 4), a decline of about 3 percent. This relative stability in a period of inflation was unprecedented. In all past episodes of inflation in this century, sharp declines in expenditures per student unit (in constant dollars) occurred. Admittedly, the financial trends in the 1970s were not buoyantly upward, but they could in no sense be interpreted as a reflection of waning public confidence in higher education.

Let me turn now to the capacity of American higher education to deliver excellent educational services. Did the quality or the performance of our colleges and universities collectively rise or fall in the 1970s? This question is perhaps the most important one that can be asked about the higher educational system, and also the most difficult to answer. My attempt to answer the question will be an exercise in social criticism, not an analysis of hard data. My thesis is that the performance of the higher educational system did slip in the 1970s in at least eight ways.

Institutional Size. The average size of institutions increased during the 1970s. The enrollment in student units grew by 39 percent. Though the number of institutions increased by somewhere between 10 and 25 percent (depending on how they are counted) the new institutions were mostly small and much of the additional enrollment was accommodated through the growth of existing institutions. The arguments about the effect of institutional size on educational quality are presented in Chapter Nine. As indicated there, the evidence suggests that the increasing size of institutions may be favorable so far as efficient allocation of resources is concerned, but possibly unfavorable from the standpoint of creating an environment conducive to the intellectual and moral growth of students.

Academic Schedules. During the 1970s, various widely adopted changes in academic schedules reduced the time that students were in contact with faculty. In general, the number of weeks in the academic year was shaved—often by substantial percentages—and the classroom and laboratory hours per week tended to be reduced at many institutions. Few if any institutions increased contact time. These changes were instituted mainly with traditional students in mind, but were implemented during a period when millions of less advantaged students were being admitted. This coincidence probably was unfortunate.

Faculty Effectiveness. Various influences affecting the faculties during the 1970s may, on balance, have impaired their effectiveness. First, however, it must be said that the faculties in the 1970s were probably the ablest and best prepared, and had the largest representation of minorities and women, in the history of American higher education. That generation of faculty was recruited mostly in the decades after World War II when the outlook for higher education was bright and many of the ablest young people chose to enter the academic profession. Their training in their various professional fields was also probably the best in our history, at least in a technical sense. As the number of these people increased and as college and university jobs became more difficult to find, these people fanned out to colleges and universities of lesser prestige enabling these institutions to gather faculties of unprecedented ability and qualifications. This dispersion continued during the 1970s, and near the end of the decade most institutions were reporting that their faculties were stronger than ever before (Minter and Bowen, 1978).

As the decade wore on, however, some countervailing forces were at work. The faculties were growing older. Also, because of a slowing in the rate of enrollment growth and because of concern about excessive tenure ratios, institutions began to recruit young faculty on temporary appointments, releasing them before they had attained tenure and replacing them with other young people who, in turn, would be released short of tenure. This "churning" of instructors and assistant professors predictably created a class of dissatisfied and frustrated academics whose chances for the permanence they had anticipated were slim. For similar reasons, colleges and universities began to employ increasing numbers of part-time faculty, many of whom were paid well below the going rate, had no claims on the institutions for fringe benefits or tenure, and did not become part of the collegial faculty responsible for the educational policy. Higher education has always used part-time faculty, and there surely is a place for them if used sparingly and wisely. They can lend flexibility and variety to staffing, bring practical knowledge and experience into the academic community, and make available the services of outstanding people who could not be employed on any other basis. But in recent years, when the reason for using part-time people often has been financial, and when many of them could bring nothing to the academic community that full-time members could not supply, the increased use of part-time staff probably represented deterioration of quality. The problem was exacerbated by the growth of adult learning. Many of these programs were conducted on a self-supporting or even profit-making basis with low-cost, part-time faculty. When adult learning was a small offshoot of the main residential instruction, the problem was not serious, but in the late 1970s, with growing numbers of adult learners, the existence of part-time faculties raised serious questions about academic quality. The nation may have been heading toward a dual system of education with one set of standards for conventional, full-time, residential students and another for part-time students.

In some other more subtle ways the effectiveness of faculties may have declined. The 1979–80 faculty, though perhaps better qualified than their predecessors in the technical aspects of their specialties, may have been less qualified in their ability to see their fields in philosophical and historical perspective, and in their concern for their students as whole persons. Many faculty members became aware of these limitations and took steps to overcome them. For example, the resurgence of interest in general education and faculty development were indicators of change. Nevertheless, over the 1970s, some educational ground was probably lost through overspecialization and overemphasis on technical study.

Finally, the morale of faculty undoubtedly declined during the 1970s. Some of this decline was induced by the failure of compensation to keep up with either the cost of living or the upward trend in the wages and salaries in the economy generally. Morale was affected adversely by a lessening of job security, by a slowing of the rate of promotion, by the prospect of hard times in case of a decline in enrollments and by unsatisfactory secondary preparation of students. In many institutions, also, the work of faculty members became less attractive because of increasing red tape connected with personnel reviews, self-studies, and compliance with bureaucratic regulations. And perhaps morale was impaired by a general sense that the efforts of academic people were less appreciated in the 1970s than they had been in earlier decades. Some of the frustration was expressed in collective bargaining, a development not likely to improve the quality of higher education.

Disadvantaged Students. During the 1970s the percentage of college students from disadvantaged backgrounds increased substantially. This increase can only be regarded as an outstanding achievement in terms of widening opportunity and making access to higher education more equitable. It is doubtful, however, that the higher educational system on the whole was able to adjust its educational methods and its way of life to meet the needs of both its traditional and its newer clienteles. The education available to both groups may have suffered. In my opinion, this slippage was not due to inattention or indifference—though more could have been done—but rather to the inherent difficulty of the problem, to limited knowledge of how to cope with it, and probably also to inadequate funds.

Inadequate Secondary Preparation of Students. Abundant evidence indicates that the secondary preparation of students admitted to college deteriorated during the 1970s. Not only did average scores on the aptitude tests of the College Board and ACT decline, but also the preparation of students in reading (Eurich, 1980), writing, and mastery of academic subject matter deteriorated (Minter and Bowen, 1980, Chapter 4). Inadequate secondary preparation has undoubtedly required colleges and universities to offer remedial programs and watered-down college courses and has impaired the academic progress of both the well-prepared and ill-prepared students.

Part-time and Nonresidential Students. Another development affecting quality over the 1970s was the vast increase in numbers of part-time and nonresidential students. Traditional higher education was built around students who devoted their full time to their studies and to the social and cultural influences of the academic community and who resided on or near the campus. These students achieved something close to total immersion and the impact of college upon them was correspondingly profound (Bowen, 1977). The literature of higher educational outcomes explicitly demonstrates that the benefits for residential students exceed those for nonresidential students. Although over the years many students have "worked their way through college," the jobs they held during the school year were usually on or near the campuses and did not divert their attention and interests from the academic community. The practice of part-time attendance was growing long before the 1970s, but during that decade attendance of part-time and nonresidential students—some of conventional college age and some older—increased substantially. For many of these students, higher education was a peripheral or incidental part of their lives. Their main interests—family, work, and community—were far removed from the campus and in some ways alien to it. Many of these students did not have access to laboratories, libraries, qualified full-time faculty, the cultural and recreational opportunities afforded by the campus, and the kinds of informal interpersonal experiences that take place spontaneously among full-time resident students. There were, of course, compensating benefits from part-time study. The part-time commuting students brought to their studies valuable practical experience from the outside world. Many of them had greater readiness for serious learning than do younger students. In any case, it was better that people participate in higher education on a part-time basis than not at all. Nevertheless, the quality of education for part-time and commuter students in 1979–80 was probably on the average not equal to traditional standards. In that sense, American higher education may have lost ground qualitatively in the 1970s.

Vocational Goals of Students and Market Orientation of Institutions. Quality may have declined during the 1970s because of the excessive vocational interests of students combined with the excessive market orientation of institutions. The worry of younger students about first jobs and future careers tempted them to choose specific vocational programs at the expense of liberal education. Similarly, the anxiety of older students about career advancement led them to seek vocational credentials in the most direct and convenient way possible. The result was a tendency toward overly vocational education, in some cases toward weakening of standards, and in a few cases toward plainly fraudulent standards.

These tendencies were accentuated by the increasing numbers of part-time, commuting, and itinerant students. Many of them were devising their own degree programs out of bits and pieces of academic work gathered from scattered off-campus courses, accreditation of independent study, and practical experience. A greal deal of education was happening without carefully designed programs, without depth or breadth of learning, and, as indicated earlier, without benefit of libraries, laboratories, the cultural ambience of the campus and the participation of fully qualified faculty. In their preoccupation with the market, some institutions all but abdicated their professional roles as designers of curriculums and as arbiters of standards. And many gave up their traditional concern for the all-round development of the human personality in favor of counting disparate credits that may or may not add up to education in its traditional meaning. The result was a serious weakening of liberal education including reduced emphasis on reading, writing, speaking, foreign languages, mathematics, history, philosphy, natural science, and other subjects essential to producing well-educated men and women.

Had the financial position of institutions been more secure, they could have resisted these tendencies. They could have discharged their professional duty as educators and protected students from their own shortsightedness by prescribing balanced or complementary programs of liberal and vocational learning. But educators were as worried about enrollments as students were anxious about careers and many institutions were tempted to cater to market demands, growing out of student preferences, by offering whatever kinds of programs would attract students.

The situation was exacerbated by a system of financing higher educational institutions that was based overwhelmingly on student-related revenues. By the end of the 1970s, most public institutions operated their educational programs almost exclusively with funds derived from tuitions and from state appropriations based on formulas in which enrollment was the dominant factor. Almost all private institutions were dependent on tuitions for the bulk of their revenues.

In addition, most federal funds and some state funds flowed to the institutions by way of grants and loans to students used to pay tuitions. In short, the institutions became utterly dependent for their financial solvency on attracting students. It is no wonder that institutions were tempted, in some cases forced, to bend their educational policies to the preferences of students that were often influenced by temporary economic conditions, by dubious labor market information, and by the desire to avoid rigorous subjects.

The system of finance that evolved during the 1970s had the great merit that it encouraged student access. Colleges and universities were given a strong incentive to extend opportunity for people of all ages, sexes, and ethnic groups to attend. It led to the growth of community colleges, night schools, store-front colleges, instruction at military bases, recognition of independent learning, and many other innovations designed to facilitate learning among those who could not or would not attend college as full-time residential students. However, it encouraged narrowly vocational education and the concomitant weakening of literacy, quantitative skills, and broad general education. At the end of the 1970s, institutions and funding agencies had great need to work together to achieve a good balance between the goals of access and educational excellence. The solutions called for financial reform to reduce the power of students over educational offerings and standards without seriously curtailing access and at the same time to reduce the competition among institutions so that reasonable educational standards could be protected.

The Erosion of Institutional Autonomy. Academic quality may have deteriorated during the 1970s by the undoubted increase in external control and bureaucratization as increasing numbers of campuses became parts of multicampus and centrally administered institutions, or came under increasingly detailed influence of statewide coordinating bodies, legislatures and their committees, state finance officers, and various federal agencies.

Concluding Comments on Quality. The main conclusion from this extended discourse on trends in the intangible assets of higher education during the 1970s is that educational quality declined. The slippage in quality was not intentional, nor due to neglect, nor the result of bad management. It did not affect all institutions. Rather, the deterioration was due to the inability of the higher educational system to adjust in a mere decade or two to the unprecedented responsibilities flowing from the vastly increased numbers and diversity of students. Even if funds had been unlimited, the higher educational system would not have been able to make the necessary adjustments instantly. The problems were enormous and the knowledge of how to cope with them inadequate. It was better to have admitted the new students and thus to have brought new social groups into the orbit of higher education, even though the results were not totally satisfactory, than to have kept the colleges and universities as preserves for full-time residential young people from upper income or culturally advantaged families. But the qualitative results have not yet matched those of traditional higher education.

One cannot prove that the supposed qualitative decline was real, nor can one assign a numerical magnitude to them. In my judgment the changes were genuine, though not catastrophic and not irreversible. But when added together they represent a significant and worrisome decline in the effectiveness of the higher educational system. In 1979–80, the system was not as good as it should have been. To restore educational quality to satisfactory levels will not be easy because both innovation and additional funds will be required. For example, large institutions should discover ways to personalize their educational programs and campus life. The amount of time when students and faculty are in fruitful contact should be increased. The status of the academic profession with respect to compensation, career potential, and teaching effectiveness should be restored. Modes of education better suited to the new students, including remedial education, should be developed. Regular faculty, library resources, laboratories, studios, and extracurricular services should be provided for part-time and commuting students. "The educated man or woman" should be restored as the basic educational ideal and this ideal should be present within both vocational and nonvocational programs.

The nation probably cannot provide education to a diverse student population of traditional and nontraditional students, doing justice to both, without additional resources per student. The needed qualitative improvements—not counting increases in staff compensation—would cost several billion dollars a year. These funds would pay for educational research and development, expanding and upgrading faculty, improving facilities and equipment, extending student services, and providing cultural and social enrichment for nontraditional students. One of the major goals of such a program would be to offer services and facilities for nontraditional students equal to, though different from, those available to full-time resident students, and to do so without lowering the quality of education for the latter.

The finances for these qualitative improvements might come from savings (in constant dollars) due to a decline in enrollments in the 1980s. If inflation persists, there can be no savings in current dollars. But with a decline in enrollment, expenditures (at the 1979–80 level of quality) might well decline in constant dollars. The savings, if any, might be used to overcome the deterioration of quality that occurred during the 1970s. Money, however, is not the only requirement for improved quality. Perhaps more important are educational vision, leadership, improved knowledge, and sound administration.

Summary and Conclusions

This chapter has reviewed the progress of the American higher educational system in the decade of the 1970s and addressed the question of how much money would be needed to conduct higher education in 1979–80 at the level of performance achieved in 1969–70. To answer the question superficially, expenditure per student unit in 1969–70 and 1979–80 were compared. This comparison revealed that the decline in per student expenditure over the decade was only 3.5 percent, from $3,333 to $3,215 (in constant 1979–80 dollars), and that only $1.4 billion of additional expenditures in 1979–80 would have brought the average up to the 1969–70 level. The weakness of this approach was that it did not take into account the sacrifices that were necessary to contain unit costs during the decade.

Another approach was to estimate the amount of money necessary to restore various parts of the higher educational budget in 1979–80 to the 1969–70 level. These estimates are assembled in the following table. They are presented not as precise figures but as informed estimates intended to convey general orders of magnitude. The figures, in billions of 1979–80 dollars, are as follows:

	Low	High
Staff compensation	$2.3	$2.3
Staff numbers		
Faculty	−0.6	−1.0
Other staff	0.4	0.5
Purchases of goods and services	0.5	0.6
Capital stock (buildings and equipment)	0.	0.
Maintenance	2.0	3.0
Socially imposed costs	1.5	2.0
Total	6.1	7.4

From the total I would be inclined to subtract 25 percent to allow for economies of scale and for squeezing out the "fat" that may have crept into the budgets during the prosperous years prior to 1969–70. The net deficiency would then be about $4.5 to $5.5 billion, or in a round number $5.0 billion.

The sum of $5.0 billion is a very rough estimate of the amount of money that would be needed to restore American higher education in 1979–80 to the level of operation it enjoyed in 1969–70. This estimate is intentionally conservative but represents an increase of about 13 percent over the amount actually expended for educational purposes in 1979–80, or an increase in the cost per student unit of about $425.

Though the base year of 1969–70 was a prosperous one for American higher education, at that time the colleges and universities were not fully engaged in the educational tasks of the 1970s which involved provision for millions of nontraditional students, some from disadvantaged backgrounds, some commuting, some attending part-time. In 1969–70, the higher educational system was not well prepared to maintain academic standards and to keep liberal learning alive in the face of intense vocational demands of students. In addition, institutions were not ready to meet the challenge of personalized education in institutions of unprecedented size and to cope with some decline in faculty effectiveness. As a result, the overall quality of the higher educational system would probably have deteriorated to some extent in the 1970s even if the funding level of 1969–70 had been maintained. Additional funds beyond the 1969–70 level would have been needed to achieve the quality for the nontraditional students that had prevailed for the traditional students in 1969–70—and at the same time to maintain that quality for the traditional students. Even with the closest attention to economy, the needed funds would undoubtedly have been an additional several billion dollars, making the total bill well over the estimated $5 billion. The amount might easily be $8 or $10 billion or 20 to 25 percent of total educational expenditures in 1979–80.

American higher education has taken on an enormous load. To carry that load at an acceptable level of quality would require substantially more funds than were available in 1979–80. If enrollments should fall in the 1980s, as is so widely predicted, the nation would have a marvellous opportunity to convert a decline in quantity into an improvement in quality—though not all needed funds could be derived from a reduction in enrollments.

11

Implications
of the Study of
Individual Institutions

In addressing the question of what higher education should cost, one might expect that a review of the data and analysis in Part Two of this book (Chapters Six to Nine) on the comparative costs of individual institutions would be relevant. If one observed strong central tendencies toward certain levels of cost, or found clear modalities in the way higher education is conducted, or could discover definite relationships between costs and educational outcomes, then one might find empirical support for particular recommendations. Unfortunately, the study of institutions did not reveal such clear-cut conclusions.

The first, and perhaps most surprising, finding from the study of individual institutions was the wide variance in educational cost per student unit. A plausible hypothesis might have been that unit cost would cluster closely around a well-defined mode representing the combined experience of many institutions that render basically similar educational services. Instead, the dispersion of costs proved to be so wide, even for ostensibly similar institutions, that the mode cannot be assumed to represent an ideal or widely accepted standard. This variance is of course consistent with the revenue theory of cost, namely, that the cost of any institution is largely determined by the amount of revenue it can raise.

A second set of findings pertained to the great differences among institutions in the way they allocate their resources among various programs, functions, and recipients (see Tables 15 and 16). Apparently, there are many ways to conduct higher education, and no one best way is so demonstrably superior as to be widely adopted. Data on resource allocations provide little guidance as to what mode of operation might be most appropriate. These data give the impression of almost centrifugal randomness. However, there were some systematic relationships between rich and poor institutions in the way they deploy their resources, and these are summarized in Table 37. In the allocation of current educational expenditures to various functions, the differences are minimal. On the average, the percentage distribution of expenditures for teaching, student services, scholarships and fellowships, and other functions are quite similar for rich and poor institutions. When allocations of expenditures among recipient groups (faculty, other staff, vendors, and students) are considered, however, some marked differences between rich and poor institutions emerge. Affluent institutions spend relatively less for faculty, for the direct teaching function, and for academic building space, and they spend relatively more for nonacademic staff, for purchased goods and services, and for student aid.

A third set of findings related to the effects of institutional expenditures on educational outcomes. The concept of educational outcomes, defined as "value added" for students as a result of the college experience, refers mainly to changes effected by colleges in the knowledge, abilities, skills, aspirations, values, attitudes, and other characteristics of students. Firm generalizations about the effects of institutional expenditures on outcomes are hard to come by. Nevertheless, some suggestive data and analysis on the relationship of expenditures and outcomes were presented in Chapters Six and Eight which led to the conclusion that there is a rather indistinct but positive relationship between institutional expenditures for education and outcomes in the form of value added. The correlations were mostly rather low and since the outcomes data were generally in ordinal form, the *amount* of value added associated with a given increase in unit cost was difficult to judge. Nevertheless, the evidence suggested that on the average increases in cost are favorable to outcomes. However, there are undoubtedly low-cost institutions that produce excellent results and high-cost institutions with mediocre performance. Good education cannot be bought with money alone. It

Table 37. Percentage allocation of educational resources, 268 representative
colleges and universities, by institutional affluence, 1976–77

	Least affluent fifth of institutions	Most affluent fifth of institutions
Percentage distribution of current educational expenditures, by programs		
Teaching	49.2%	44.6%
Student services	7.4	8.0
Scholarships and fellowships	7.9	12.4
Academic support	7.7	7.6
Institutional support	15.3	15.8
Operation and maintenance of plant	11.1	10.3
Mandatory transfers and other	1.4	1.3
	100.0%	100.0%
Percentage distribution of current educational expenditures, by categories of recipients		
Faculty (compensation)	51%	36%
Other staff (compensation)	28	33
Vendors of goods and services (purchases)	13	19
Students (scholarships and fellowships)	8	12
	100%	100%
Capital		
Campus building space per student unit	80 sq. ft.	180 sq. ft.
Expenditures for additions to physical plant as percentages of total Educational and General expenditures	16%	10%
Building space assigned to classrooms as percentage of total building space	14%	10%
Average endowment at market value per student unit	$1,280	$20,040

Source: These figures are derived from data presented in Tables 17, 23, 24, 25.

requires also intangible qualities such as clarity of purpose, dedication, sense of community, love of learning and teaching, personal interest in students, and prudent administration. Money can be wasted in higher education as well as in families, businesses, and government agencies. Caution is advisable when making claims that increasing amounts of money will bring about proportionate improvements in outcomes; yet, on the average other things being equal, money does make a difference. Doubtless, if outcomes such as the consumer benefits to individuals and the social benefits of higher education could be fully measured, the ratio of benefits to cost might be higher than those found in this study.

From these findings, two inferences may be drawn about what higher education *should* cost. First, institutions differ widely in the efficiency with which they carry out their missions. This being so, many institutions could improve their efficiency. Second, hundreds of colleges and universities, both public and private, are seriously underfinanced. The remainder of the chapter will be devoted to these two inferences.

Efficiency

The degree of efficiency in any human undertaking is discovered by comparing means and ends. It is measured as a ratio between the two. The greater the ends achieved with given means, or the fewer the means used to achieve given ends, the greater the efficiency. Such comparisons of means and ends are commonly expressed by pairs of words such as resources-outcomes, input-output, cost-benefit, or cost-effectiveness. Regardless of the terminology, the underlying concepts are: (1) that the use of resources involves an opportunity cost and results in an outcome, and (2) that efficiency is measured or judged as a *ratio* between the outcome and the cost.

In many discussions of efficiency in higher education, two frequent errors are committed. The first, common to critics of higher education, is to judge efficiency only in relation to cost. It is assumed that an institution that can educate a student for $2,000 a year is more efficient than one which spends $3,000 per student. Clearly, the question of which is more efficient can be answered only when something is known about the outcomes. The second error, common to the proponents of higher education, is to judge efficiency only in relation to outcomes. It is assumed that improved outcomes are desirable regardless of cost. Both of these approaches fail to recognize that efficiency is a relationship between two variables, cost and outcomes. To cut costs would not be efficient if the outcomes sacrificed were more valuable than the opportunity cost of the resources saved; however, to add to cost would not be efficient if the outcomes added were less valuable than the forgone benefits of employing the resources in another use. Higher education has no claim on resources that produce only minor gains in outcomes at the expense of major sacrifices of other goods.

The matter of efficiency is often confused, also, by failure to distinguish clearly between resource inputs and outcomes. Higher educational systems and institutions are often judged by such criteria as faculty-student ratios, building space, equipment, number of library books, admissions test scores, eminence of faculty, and so on. These are all inputs reflecting costs and reveal nothing about outcomes except insofar as such inputs are assumed to be closely correlated with outcomes, a questionable assumption. Sometimes, also, the outcomes of colleges and universities are judged by "processes" such as methods of teaching and extracurricular experiences of students. These are, strictly speaking, technologies by which resources are transformed into outcomes, and not outcomes proper. The reason that higher education is so often judged by inputs or processes is, of course, that educators are so helpless when confronted with the task of assessing true outcomes. They revert to inputs and processes in the desperate but unsubstantiated hope that these will be closely correlated with true outcomes. They are in a sense saying that the higher the cost the greater the efficiency.

The statement that institutions differ widely in their efficiency means not merely that they differ in their costs, or that they differ in their outcomes, but rather that they differ in the ratio of their outcomes to their costs. A high-cost institution may be very efficient if it is producing commensurate outcomes; and a low-cost institution may be very inefficient if its outcomes are negligible or even negative. When the data show vastly different unit costs among institutions that seem to be providing about the same services with about the same outcomes, or widely different outcomes among institutions that are operating at about the same costs, the logical inference is that some institutions are considerably more efficient than others, and that the higher educational system as a whole could be more efficient if the institutions of low efficiency could raise the efficiency.

In profit-making organizations operating in a competitive market, strong incentives would prevail for inefficient organizations to improve. Return on the investment and even survival would depend on it. But given the not-for-profit atmosphere and the highly differentiated products of higher education, incentives for efficiency are weak and the result is the wide variance in efficiency that is readily observed.

The way to improved efficiency is to achieve greater knowledge of outcomes. At present, educators know little about their results and next to nothing about the effects of changes in their procedures and methods on their results. They do not know whether they are efficient or not. There have been some sporadic one-time studies of outcomes in particular institutions and a number of one-time studies of small samples of institutions such as were presented in Chapter Eight. From these studies it seems probable that the higher education system as a whole produces significant and beneficial results (Bowen, 1977). But there have been few systematic ongoing efforts to assess outcomes of particular institutions and certainly few cases where the study of outcomes has been linked with managerial decisions or accountability. Without such knowledge, higher education is destined to fly blind. There is little doubt that efforts to evaluate outcomes and to judge, if not measure, efficiency on the basis of facts and evidence could over time contribute to improvement in the efficiency of the higher educational system. The techniques for evaluating educational results are becoming available. They should be further developed and utilized.

Minimal Standards

The second inference from the study of institutions—and perhaps the most important one—is that, given the wide range of cost differences, many colleges and universities are seriously underfinanced. Even if they were operated with great efficiency, they would still lack the resources necessary for delivering acceptable higher education. As shown in Chapter Six, many institutions were operating in 1976–77 with cost per student unit in the range of $1,000 to $1,700—well below the average expenditure per pupil for elementary and secondary education ($1,782 in the same year). In twelve states expenditures per student unit in all state institutions averaged below $1,700 (see Table 14). Several million students are served by colleges and universities with patently inadequate resources.

To illustrate what is meant by inadequacy, the actual operating budgets of a low-cost institution may be revealing. It is a state college of 4,871 student units located in a wealthy industrial state of the northeast. The figures, expressed per thousand student units, are as follows:

Number of faculty	33	
Average faculty compensation	$13,000	
Total cost of faculty		$ 429,000
Number of support staff	51	
Average compensation of support staff	$10,000	
Total cost of support staff		$ 510,000
Scholarships and fellowships		$ 105,000
Purchases of goods and services		$ 136,000
Total educational expenditures		$1,180,000
Educational expenditures per student unit	$ 1,180	

The results of inadequate financing in this institution are a pitifully small faculty and support staff, low compensation, and minimal amounts available for student aid and purchased goods and services.

No one knows, of course, just what would be an acceptable minimum for unit costs in higher education. There can be legitimate differences of opinion on this question. Ultimately, like most educational questions, it is a moral question, not a technical one, and I shall approach it accordingly. A starting place might be two eloquent statements about the nature of good education, one by an elitist and the other by an egalitarian. Cardinal Newman observed that "A university is . . . an Alma Mater, knowing her children one by one, not a foundry, or a mint, or a treadmill." Similarly, John Dewey wrote that "What the best and wisest parent wants for a child, that must the community want for all its children. Any other ideal for our schools is narrow and unlovely; acted upon it destroys our democracy."

Perhaps the moral wisdom of these two great men will help in reaching estimates of what higher education should cost. A standard of minimal cost might be approached by asking: How do we want our children and grandchildren to be educated? And in this day of expanding adult education we must ask also a second question: How do we want our fellow citizens to be educated? Each of us, in evaluating a particular college or university, must ask: Would I want my children to attend this institution or would I recommend this institution to a colleague or friend? If the answer is no, we are then morally bound to conclude that neither would we want anyone else's child or anyone else's colleague or friend to attend. And in evaluating the system of higher education, each of us must ask: Are these the kinds of institutions where we want the next generation of our fellow citizens to be educated? Are these places fit to be the matrix in which the civilization of the twenty-first century is to be formed? If the answer is no, we are morally bound as citizens to strive for improvement.

With these questions in mind, perhaps one can describe the characteristics of an institution that would be regarded as near the margin between inadequacy and acceptability:

1. It would have a capable faculty of well-educated and cultivated men and women who are proficient in their fields, who have broad interests, and many of whom are suitable role models worthy of emulation. The conditions for assembling such a faculty would be adequate compensation in all its forms (monetary and non-monetary) to attract and hold persons qualified for comparable positions in other industries and professions; and working conditions—facilities, teaching loads, clerical and laboratory assistance, intellectual freedoms, and stimulation of colleagues—sufficient to enable faculty members to be lifelong learners and scholars (though not necessarily authors of numerous publications).

2. The institution would have adequate but not necessarily luxurious facilities for student learning such as libraries, laboratories, and studios. These would be available to all students, residential and commuting, full-time and part-time.

3. It would offer a reasonable range of choice of academic fields and interests for students.

4. It would offer cultural opportunities through a tasteful and well-ordered (though not necessarily luxurious or monumental) campus, extracurricular programs relating to the arts and ideas, and a cosmopolitan outlook.

5. It would be a *community* in which respect for persons, social life, recreation, discussion, and participation would flourish.

6. It would welcome students of varied geographical, racial, ethnic, religious, and family origins.

7. The standard of living as to food, lodging, clothing, social life, and transportation would be simple but related to the prevailing standard of living in the general society.

These standards fulfill two objectives. They would provide the conditions essential to significant educational outcomes, and they would offer students an experience that would be rewarding in its own right, irrespective of ulterior ends. The college years are a substantial fraction of life and should be reasonably absorbing and agreeable. But this goal can be achieved under conditions of austerity and simplicity and does not call for luxury and complexity. The question of just where this critical point between adequacy and inadequacy lies is a matter of judgment. It is related to the prevailing standard of living in the society generally, to what is psychologically acceptable to students, and ultimately to the way we want the personality and character of our children and our fellow citizens to be formed.

What would it cost to provide higher education that meets this minimal standard? To calculate the cost, we need consider only a few significant variables which encompass the entire current budget:

- The ratio of faculty to students: number of full-time-equivalent faculty per 1,000 student units
- Average annual compensation of faculty
- The ratio of supporting staff to students: number of full-time-equivalent staff per 1,000 student units
- Average compensation of supporting staff
- Payments for scholarships and fellowships per 1,000 student units
- Purchases of goods and services from outside vendors per 1,000 student units

The next step then is to assign to each of these variables values that are consistent with the concept of an institution that barely meets the educational characteristics specified. (Since available institutional data are expressed in 1976–77 dollars, the estimates are stated in terms of that year.)

Faculty-Student Ratio. In 1976–77, there were about 1,566,000 full-time-equivalent workers in higher education. Of these, about 591,000 were faculty members engaged in instruction. In the same year, there were 8,313,000 full-time-equivalent students or 11,513,000 student units. Thus, faculty per thousand student units numbered about fifty-one. This number was of course higher than that for many of the less affluent institutions. What number would be needed to meet the minimal standard I have proposed?

One answer might be derived from a study of *Efficiency in Liberal Education* in which the costs of various modes of undergraduate instruction and the faculty-student ratio required for each were estimated (Bowen and Douglass, 1971). This study explored the effects of varying such factors as teaching loads, curricular proliferation, distributions of courses by subject fields, and instructional methods such as lecture, lecture-discussion, tutorials, independent study, and mechanically assisted instruction. By manipulating these variables the number of faculty required for an institution of given size could vary widely. The authors experimented with combinations that would require as few as twenty-seven faculty members per thousand student units, others that would require as many as ninety-one faculty per thousand, with many possibilities between the extremes. The final recommendation was an eclectic plan that drew on all the various modes of instruction. When this plan was combined with an average faculty teaching load of six four-credit courses a year, and a somewhat streamlined curriculum, it was found that at least forty-five full-time-equivalent faculty members per thousand student units would be required. When to these faculty members was added a small complement of persons engaged in extracurricular activities such as athletics, drama, and music, the minimum number would come close to fifty-five per thousand student units. This figure was lower than the average faculty-student ratio in the more affluent private universities and liberal arts colleges (see Tables 19 and 20), but somewhat higher than the average for all public institutions. From these calculations, one might judge that a faculty of around forty-five to forty-nine full-time-equivalent persons per thousand student units would be near the bare minimum that would meet the proposed standard. In conventional terms, that would be the equivalent of an ordinary faculty-student ratio (in full-time-equivalents) of one to fifteen or sixteen.

Faculty Compensation. As indicated in Chapter Three, average faculty compensation in 1976–77 was fairly satisfactory, that is, reasonably competitive with compensation in other industries and occupations employing workers of similar qualifications. In that year average faculty compensation for persons on academic year appointments was $20,234. Moreover, the range of compensation between more affluent and less affluent institutions was quite narrow. As shown in Table 21, average faculty salaries in the most affluent fifth of institutions of various types were from 5 to 26 percent higher than those in comparable institutions of the least affluent fifth. An institution attempting to maintain a faculty that would meet the minimum standards specified would probably have had to pay at least 85 to 90 percent of the average compensation or $17,000 to $18,000. However, if all such institutions met this standard, the average of compensation would increase and the level needed for competitiveness also would rise. A better final estimate might therefore be $17,500 to $18,500.

Ratio of Support Staff to Students. The support staff of colleges and universities includes a great variety of workers such as administrative officials, professional persons, technicians, secretarial and clerical workers, physical plant workers, and many others. In general, less affluent institutions tend to hold down the number of support staff relative to faculty; as institutions become more affluent they tend to increase the support staff more than they increase the number of faculty. The least affluent institutions employ about 68 support staff for each thousand student units and the most affluent ones about 166 (Table 19). On the basis of these figures, a barely adequate institution might employ considerably fewer support staff than the national average, perhaps 70 to 72 per thousand student units.

Compensation of Support Staff. Institutions regardless of affluence compete in the general labor market for personnel managers, accountants, secretaries, mechanics, technicians, and most other support staff members. Therefore they do not have a great deal of latitude in setting compensation. In 1976–77, the average pay for these persons was around $13,400 (Bowen, 1978a, p. 27) and marginal institutions would have to meet an average of at least $12,500 to $13,000 to obtain an efficient work force.

Scholarships and Fellowships. If an institution is to be able to welcome students of varied backgrounds and financial status, it will need some scholarship and fellowship funds. This need will be greater in private institutions with their high tuitions than in more moderately priced public institutions. Actual expenditures for scholarships and fellowships in 1976–77 for private institutions were, at the median, about 11 percent of total educational expenditures and for public institutions about 4 percent, and at the lower quartile 8 and 1 percent, respectively. For minimally adequate institutions, these percentages might be set at 9 percent for private institutions and 2 percent for public institutions. The cost per thousand student units would be around $350,000 in private institutions, $45,000 in public institutions.

Purchases of Goods and Services. The final component of the current educational budget is goods and services purchased from outside vendors. About 20 percent of all current educational expenditures are devoted to such purchases, but the percentage is considerably lower for less affluent than for more affluent ones. A marginally adequate institution might allow 16 percent of total current educational expenditures for purchases, or $200,000 to $230,000 per thousand students.

Estimate of Total Cost. Taken together, the estimates of the several budgetary items for a minimally adequate institution yield the following figures for cost per thousand student units in 1976–77:

Total cost for faculty (45 to 50 persons at $17,500 to $18,500)	$788,000	to	$925,000
Total cost of support staff (67 to 75 persons at $12,000 to $13,000)	804,000		975,000
Scholarships and fellowships	37,000		210,000
Purchased goods and services	200,000		230,000
Total expenditures per thousand student units	$1,829,000		$2,340,000
Cost per student unit	$1,829		$2,340

Generally speaking, the costs of private institutions are higher than those of public institutions. Private institutions inescapably incur relatively high costs for fund-raising, student recruitment, and scholarships and fellowships. They also tend to be smaller than public institutions and thus to reap fewer economies of scale. Therefore, the upper cost estimate of $2,340 per student unit might be thought of as a minimum for private institutions whereas the lower estimate of $1,829 might be regarded as a minimum for public institutions.

These estimates may be compared with the distribution of costs for all institutions, which were as follows (from Table 12):

	Minimum	First quartile	Median	Third quartile	Maximum
Public	$1,076	$1,727	$2,020	$2,848	$4,786
Private	824	2,149	2,813	3,458	8,039
Total	824	1,938	2,545	3,286	8,039

The estimated unit costs of minimally adequate institutions, $1,829 for a public institution and $2,340 for a private institution, lie between the first quartile and the median for all institutions.

These data suggest that probably one-third of all institutions were operating in 1976–77 with unit costs below the assumed level of minimal adequacy. This would include about 1,000 institutions serving several million students. It goes without saying that this conclusion is subject to reservation because the data on which it is based are only rough estimates. Another investigator might well have produced different figures either lower or higher. In particular, there is no implication in these figures that every institution with unit costs below $1,829 to $2,340 is educationally inadequate. Every careful observer of American higher education is impressed by the remarkable performance of many impoverished institutions whose good work is achieved by unusual dedication and sacrifice often reinforced by a rich tradition of concern for students and of integrity. Nor is there any suggestion that every institution with resources above these figures is adequate. Good education requires much more than money. Nevertheless, the standards proposed are in my judgment truly minimal—probably too low—in the spirit of Cardinal Newman's and John Dewey's moral precepts. They represent, in a sense, a tentative definition of the responsibility of American society toward its students young and old. These estimates imply, indeed proclaim, that American higher education is unconscionably underfinanced in the sense that hundreds of institutions lack the resources to provide education of acceptable quality. To raise these institutions to the minimal standard would probably require at least $2 billion of additional current expenditures. The $2 billion is expressed in 1976–77 dollars. When converted to 1979–80 dollars, the figure would be around $2.7 billion, or an increase of about 7 percent in total educational costs for 1979–80. The need for these additional resources is especially urgent because a majority of students of disadvantaged backgrounds attend low-budget institutions. Their educational and cultural needs are more, not less, than those of more privileged students.

Frequently, in discussions of efficiency in higher education, it is suggested that there is a great deal of waste in colleges and universities and that this waste should be squeezed out by reducing total unit costs. Once it is realized that perhaps as many as one third of the institutions—both public and private—have less money than they ought to have to provide acceptable education, one can only conclude that across-the-board cuts are inappropriate. It may be appropriate to suggest reallocation of resources within low-budget institutions to achieve better results for given expenditures, but not to advocate overall cost reduction.

Equity Among Persons

Just as many institutions, perhaps a third, are operating with unit costs below an acceptable level, others operate with unit costs well above what are needed for minimally acceptable educational performance. An immediate reaction to this state of affairs is that the costs of the more affluent institutions should be reduced and the savings distributed to the low-cost institutions. This redistribution might be advocated on grounds of both efficiency and equity. For many reasons, however, such a simple redistribution of resources among institutions would be neither desirable nor feasible.

Many colleges and universities whose unit costs may be above the minimum exceed it by only a narrow margin and to force them down to an arbitrary bare minimum would be absurd. Some high-cost institutions are heavily engaged in exceptionally expensive fields such as medicine, science, engineering, fine arts, and the like, and their high costs may be inevitable. Many of them perform valuable functions other than the instruction of students. For example, some give strong support to research through low departmental teaching loads; some make substantial social contributions by maintaining distinguished faculty members who are available on call for public service activities; some provide important cultural facilities for the surrounding community; some contribute educational experimentation and innovation and thus provide educational leadership of value to the entire higher educational community; some lend diversification to the higher educational system so that the system can more effectively serve students of varied interests and backgrounds.

Relatively high-cost institutions may be defended also on grounds of academic autonomy and freedom. With autonomy goes the freedom of institutions to raise funds wherever and however they can legally find them. This freedom produces differences among institutions in financial position, but it also enables institutions to respond to the interests of different segments of society. If ultimate control were exercised over the amount of money institutions could acquire, the freedom and responsiveness of the higher educational system would be greatly restricted.

Finally, relatively high-cost institutions may be defended either on the ground that they assume an exceptionally heavy burden of disadvantaged students who require extra educational services, or on the ground that they attract large numbers of gifted students whose talents entitle them to education of exceptional quality and high cost. In fact, most high-cost institutions do not admit exceptionally large numbers of disadvantaged students, but they do admit relatively many gifted students. The question, then, is whether more resources per student should be invested in the education of gifted students than in the education of those with less aptitude. When the matter is considered in terms of broad social efficiency, the objective being to maximize in the next generation such values as national economic growth, cultural advancement, and national power, then gifted persons may have a greater claim on resources than the disadvantaged. The American higher educational system has been traditionally based on a meritocratic philosophy, which favors relatively heavy educational investments in the gifted. The meritocratic principle is perhaps not as widely accepted as it once was; the balance has tipped to some extent toward egalitarian values. Nevertheless, the meritocratic perspective still prevails and the higher educational system still is geared to providing more resources for the gifted than for the disadvantaged.

Though the case for tolerating wide differences among institutions in unit costs is on the whole persuasive, there are also powerful counter arguments. One is that differences in cost lead to serious inequities among social classes in the educational opportunities afforded. Well-to-do institutions such as the major private universities, the flagship state universities, and some liberal arts colleges tend to draw disproportionate shares of students of privileged backgrounds. Students of more limited backgrounds tend to find their way to low-cost institutions where the staff, facilities, and amenities often compare unfavorably with those in the more affluent institutions (see Table 38). This stratification occurs for a variety of reasons. Institutions that are financially well-off offer more facilities and amenities and therefore receive more applicants than other institutions. They therefore can be more selective and also can charge higher tuitions, thereby further improving their financial position. They also can attract gifted students by offering more financial aid than less affluent institutions can afford. At the same time students from disadvantaged backgrounds are less likely to seek admission to the "best" institutions—some because of lack of sophistication about colleges and universities, others because of lack of funds to attend distant institutions or because they are working part or full-time and must attend institutions near their jobs. If they do apply to the "best" institutions, they are less likely to gain admission because of their limited backgrounds.

For all of these reasons, institutional affluence and selectivity of students are strongly correlated. The correlation is so high that many scholars of higher education equate selectivity of institutions with educational quality. For example, average scores of entering students on Scholastic Aptitude Tests are often taken as proxies for educational excellence.

Wide cost differences among institutions can also be questioned on grounds of discrimination among geographic regions. Most students attend colleges or universities near their homes (Anderson, Bowman, and Tinto, 1972). In general, students who attend distant institutions are members of families with above-average incomes and some sophistication about higher education or are qualified for exceptional financial aid. Therefore, regional differences in cost tend

**Table 38. Institutional expenditures and students' economic background,
by type of institution, 1975–76**

	Educational and general expenditures per full-time-equivalent student	*Median income of parents of entering freshman*
Public Institutions		
Two-year colleges	$1,778	$13,579
Four-year colleges		
Low selectivity	1,741	13,895
Medium selectivity	2,071	16,593
High selectivity	3,888	17,802
Universities		
Low selectivity	2,678	17,813
Medium selectivity	3,086	18,618
High selectivity	4,153	21,946
Private institutions		
Four-year nonsectarian colleges		
Low selectivity	2,627	13,978
Medium selectivity	2,485	17,977
High selectivity	2,835	20,150
Very high selectivity	4,275	26,117
Universities		
Low selectivity	2,142	20,977
Medium selectivity	3,514	27,986
High selectivity	5,954	23,573

Source: Unpublished data derived from the files of the Higher Education Research
Institute and kindly made available to the author by Alexander W. Astin.

to restrict educational opportunity for those who live in areas of the
country with relatively limited support for higher education. As
noted earlier (see Table 14), the differences among the states in expenditures per student in public institutions are striking, and regional
differences among private colleges are probably equally large. Regional discrimination has long been a major legal issue in the financing of public elementary and secondary education. This issue came to
a climax in a famous 1971 California judicial decision in the case of
Serrano v. *Priest.* In this decision, the California Supreme Court
ruled that the state system of financing elementary and secondary
education produced wide disparities among school districts in rev-

enues per pupil, and that these disparities violated the constitutional rights to equal educational opportunity of pupils who lived in school districts with low tax bases (Carroll, 1979). The facts and the legal issues are quite different for higher education than for elementary and secondary education; nevertheless, the principle enunciated in *Serrano* v. *Priest* is not totally irrelevant to higher education.

Concluding Comments

The study of the costs of individual institutions presented in Part Two and reviewed in this chapter have suggested several conclusions of great importance:

The variance in unit cost among institutions is far wider than it should be in a democratic society. Educational expenditures per student unit vary from $1,612 for the least affluent fifth of institutions to $4,599 for the most affluent fifth of institutions, a ratio of nearly 1 to 3 (Table 17). Such wide variance clearly implies that institutions at the lower end of the distribution are inadequately financed. American society is providing millions of its students with a college education that falls short of the standard enunciated by Cardinal Newman or John Dewey. A large proportion of the least advantaged students—the very ones who need individual attention and adequate facilities—attend underfinanced institutions. Our nation is concentrating its higher educational resources on institutions attended largely by students of privileged backgrounds, among whom a great deal of the nation's aptitude and readiness for higher education is to be found.

Over a single generation, the returns to higher education in the form of national economic growth, cultural development, and world influence may be maximized when resources are concentrated on students from privileged backgrounds. The returns from education for people with less privileged backgrounds, and therefore with less readiness for higher education, may take more than a single generation to materialize. But in the long run, the overall advancement of the nation may be facilitated as much by spreading the resources more widely to encourage personal development and enriched cultural opportunities for people of all classes as by concentrating them on the more privileged groups. There is much potential talent to be recruited and nurtured in all parts of the population. Fortunately there is no inherent conflict between the education of an elite and the education to cultivate the potentials of the less privileged social classes. Given modest increases in resources, both can be accomplished at the same time.

Many institutions, often the very ones where large numbers of the less privileged students are found, do not have the resources to provide an acceptable education. To meet rather modest minimal standards of education might require an expenditure per student unit of around $2,500 for public institutions and $3,200 for private institutions (in 1979–80 dollars). Observers may debate whether the minimum is too austere or too generous, but clearly the present unit costs of many institutions fall short of the spirit of Newman and Dewey. The overwhelming problem for much of American higher education, then, is not inefficiency or waste but sheer undernourishment. No doubt some institutions could allocate their resources more efficiently, but the potential for solving the educational and financial problems of the less affluent institutions through improved efficiency is trivial compared with the need for additional funds. Only a major infusion of funds would bring the less affluent colleges and universities up to an acceptable standard.

12

Final Observations

At the outset of this study, I had no clear-cut hypotheses, little fore-warning of what I might find, and certainly no intimation of the kinds of conclusions that might emerge. In the course of the study, I was often surprised by the findings and genuinely puzzled about their implications. My intention was to learn as much about institutional costs as I could with the ultimate purpose of addressing the question: How much should higher education cost? I understood, of course, that this was a normative question and I was not sure whether facts and analysis about costs would lead toward the answer. To a limited extent they did, but in the end I was forced to inject my own values into the proceedings. In the case of the longitudinal study of long-term trends in costs, my value judgments entered prominently into the assessment of educational and financial trends in the 1970s and into my attempt to judge how much higher education would cost in 1979–80 if conducted at the level of quality achieved in 1969–70. In the case of the cross-sectional study of 268 individual institutions, a value judgment entered when I relied on my interpretation of the educational philosophies of Cardinal Newman and John Dewey to set a standard of cost per student. Having adopted that standard, I then estimated what it would cost to bring low-budget institutions up to par.

The longitudinal investigation led me to conclude that to re-store the higher educational system in 1979–80 to the level of performance it had attained in 1969–70 would take about $5 billion of additional expenditures plus unknown but substantial amounts of further resources if qualitative deficiencies were to be overcome. From the cross-sectional investigation I estimated that to bring substandard institutions up to a level of minimal adequacy would require about $2.7 billion. Though these two estimates do not measure the same thing, there is some overlap between them. If $5 billion were spent to raise the whole higher educational system to the 1969–70 level, this expenditure would benefit some or all of the substandard colleges and universities and therefore reduce the $2.7 billion needed to raise these institutions up to the Newman-Dewey standard. Allowing for this overlap, the combined total would be perhaps of the order of $6 to $7 billion—plus substantial amounts to overcome the qualitative deterioration that occurred during the 1970s. The grand total might be as much as $10 to $12 billion.

These figures refer only to current expenditures for educational purposes in 1979–80. They do not include outlays for organized research and public service, auxiliary enterprises, hospitals, independent operations, or capital expenditures. In 1979–80 actual current expenditures for educational purposes were about $38 billion. To add $6 to $7 billion would increase the total cost of higher education by about 16 to 18 percent. To raise the figure to the $10 to $12 billion needed to overcome qualitative deterioration would increase total cost by about 25 percent. These are conservative estimates of what would be involved in bringing the system up to an acceptable level of performance.

Admittedly, these estimates are far from precise. Other observers might well have assigned different magnitudes to the various ingredients of the estimates. Value judgments different from those I adopted might have yielded substantially lower or higher estimates. In any event, precise figures are not important. I would submit, however, that any careful observer of the current condition of higher education would conclude: (1) that its performance deteriorated in the 1970s, and (2) that at both the beginning and the end of the decade a substantial proportion of institutions were operating below minimally acceptable standards. The remedy, of course, is not money alone. But a substantial infusion of money would be needed to reverse ominous trends and to raise the performance of the many substandard institutions.

At the end of the 1970s the vast majority of American colleges and universities were by no means educationally or financially bankrupt. The legacy of the golden years had not been wholly eroded. But slow attrition of quality did occur in the 1970s and a continuation of the trends of that decade would be disastrous. There were serious deficiencies not only at the less affluent end of the institutional spectrum but also at the more affluent end.

The less affluent institutions are an indispensable part of the higher educational system. Many of them—though by no means all—are small and provide a personalized atmosphere. Many serve nearby students who could not or would not attend distant institutions. Their styles are varied and many serve special clienteles differentiated by age, sex, ethnicity, religion, and readiness for higher education. And many provide much needed remedial work that is not readily available elsewhere. Perhaps more important, they simply carry a huge part of the nation's educational load. These institutions sometimes lack glamour, they seldom make headlines on the sports pages, they do not produce Nobel Prize winners, they seldom have luxurious campuses and ancient traditions, and they do not have large numbers of influential alumni or political clout. But they consistently carry on important educational work—often under great handicaps and without the public appreciation that is their due.

There are strong arguments also for maintaining and strengthening the affluent colleges and universities. Nothing said here is intended to suggest a tearing down of the more affluent institutions. However, affluence does confer upon colleges and universities heavy responsibilities to use their educational resources efficiently in the broad social interest and not waste them through slackness, in quest of institutional vanity, or by trying to provide a needlessly high standard of institutional living. The dilemma of the rich institutions is that the relationship between resources and educational outcomes is at best uncertain. No one can be sure that richer institutions are performing with a degree of excellence consistent with their resources. Indeed, many institutions, if they looked around them, would find that there are poorer institutions with outcomes equal to or even better than their own. Any institution would be well advised to compare its performance with that of others and perhaps to discover how to accomplish more with the same money, or to accomplish the same results with less money.

As noted in Chapter Eight, one of the greatest needs of higher education is better information about its outcomes. Both public policy and institutional administration are gravely handicapped by their scant knowledge of the results of education. To identify and measure all the outcomes of higher education may never be possible. Higher education has many of the qualities of an art form rather than of a science. Yet we can learn much more about the results than we now know. New methods for the purpose are steadily being devised and there is need of much experimentation and discovery by individual institutions. Only with greater knowledge of results, and of the relationship of resources to results, will the search for greater efficiency be productive.

Higher Education: A Growth Industry?

To argue that higher education needs more money may well be dismissed as useless in the 1980s when the competition for public and philanthropic funds may be so keen that any substantial increases in expenditures for higher education (other than cost of living increases) will be ruled out. I offer no predictions for what may turn out to be a turbulent period full of surprises. Higher education may be fated to lose ground educationally and financially in the late twentieth century as it has done in previous eras. However, emerging conditions or possibilities may lead the nation to increase its support for higher education.

The traditional American style of life, with its heavy use and consumption of physical goods, will gradually be forced to change. Natural resources, not only energy but also many others, may be in short supply. And even if resources should be plentiful, as some believe (Barnett and Morse, 1963; Johnson and Bennett, 1980), the environment will lack the capacity to absorb the pollution connected with ever-increasing production and consumption of physical things. Perhaps more important, people will lack the time to use the ever-multiplying products. Moreover, increasing numbers of people are finding that the proliferation of physical things does not lead to an especially satisfying way of life and may even be associated with personal alienation and social unrest. In the years ahead, therefore, people may turn to new ways of life that are less taxing on resources, less destructive to the environment, and more satisfying of deep human needs. Education has an important place in this way of life for people of all ages. It uses little energy or other natural resources, it places minimal strain on the environment, and millions of people find that it is an intrinsically rewarding activity and that it contributes to their lives. In an era of retrenchment in the production of things, higher education could well become one of the growth industries of the future.

To speak of higher education as a growth industry at the brink of a decline in the number of persons between the ages of eighteen and twenty-one may seem absurd. But the potential students are of all ages. The number of people who could benefit from higher education is enormous. To cite a few figures, only 17.5 million persons or 14.7 percent of the adult population (twenty-five years of age and over) are college graduates; another 15.5 million have attended college without graduating; and 85.8 million over the age of twenty-five, or nearly three-fourths of the adult population, have never been to college. Even in the group from eighteen to twenty-four, only about half ever attend and only a fourth ever graduate from college. There are vast numbers of persons who are potential candidates for further higher education. The numbers are so large that only small changes in the percentages attending would make enormous differences in enrollments. For example, each increase of one percent in the number of persons over the age of twenty-four attending college would add a half-million full-time-equivalent enrollments (Bowen, 1980).

But assuming that enrollments do fall sharply in the 1980s, and I am by no means ruling out that possibility, there are at least four options: (1) to redirect higher educational resources toward improved quality; (2) to redirect resources toward research and public service; (3) to redirect resources toward new clienteles; and (4) to retrench, that is, to shift resources from higher education to other parts of the economy. A strong case can be made for any one of these options, or perhaps for a combination of several (Bowen, 1980). But in view of the subtle slippages in the quality of American higher education over the past decade and the presence of hundreds of institutions that are underfinanced, a decline in enrollment could present a welcome opportunity for the nation to redirect resources specifically toward the improvement of educational performance.

Postscript on Finance

Having presented the case for increased funding of American higher education, I am tempted to launch into a full-scale discussion of the financing of higher education for the 1980s and beyond. I shall resist that temptation; to do so would require another book. But perhaps I can suggest the bare outlines of some appropriate policies.

In the intense national debates on higher educational finance in the late 1960s, attention was focused on two competing goals: the developing and improving of institutions versus facilitating the access of students. The outcome of the debate was a major shift of emphasis toward the goal of student access. The Congress of the United States elected to concentrate its support for higher education on financial aid to students and to leave institutional support largely to the states and to private donors. Meanwhile the state governments tied their support of institutions overwhelmingly to formulas in which enrollment was the principal factor. At the same time but for other reasons, private institutions became increasingly dependent on tuitions. Thus, without anyone planning it that way, the American higher educational system became almost wholly reliant on enrollments for its support. Educational finance became a kind of *laissez-faire* market system in which the fate of institutions is dictated by student decisions some of which may or may not be consistent with either their own long-range interests or with the public interest. There was a massive shift of power to students who carried with them, directly or indirectly, the bulk of the revenues for higher education.

This financial system has been enormously successful and effective in facilitating access. It has provided funds to students of low-income families and has given the strongest possible incentives to institutions to increase their enrollments. This mode of finance may have worked reasonably well for the institutions during the period of rapidly rising enrollments. But it has been working badly as enrollment growth has tapered off. And it may become catastrophic if enrollments should decline sharply. Already it has led to intense and unhealthy competition for students. As a result, it has tended to undermine general education, to erode academic standards, and to produce an unseemly atmosphere of hucksterism in the conduct of higher education. Although these effects have been especially pronounced in the less affluent institutions, almost no part of higher education has been exempt. The dilemma of many of the less affluent institutions is that they cannot get additional resources because they cannot attract more students, and they cannot compete for students because of inadequate resources.

The nation is in great need of new financial policies directed toward the strengthening of institutions. Such policies would provide basic financial support calculated to shore up institutions, both public and private, without inviting heavy-handed external control.

Several obvious examples of such aid may be mentioned. One, familiar to both federal and state governments, is grants for capital improvement, expansion, and maintenance. The colleges and universities are short of capital. The plant and equipment acquired in the 1950s and 1960s or before are aging and in need of accelerated maintenance and remodeling and in some cases replacement. Library collections have deteriorated through decelerated purchases and inadequate operating funds. Equipment is needed for replacement and also to accommodate essential new programs.

A second possibility is federal incentive grants to the states to encourage adequate state funding of institutions and possibly to reduce regional differences in support levels for higher education.

Third, the states should find ways to reduce the amplitude of revenue fluctuations associated with changes in enrollment. There are several ways of achieving this objective. One would be to provide a significant part of state appropriation in the form of block grants to institutions. Another would be to use a moving average of enrollments over several years in determining the amount of grants based on enrollments.

Fourth, grants could be made by either the federal or state governments to help finance educational research and development within the institutions. Institutions might be encouraged especially to assess their educational outcomes and to strengthen faculty development.

Fifth, and not necessarily least, some student aid funds might be shifted to the institutions for administration by them.

Finally, federal direct grants to institutions, as were widely advocated in the late 1960s, are still a possibility, though the higher educational community today is much more wary of federal control than they were a decade ago.

These suggestions do not constitute a financial program, but they show that there are numerous ways to restore some of the internal integrity of institutions that was lost when higher education became so heavily dependent on funds delivered directly or indirectly by students. At the very least, the amplitude of fluctuations in revenues should be reduced so that institutions can plan ahead and make orderly adjustments to changes in enrollments and other conditions.

In devising a financial program, special concern is due the private sector of higher education which under some conditions could bear the brunt of the decline in numbers of college-age students. I am not suggesting a bailout of particular institutions in distress (a la Chrysler, Penn-Central, or Lockheed) but rather the creation of an environment favorable to the survival of an effective private sector.

Our nation urgently needs a change in financial policy that gives greater attention to the development and maintenance of *institutions* both public and private. Educational opportunity for the American people of all ages calls not only for access but also for institutions that are worthy of access, institutions that meet the standards of Cardinal Newman and John Dewey.

Appendix A

Sources and Methods for Allocating Total Expenditures

This appendix is an extended footnote to Table 1, page 7. Some of the percentage distributions in Table 1 are fairly accurate, others are rough estimates. The vertical distribution by administrative divisions is consistent with data on the distribution of total expenditures for all U.S. institutions as reported by the National Center for Education Statistics in its *Digest of Education Statistics* (1976, p. 141). The horizontal distribution by expenditure categories is based on data from a wide variety of sources, including Halstead, (1977), Jenny (1979), and financing reports and special tabulations supplied by numerous colleges and universities.

The total dollar amount distributed among the various cells in Table 1 is $40.974 billion. This total includes expenditures for all purposes except those for independent operations, which are primarily federally financed research and development centers (such as the Argonne National Laboratory or Jet Propulsion Laboratory) that are loosely affiliated with universities.

The following definitions were used in computing the data presented in Table 1. "Faculty" includes academic deans as well as faculty members. "Other Professional Staff" includes professional persons employed in academic support, student services, institutional support, operation and maintenance of plant, auxiliary enterprises, and hospitals.

"Capital Costs" includes all capital costs, although colleges and universities do not ordinarily include the use of capital (except interest expense) among their costs. Capital costs may be measured either (1) by amortizing capital assets over their expected useful lifetimes and adding an imputed interest cost or (2) by imputing capital cost as the rental value of comparable land, buildings, and equipment in the private market economy. The second option was chosen in this table. The assignable area of plant employed in the several administrative divisions of higher education was estimated partly on the basis of data on selected institutions from the Higher Education General Information Survey of the U.S. Department of Health, Education, and Welfare. The rental value for 1974–75 was computed at the rate of $5.00 a square foot (not including utilities) based on the advice of several commercial real estate brokers. The resulting data were adjusted upward to include equipment. For further discussion of computing capital costs, see Bowen and Douglass (1971), O'Neill (1971).

In the classification by administrative divisions, "Academic support" includes support services (such as libraries, computer services, museums) for instruction, research, and public service. "Institutional support" includes general administrative, financial, and public relations activities. "Public service" pertains to activities providing noninstructional services to individuals and groups external to the institution. "Auxiliary enterprises" includes residence halls, student unions, food services, book stores, and other self-supporting enterprises operated by colleges and universities.

Appendix B

Historical Trends in the Costs of Higher Educational Institutions

---

This appendix presents basic data and documentation relating to estimates of long-term trends in institutional costs as presented in Chapter Two. Historical data in the form needed for the purposes of this study are not readily available, thus some figures were derived by inference and can be regarded only as rough but reasonable estimates. On the whole, they probably are of sufficient reliability to justify the conclusions drawn from them, as experiments with different sources and different methods of constructing the data yielded similar conclusions. Most of the data were gathered for each year from 1929-30 to 1977-78, though only decennial figures are shown here.

The objective was to produce credible information on trends in average cost per unit for the education of students in American colleges and universities. *Education* was defined to include the various services rendered by institutions of higher education for the benefit of students. As so defined, it included direct instruction and departmental research, student services, and a prorated share of expenditures for academic support, general administration, and plant operation and maintenance. Departmental research was included because it is supplemental to and supportive of instruction, and therefore it represents part of the cost of educating students. This inclusion of departmental research may dissatisfy some observers. James (1978) has argued that the proportion of resources devoted to departmental research has increased substantially over recent decades—more than most available data would indicate. It may well be that some departments have been steadily reallocating funds from education to research. But when we consider all types of institutions, including community colleges and state colleges, any such shift will seem relatively small. In any case, although some may interpret this reallocation as a decrease in educational resources, I chose to interpret it as an improvement in educational quality flowing from the increased opportunity for faculty to engage in creative, intellectual, and artistic activity. Given this interpretation, the expenditures for education (including departmental research) were then isolated and related to enrollment.

Table 39 presents estimates of expenditures for education over the years from 1929–30 to 1977–78. Current (operating) expenditures of all institutions of higher education in the United States were obtained for the period 1929–30 to 1975–76; figures for later years are the author's estimates. From these figures, expenditures for auxiliary enterprises and student financial aid were subtracted, the remainder being what is ordinarily called *educational and general expenditures.* Next, data on capital expenditures (for buildings and durable equipment) exclusive of those for auxiliary enterprises were assembled, and these were prorated to research and public service and to education. The educational and general expenditures and the capital expenditures were then combined to show total expenditures for research and public service and for education.

The next step was to adjust these figures for changes in the general price level. The deflator for current operating expenditures was the Consumer Price Index of the U.S. Bureau of Labor Statistics, and the deflator for capital expenditures was an index of construction and equipment price. The deflated expenditure figures and the price indexes are shown in Table 40.

The number of full-time-equivalent students during this period was estimated by using mostly official data. Over the years, however, the relative numbers of graduate, upper division undergraduate, and lower division undergraduate students changed. Because instructional costs are higher for advanced students than for beginners, the basic enrollment figures were converted into student units by assigning heavier weights to advanced students than to beginners. The results are shown in Table 41.

Table 39. Estimates of institutional expenditures for education, all U.S. institutions of higher education, 1929–30 to 1977–78 (in millions of dollars)

	1929–30	1939–40	1949–50	1959–60	1969–70	1977–78
Current (operating) expenditures, total	507	675	2,246	5,601	21,043	—
Educational and general expenditures[a]						
Instruction and departmental research	221	280	781	1,793	7,653	17,385[b]
Organized activities of educational departments	—	27	119	303	741	1,447[b]
Sponsored research and other separately budgeted research	18	27	225	1,022	3,090	4,921[b]
Extension and public service	25	35	87	206	682	1,447[b]
General administration and general expense	43	63	213	583	2,628	6,643[b]
Libraries	10	19	56	135	653	1,261[b]
Plant operation and maintenance	61	70	225	470	1,542	4,008[b]
Educational and general expenditures, total	378	522	1,706	4,513	16,989	37,112[b]
Allocated to research and public service[c]	62	87	439	1,666	5,267	9,382
Allocated to education[c]	316	435	1,267	2,847	11,722	27,730
Capital expenditures, total[d]	103	68	325	1,092	3,573	4,659
Allocated to research and public service	17	11	83	402	1,108	1,179
Allocated to education[e]	86	57	242	690	2,465	3,480
Educational and general and capital expenditures, total	481	590	2,031	5,605	20,562	41,771
Allocated to research and public service	79	98	522	2,068	6,375	10,561
Allocated to education	402	492	1,509	3,537	14,187	31,210

[a] Basic source for 1929–30 to 1969–70: U.S. Bureau of the Census, *Historical Statistics of the United States*, vol. 1, p. 384; for later years, National Center for Education Statistics, *Digest of Education Statistics*, 1976, p. 142; 1978, pp. 134–135. The classification of expenditure is that in effect prior to 1974–75. In 1974–75, the National Center for Education Statistics adopted a new chart of accounts. However, for the sake of continuity, the old classifications are used throughout.

[b] Estimated by the author. Serious complications arise in compiling consistent series because the classification of accounts as determined by the National Center for Education Statistics changed in 1969–70, when major public service programs were transferred out of educational and general expenditures, and again in 1974–75, when a substantial rearrangement of accounts was made and "mandatory transfers" were added. The following publications of the National Center for Education Statistics were used in making these estimates: *Digest of Education Statistics*, 1976, pp. 140–142 and 1978, pp. 134–135; *Projections of Education Statistics*, 1978, pp. 96–103; *Financial Statistics of Colleges and Universities*, 1977, *Preliminary Tabulations*, 1978. For consistency, definitions in use before 1969–70 were applied to the data for 1969–70 and 1977–78.

[c] The allocation of educational and general expenditures between education and research was accomplished as follows: "instruction and departmental research" and "organized activities of educational departments" were assigned to education; "separately organized research" and "extension and public services" were assigned to research and public service; "general administration and general expense," "libraries," and "plant operation and maintenance" were divided between education and research in proportion to the previously mentioned expenditures for each.

[d] Total capital expenditures were derived from U.S. Bureau of the Census, *Historical Statistics of the United States*, vol. 1, p. 385; *Statistical Abstract of the United States*, various years, for example, 1976, p. 145; National Center for Education Statistics, *Digest of Education Statistics*, 1978, pp. 134–135. A theoretically superior approach to calculating capital cost is to estimate the value of the capital assets used in higher education each year and then estimate the amount required each year for interest and depreciation (see O'Neill, 1971, pp. 28–35 and 85–90). This approach, however, involves a number of serious problems, namely, the estimation of the value of the capital assets and the selection of interest and depreciation rates. I opted for a much simpler approach which treats capital expenditures as expenses. The main drawback of this method is that it produces somewhat wider annual variations in estimated capital cost. The advantage is that the amounts shown are actual expenditures.

[e] Total capital expenditures were allocated to instruction, research and public service, and auxiliary and other—in proportion to current expenditures for each of these three categories. Only the portions allocated to instruction and to research and public service are included here.

Table 40. Total expenditures allocated to education in constant dollars and price indexes used for deflation, 1929–30 to 1977–78

	1929–30	1939–40	1949–50	1959–60	1969–70	1975–76	1977–78
Total expenditures allocated to education in billions of constant (1967) dollars[a]	917	1,234	2,161	4,072	12,465	—	16,279
Consumer Price Index[b]	50.3	41.8	71.8	88.0	113.1	165.9	188.4
Higher Education Price Index[c]	33.6	31.3	51.3	75.7	121.0	177.2	201.3
Index of Construction and Equipment Prices[d]	29.8	29.5	61.0	82.4	117.3	192.3	223.1

[a] Educational and general expenditures allocated to education (as shown in Table 39) deflated using Consumer Price Index for current expenditures and Index of Construction and Equipment Prices for capital expenditures.

[b] U.S. Bureau of Labor Statistics, two-year moving average.

[c] Source for 1929–30 to 1961–62 data is O'Neill, 1971, p. 81; for 1963–64 to 1977–78, Halstead, 1975, p. 9 and 1976, p. 10; *Chronicle of Higher Education*, September 24, 1979, p. 9. The Halstead data were linked to the O'Neill data.

[d] Source for 1929–30 to 1963–64 is O'Neill, 1971, p. 91; for 1964–65, Halstead, 1975, p. 92; for 1974–75 to 1977–78, Halstead's data projected on the basis of the Boeckh Index of Construction Cost of Apartments, Hotels, and Office Buildings, *Survey of Current Business, monthly issues, p. S10.*

Table 41. Enrollments, all U.S. institutions of higher education, 1929–30 to 1977–78 (in thousands)

	1929–30	1939–40	1949–50	1959–60	1969–70	1977–78
Full-time-equivalent students, total[a]	890	1,202	2,145	2,775	6,319	8,560
Public institutions, subtotal	447	656	1,127	1,647	4,564	6,511
Universities	247	332	574	773	1,871	2,307
Other four-year institutions	172	231	400	591	1,602	2,135
Two-year institutions	28	93	153	283	1,091	2,069
Private institutions, subtotal	443	546	1,018	1,128	1,755	2,049
Universities	199	240	417	391	599	642
Other four-year institutions	224	269	546	672	1,052	1,302
Two-year institutions	20	37	55	65	104	105
Full-time-equivalent students by academic level of students, total[b]	890	1,202	2,145	2,775	6,319	8,560
Undergraduates—freshmen and sophomores	530	722	1,256	1,639	3,777	5,333
Undergraduates—juniors and seniors	322	395	698	861	1,721	2,106
Graduate and advanced professional students	38	85	191	275	821	1,121
Full-time-equivalent students, total, adjusted for academic level[c]	1,127	1,570	2,876	3,756	8,822	11,855

[a] These estimates are based on the following sources: U.S. Bureau of the Census, *Historical Statistics of the United States*, vol. 1, pp. 382–383; O'Neill, 1971, pp. 71–75; National Center for Education Statistics, *Projections of Education Statistics*, 1974, p. 76; 1975, p. 79; 1976, p. 86; American Council on Education, *A Fact Book on Higher Education*, no. 2, 1976, p. 77; *Chronicle of Higher Education*, September 19, 1977, p. 8 and January 9, 1978, p. 10.

[b] These estimates are based on data from several sources, especially American Council on Education, *A Fact Book on Higher Education*, no. 2, 1976, p. 117 and no. 4, 1976, p. 228; O'Neill, 1971, pp. 71–76.

[c] Computed from data on full-time-equivalent enrollment by academic level of students. The weights, based on estimated cost of instruction per student, are: freshmen and sophomores, 1.00; juniors and seniors, 1.50; graduate and advanced professional students, 3.00. (See O'Neill, 1971, p. 78.) These weights are slightly different from those used in the cost comparisons among institutions in Part Two, because detailed data by types of students were not available for the entire period under study here. For a fuller discussion of the weights used in Part Two, see Appendix C.

Finally, instructional expenditures per student were computed from the data on deflated expenditures and both unadjusted and adjusted figures on enrollment. These results are shown in Chapter Two, Table 4.

Appendix C

Sources and Methods
of Analysis for Data
on Institutional Costs

Part Two, Chapters Six through Nine, is based primarily on data regarding institutional costs for a representative sample of colleges and universities. This appendix explains in some detail how these data were gathered and analyzed.

Source of Data. The data were derived from unpublished reports by the Higher Education General Information Survey (HEGIS) of the U.S. Department of Health, Education, and Welfare.

The Sample. The sample consists of 268 accredited institutions stratified by size, as measured by total enrollment; by geographical region, as defined by four quadrants of the country having roughly equal numbers of institutions; by public and private control; and by the Carnegie Council's classification of institutional type (Carnegie Council on Policy Studies in Higher Education, 1976). Independent professional schools not affiliated with universities are not included.

In selecting the sample there was one deviation from the rule of randomness. Within each cell, some institutions were substituted for selected institutions whose data were incomplete or otherwise unusable. Thus, the sample is biased in favor of institutions that reported complete and consistent data.

Educational Expenditures. Comparisons among colleges and universities were difficult because of wide differences in the range of their activities and, therefore, in the amounts they spend. Institutions differ especially in their involvement in research and public service, in the extent of their auxiliary enterprises such as residence halls, food service facilities, student unions, and bookstores, in their provision of health care through teaching hospitals, and in their spending for capital purposes. Moreover, for some of these activities—especially separately budgeted research and public service—no obvious units of service are available against which to measure expenditures. To achieve reasonable comparability among institutions, it was expedient, though not ideal, to exclude expenditures for these activities and to concentrate on expenditures for the education of students. Education is the main business of virtually all colleges and universities, and educational expenditures can be conveniently compared to units of service, namely student units.

Absolutely accurate figures on educational expenditures cannot be deduced from available data. The procedures for estimating educational expenditures are described in Appendix B.

As in all cost accounting, the allocation of joint costs to particular outputs tends to be arbitrary. The effort to isolate Educational Expenditures in this study was no exception. I can only say that the results—especially as shown in Table 12—seem plausible. One controversial aspect of the allocation was the inclusion of departmental research as part of the cost of education. I believe this is justified, in part at least, by the contribution of research and a research environment, to the education of students. Much of the distortion due to the inclusion of departmental research is overcome by the classification of institutions by type.

Student Units. The enrollments of colleges and universities differ not only in the total number of students in attendance but also in the proportion of students who are full-time or part-time and the academic level of these students. Because the cost of educating advanced students is generally higher than that of educating freshmen and sophomores, a simple count of full-time-equivalent students is inadequate. Therefore, I converted the number of full-time-equivalent students into student units by assigning weights to various academic levels. The weights used for this purpose are:

Lower-division students (freshmen and sophomores)	1.0
Upper-division students (juniors and seniors, and unclassified undergraduates)	1.5
Professional students (students in professional programs which require at least two academic years of college work for entrance and a total of at least six years for a degree; for example, architecture, graduate business, dentistry, law, medicine, social work, and theology)	2.5
Graduate students: first year and unclassified postbaccalaureate students	2.1
Graduate students: beyond first year	3.0

Using these weights, I expressed the enrollment for each institution in units of full-time lower-division students, or *student units*. For all institutions except two-year colleges, the number of student units was larger than the number of full-time-equivalent students since advanced students counted for more than one.

The weights assigned to students of various academic levels were based on cost studies made by many institutions and by several state systems of higher education. The sources from which these estimates were derived include: Carnegie Commission on Higher Education, 1972, pp. 36–38, 65; Ehrlich and Moeller, 1975; Froomkin, 1970, pp. 35–61; Halstead, 1974, pp. 672–676; Meisinger, 1976, pp. 245–262; Mushkin and McLoone, 1960; O'Neill, 1971, pp. 14, 78; Illinois Board of Higher Education, 1969; Michigan Council of State College Presidents, 1968; State University System of Florida, 1961; Southern Association of Colleges and Schools, 1975; Tennessee Higher Education Commission, 1971; University of Iowa, 1968; Washington Council for Postsecondary Education, 1977; and Unpublished data for the Claremont Colleges.

Affluence. A primary concept in the analysis of costs is institutional affluence. The analysis in Part Two shows how institutional affluence affects the allocation of expenditures among various functions and recipients. Affluence is measured by dividing an institution's total educational expenditures by the number of student units served and thus calculating the institution's expenditures per student unit.

References

Akin, J. S., and Garfinkel, I. "School Expenditures and Economic Returns to Schooling." *Journal of Human Resources*, Fall 1977, pp. 460–481.

Alfred, B. M., and Gray, G. A. "Academic Time Allocation Reliability Study, 1968–69." In Association of Universities and Colleges of Canada, *An Exploratory Cost Analysis of Some Canadian Universities*. Ottawa, Ontario: Association of Universities and Colleges of Canada, 1970.

American Association of University Professors. "The Economic Status of the Profession." Annual reports of Committee Z, *AAUP Bulletin*, Summer issues, 1959–60 through 1978–79.

American Council on Education. *A Fact Book on Higher Education*. Washington, D.C.: American Council on Education, quarterly issues.

American Management Association, Executive Compensation Service. *Professional and Scientific Report*. (3rd ed.) New York: American Management Association, 1976–77.

American Management Association, Executive Compensation Service. *Middle Management Report*. (26th ed.) New York: American Management Association, 1977–78a.

American Management Association, Executive Compensation Service. *Supervisory Management Report*. (22nd ed.) New York: American Management Association, 1977–78b.

American Management Association, Executive Compensation Service. *Technician Report*. (5th ed.) New York, 1977–78c.

American Management Association, Executive Compensation Service. *Top Management Report*. (28th ed.) New York: American Management Association, 1977–78d.

Anderson, C. A., Bowman, M. J., and Tinto, V. *Where Colleges Are and Who Attends*. New York: McGraw-Hill, 1972.

Anderson, R. E. *Strategic Policy Changes at Private Colleges*. New York: Teachers College Press, 1977.

Andringa, R. C. "New Demands by Government for More Information from Postsecondary Education." Address delivered at 2nd forum on New Planning and Management Practices in Postsecondary Education, Chicago, November 16, 1973.

Andringa, R. C. "The View from the Hill." *Change*, April 1976, pp. 26–30.

"Another Campus Revolt—This Time Against Washington." *U.S. News and World Report,* July 5, 1976, pp. 91–94.

Association of American Colleges. *A National Policy for Private Higher Education.* Washington, D.C.: Association of American Colleges, 1974.

Association of Physical Plant Administrators of Universities and Colleges. *Comparative Unit Cost and Wage Report on Maintenance and Operations of Physical Plants of Colleges and Universities.* Washington, D.C.: Association of Physical Plant Administrators of Universities and Colleges, 1971, 1973, 1976.

Association of Universities and Colleges in Canada. *An Exploratory Cost Analysis of Some Canadian Universities.* Ottawa, Ontario: Association of Universities and Colleges in Canada, 1970.

Astin, A. W. "The Measured Effects of Higher Education." *The Annals of the American Academy of Political and Social Science,* November 1972, pp. 1–20.

Balderston, F. E. *Managing Today's University.* San Francisco: Jossey-Bass, 1974.

Barnett, H. J., and Morse, C. *Scarcity and Growth: The Economics of Natural Resource Availability.* Baltimore: Johns Hopkins University Press, 1963.

Baumol, W. J., and Bowen, W. G. *Performing Arts: The Economic Dilemma.* New York: Twentieth Century Fund, 1966.

Baumol, W. J., and Marcus, M. *Economics of Academic Libraries.* Washington, D.C.: American Council on Education, 1973.

Bayer, A. E. *Teaching Faculty in Academe: 1972–73.* Research Reports, Vol. 8, No. 2. Washington, D.C.: American Council on Education, 1973.

Bayer, A. E. "Faculty Composition, Institutional Structure, and Students' College Environment." *Journal of Higher Education,* September–October 1975, pp. 549–565.

Beatty, G., Jr., Gulko, W. W., and Sheehan, B. S. *The Instructional Cost Index: A Simplified Approach to International Cost Comparison.* Amherst: University of Massachusetts, 1974.

Becher, T., Embling, J., and Kogan, M. *Systems of Higher Education: United Kingdom.* New York: International Council for Educational Development, 1978.

Bender, L. W. *Federal Regulation and Higher Education.* Washington, D.C.: American Association for Higher Education, 1977.

Bennett, J. T., and Johnson, M. H. "Paperwork and Bureaucracy." *Economic Inquiry,* July 1979, pp. 435–451.

Birnbaum, R. "Unionization and Faculty Compensation: Part II." *Educational Record,* Spring 1976, pp. 116–118.

Blaug, M. *The Economics of the Arts.* London: Martin Robinson, 1976.

Bok, D. C. *Harvard University: The President's Report, 1974–75.* Cambridge, Mass.: Harvard University, 1976.

Bok, D. C. "The Federal Government and the University." *The Public Interest,* Winter 1980, pp. 80–101.

Bokelman, W., D'Amico, L. A., and Holbrook, A. J. *A Half-Century of Salaries at Land-Grant Institutions.* OE-52004-3. Washington, D.C.: U.S. Office of Education, Department of Health, Education, and Welfare, 1962.

Bork, R. H. "Can Universities Escape the Regulation They Prescribe for

All Other Institutions?" *The Alternative: An American Spectator,* April 1977.

Bowen, H. R. "Faculty Salaries: Past and Future." *Educational Record,* Winter 1968a, pp. 9–21.

Bowen, H. R. *The Finance of Higher Education.* New York: McGraw-Hill, 1968b.

Bowen, H. R. "Financial Needs of the Campus." *The Corporation and the Campus.* New York: Academy of Political Science, 1970.

Bowen, H. R. *Investment in Learning. The Individual and Social Value of American Higher Education.* San Francisco: Jossey-Bass, 1977.

Bowen, H. R. *Academic Compensation: Are Faculty and Staff in American Higher Education Adequately Paid?* New York: Teachers Insurance and Annuity Association and College Retirement Equities Fund, 1978a. (Order from the publisher, 730 Third Avenue, N.Y., N.Y. 10017. $2.00 postpaid.)

Bowen, H. R. *Socially Imposed Costs of Higher Education.* Chicago: University of Illinois, 1978b.

Bowen, H. R. "Social Responsibility of the Businessman—Twenty Years Later." In E. M. Epstein and D. Votaw (Eds.), *Rationality, Legitimacy, Responsibility: Search for New Directions in Business and Society.* Santa Monica, Calif.: Goodyear Publishing, 1978c.

Bowen, H. R. "Outcomes Planning: Solution or Dream?" In National Center for Higher Education Management Systems, *Proceedings of the 1977 NCHEMS National Assembly.* Boulder, Colo: National Center for Higher Education Management Systems, 1978d.

Bowen, H. R. *Adult Learning, Higher Education, and the Economies of Unused Capacity.* New York: College Entrance Examination Board, 1980.

Bowen, H. R., and Douglass, G. K. *Efficiency in Liberal Education.* New York: McGraw-Hill, 1971.

Bowen, H. R., and Minter, W. J. *Private Higher Education, Annual Reports on Financial and Educational Trends in the Private Sector of American Higher Education.* Washington, D.C.: Association of American Colleges, 1975, 1976, 1977.

Bowen, H. R., and Minter, W. J. *Independent Higher Education.* Washington, D.C.: National Association of Independent Colleges and Universities, 1978, 1980.

Bowen, W. G. *The Economics of the Major Private Universities.* Berkeley: Carnegie Commission on the Future of Higher Education, 1968.

Brewster, K. "Higher Education and the Federal Government." *Congressional Record,* March 10, 1975, pp. S3515-3517.

Brinkman, P. "Factors Affecting Instructional Costs at Major Research Universities." Unpublished manuscript, 1980.

Brown, W. W., and Stone, C. C. "Academic Unions in Higher Education." *Economic Inquiry,* July 1977, pp. 385-396.

Cameron, K. "Organizational Effectiveness in Higher Education, Feedback Report." Unpublished paper, 1977.

Cameron, K. "Measuring Organizational Effectiveness in Institutions of Higher Education." *Administrative Science Quarterly,* December 1978, pp. 604-632.

Canada, Dominion Government. "An Exploratory Cost Analysis of Some Canadian Universities." Unpublished report, Ottawa, Ontario, 1970.

Carlson, D. E. "The Production and Cost Behavior of Higher Education." Paper-P-36, Ford Foundation Program for Research in University Administration. Berkeley: Office of the Vice-President, Planning, University of California, 1972.

Carlson, D. E. *A Review of Production Function Estimation for Higher Education Institutions.* Cambridge, Mass.: Graduate School of Education, Harvard University, 1977.

Carnegie Commission on Higher Education. *New Students and New Places.* New York: McGraw-Hill, 1971.

Carnegie Commission on Higher Education. *The More Effective Use of Resources.* New York: McGraw-Hill, 1972.

Carnegie Council on Policy Studies in Higher Education. *A Classification of Institutions of Higher Education* (Rev. ed.) Berkeley: Carnegie Council, 1976.

Carnegie Council on Policy Studies in Higher Education. *The States and Private Higher Education: Problems and Policies in a New Era.* San Francisco: Jossey-Bass, 1977.

Carnegie Council on Policy Studies in Higher Education. *Three Thousand Futures: The Next Twenty Years for Higher Education.* San Francisco: Jossey-Bass, 1980.

Carroll, S. J. *The Search for Equity in School Finance: Summary and Conclusions.* Santa Monica, Calif.: Rand Corporation, 1979.

Cartter, A. M. *Ph.D.'s and the Academic Labor Market.* New York: McGraw-Hill, 1976.

Cartter, A. M., and Solmon, L. C. "Implications for Faculty." *Change,* September 1976, pp. 37–38.

Chambers, M. M. *Should State Legislatures Insist on Appropriating Federal Funds?* Normal, Ill., 1977.

Cheit, E. F. "What Price Accountability?" *Change,* November 1975, pp. 30–34, 60.

Cheit, E. F. "The Benefits and Burdens of Federal Financial Assistance to Higher Education." *American Economic Review,* February 1977, pp. 90–95.

Chickering, A. W. "Institutional Size and Student Development." Paper presented at the Council for the Advancement of Small Colleges Conference on Factors Affecting Student Development in College, 1965.

Chickering, A. W. "The Best Colleges Have the Least Effect." *Saturday Review,* January 16, 1971, pp. 48–50.

Chronicle of Higher Education, Sept. 19, 1977, p. 8.

Chronicle of Higher Education, Jan. 9, 1978, p. 10.

Chronicle of Higher Education, Sept. 24, 1979, p. 9.

Chronicle of Higher Education, Oct. 15, 1979, p. 8.

Clark, B. R. "The Wesleyan Story: The Importance of Moral Capital." In D. Riesman and V. A. Stadtman (Eds.), *Academic Transformation: Seventeen Institutions Under Pressure.* New York: McGraw-Hill, 1973.

Clark, B. R. "The Insulated Americans: Five Lessons from Abroad." *Change,* November 1978, pp. 24–30.

Clark, B. R., and others. *Students and Colleges: Interaction and Change.* Berkeley: Center for Research and Development in Higher Education, University of California, 1972.

College and University Personnel Association. *1976–77 Administrative*

Compensation Survey. Washington, D.C.: College and University Personnel Association, 1977.

Columbia Research Associates. *The Cost of College*. Report Prepared for the Office of Program Planning and Evaluation, U.S. Office of Education. Cambridge, Mass.: Columbia Research Associates, 1971. (Also supplements 1972 and 1975.)

Commission on Federal Paperwork. *Education*. Washington, D.C.: U.S. Government Printing Office, 1977.

Committee for Economic Development. *Redefining Government's Role in the Market System*. New York: Committee for Economic Development, 1979.

Conference Board. *Top Executive Compensation*. New York: Conference Board, 1976.

Cook, T. J., and Zucchi, D. M. *College and University Employee Benefits Cost Survey*. New York: Teachers Insurance and Annuity Association and College Retirement Equities Fund, 1979.

Corrallo, S. "An Analysis of Instructional Expenditures for Institutions of Higher Education in the Northeast United States." Unpublished doctoral dissertation, State University of New York, Buffalo, 1970.

Council for Financial Aid to Education. *Voluntary Support of Education, 1977-78*. New York: Council for Financial Aid to Education, 1979.

Council of Economic Advisers, Executive Office of the President. *Economic Report of the President*. Washington: U.S. Government Printing Office, annual.

Czajkowski, P. J. *Some Observations Based upon the Results of the Application of IEP (Information Exchange Procedures) to MRU (Major Research Universities)*. Urbana: University Office for Planning, University of Illinois, 1979.

Dainton, F. "Universities and the State: Securing Responsive and Responsible Academic Freedom." In J. L. Schaubhut (Ed.), *The Past, Present and Future of Higher Education*. Washington, D.C.: Society for College and University Planning, 1978.

Dearden, J. "Cost Accounting Comes to Service Industries." *Harvard Business Review*, September–October 1978, pp. 132–140.

Deitch, K. M. *Some Aspects of the Economics of American Higher Education*. Cambridge, Mass.: Sloan Commission on Government and Higher Education, January 1978a. (Working Paper.)

Deitch, K. M. *Financial Aid: A Resource for Improving Educational Opportunities*. Cambridge, Mass.: Sloan Commission on Government and Higher Education, March 1978b. (Working Paper.)

Dickmeyer, N., and Hughes, K. S. *Comparative Financial Statistics for Community and Junior Colleges, 1977-78*. Washington, D.C.: National Association of College and University Business Officers, 1979.

Dillon, K. "The Rising Costs of Higher Education: 1946-1977." Unpublished doctoral dissertation, Claremont Graduate School, 1979.

"Do Unionized Faculty Members Get Bigger Pay Increases?" *Chronicle of Higher Education*, December 6, 1976.

Dunham, R. E., Wright, P. S., and Chandler, M. O. *Teaching Faculty in Universities and Four-Year Colleges*. Washington, D.C.: U.S. Office of Education, 1966.

Editorial Projects for Education. *EPE 15 Minute Reports*, Feb. 1980, pp. 1–2.

Ehrlich, E. J., and Moeller, A. *An Analysis of 1973–74 Costs at the University of Nebraska and Selected Big Eight Universities.* Lincoln: State of Nebraska, Legislative Fiscal Office, 1975.

Employment Standards Administration, U.S. Department of Labor. *Minimum Wages and Maximum Hours Standards Under Fair Labor Standards Act.* Washington, D.C.: U.S. Government Printing Office, 1976.

Enarson, H. L. "Restoring the Partnership." Columbus: Ohio State University, 1976.

Enarson, H. L. "The Common Good: Foundation for Partnership." *Educational Record,* Spring 1977, pp. 123–131.

Eurich, A. C. "Student Readers: The 50-Year Difference." *Change,* April 1980, pp. 13–15.

Feldman, K. A., and Newcomb, T. M. *The Impact of College on Students.* San Francisco: Jossey-Bass, 1969.

Fincher, C. "On the Study of Cost Studies." *Research in Higher Education,* 1978, pp. 93–96.

Finn, C. E., Jr. "Federalism and the Universities: The Balance Shifts." *Change,* Winter 1975–1976, pp. 24–29, 63.

Froomkin, J. T. *Aspirations, Enrollments, and Resources: The Challenge to Higher Education in the Seventies.* Washington, D.C.: U.S. Office of Education, U.S. Government Printing Office, 1970.

Froomkin, J. T., Jamison, D. T., and Radner, R. (Eds.). *Education as an Industry.* Cambridge, Mass.: Ballinger, 1976.

Fuchs, V. "The Earnings of Allied Health Personnel—Are Health Workers Underpaid?" *Explorations in Economic Research,* Summer 1976, pp. 408–432.

Gallant, J. A., and Prothero, J. W. "Weight-Watching at the University: The Consequences of Growth." *Science,* Jan. 28, 1972, pp. 381–388.

Glenny, L. "Allocation of Resources to Higher Education in the United States." In B. B. Burn (Ed.), *Access, Systems, Youth and Employment.* New York: International Council for Educational Development, 1977.

Gourman, J. *The Gourman Report.* Los Angeles: National Educational Standards, 1978.

"The Gourman Report: A Mysterious Rating of Universities." *Chronicle of Higher Education,* May 8, 1978, p. 5.

Halstead, D. K. *Statewide Planning in Higher Education.* Washington, D.C.: Office of Education, U.S. Department of Health, Education, and Welfare, U.S. Government Printing Office, 1974.

Halstead, D. K. *Higher Education Prices and Price Indexes.* DHEW Publication No. OE 75-17005. Washington, D.C.: U.S. Government Printing Office, 1975. (Also annual supplements 1975, 1976, 1977, and 1978.)

Harcleroad, F. F. *Institutional Efficiency in State Systems of Public Higher Education.* Tucson: Higher Education Program, College of Education, University of Arizona, 1975.

Heyns, R. W. "Our Best Defense Against Regulation." *AGB Reports,* May–June 1977, pp. 9–13.

Houthakker, H. S. "An International Comparison of Household Expenditure Patterns, Commemorating the Centenary of Engel's Law." *Econometrica,* 1957, 25, 32–51.

Hyde, W. L. "Proved at Last: One Physics Major Equals 1.34 Chemistry Major or 1.66 Economics Major." *Educational Record*, Fall 1974, pp. 286–290.

Illinois Board of Higher Education. *Report of Continuing Studies of Costs in Illinois Public Senior Institutions*. Springfield: Illinois Board of Higher Education, 1969.

Imlah, A. H., Hanna, F. A., and Lee, H. N. "Instructional Salaries in 41 Selected Colleges and Universities for the Academic Year 1961–62." *AAUP Bulletin*, Spring 1962, pp. 19–42.

Ingraham, M. H. *The Outer Fringe: Faculty Benefits Other than Annuities and Insurance*. Madison: University of Wisconsin Press, 1965.

Ingraham, M. H. *The Mirror of Brass: The Compensation and Working Conditions of College and University Administrators*. Madison: University of Wisconsin Press, 1968.

Interagency Task Force on Higher Education Burden Reduction, U.S. Government. "Report." Mimeograph, December 14, 1976.

Jacobson, R. L. "Professional Growth, Job Security Concern Campus Administrators." *The Chronicle of Higher Education*, August 13, 1979.

James, E. "Product Mix and Cost Disaggregation: A Reinterpretation of the Economics of Higher Education." *The Journal of Human Resources*, Spring 1978, pp. 157–186.

Jellema, W. W. "Study of Independent Higher Education in Indiana: Cost of Instruction." Unpublished paper, 1975.

Jenny, H. H. "The Bottom Line." Unpublished paper, College of Wooster, 1979.

Jenny, H., and Wynn, G. R. *The Golden Years*. Wooster, Ohio: College of Wooster, 1970.

Jenny, H., and Wynn, G. R. *The Turning Point*. Wooster, Ohio: College of Wooster, 1972.

Jenny, H., and Wynn, G. R. *Short-Run Cost Variations in Institutions of Higher Learning*. Wooster, Ohio: College of Wooster, 1973.

Johnson, G. E., and Stafford, F. P. "Lifetime Earnings in a Professional Labor Market: Academic Economists." *AAUP Bulletin*, Winter 1972–73, p. 204.

Johnson, M. H., and Bennett, J. T. "Increasing Resource Scarcity: Further Evidence." *Quarterly Review of Economics and Business*, Spring 1980, pp. 42–48.

Kaiser, H. H. *Mortgaging the Future: The Cost of Deferred Maintenance*. Washington, D.C.: Association of Physical Plant Administrators, 1979.

Kemeny, J. G. "Private Higher Education: Today and Tomorrow." *Educational Record*, Summer 1977, pp. 194–196.

Kerr, C., and others. *12 Systems of Higher Education: 6 Decisive Issues*. New York: International Council for Educational Development, 1978.

Keynes, J. M. *The General Theory of Employment, Interest, and Money*. London: Macmillan, 1936.

Kress, S. E. "Economies of Scale and the Form of Expenditure Functions in Education: An Econometric Study of California Community Colleges." Unpublished doctoral dissertation, University of California, Berkeley, 1977.

Krueger, A. O. "The Changing Economic Status of the Profession and the Impact of Inflation." *Academe,* December 1979, pp. 487-492.

Ladd, E. C., Jr. "The Economic Position of the American Professoriate." Paper presented at a conference, University of Southern California, January 25-27, 1978.

Lawrence, G. B., and Service, A. L. (Eds.). *Quantitative Approaches to Higher Education Management.* Washington, D.C.: American Association for Higher Education, 1977.

Legislative Analyst, State of California. *Report on California State Universities and Colleges Growth in Expenditures for Administration Compared to Growth for Instruction.* Sacramento: Legislative Analyst, 1977.

Leiter, R. D. (Ed.). *Costs and Benefits of Education.* Boston: Twayne, 1975.

Lilley, W., III, and Miller, J. C., III. "The New 'Social Regulation.'" *The Public Interest,* Spring 1977, pp. 49-61.

Linder, S. B. *The Harried Leisure Class.* New York: Columbia University Press, 1970.

Longenecker, H. E. *University Faculty Compensation Policies and Practices in the United States.* Urbana: University of Illinois Press, 1956.

Lupton, A. H., and Moses, K. D. *Admissions/Recruitment: A Study of Costs and Practices in Independent Higher Education Institutions.* New York: Academy for Educational Development, 1978.

McGill, W. J. "The University and the State." *Educational Record,* Spring 1977, pp. 132-145.

McKinsey and Company. *The Twelve College Cost-Quality Study.* Washington, D.C.: McKinsey and Company, 1972.

McKinsey and Company. *The McKinsey Quarterly,* annual autumn issues.

McKnew, C. R., Jr., and Tuerck, D. G. "On the Irrelevance of Educational Opportunity Costs." In R. D. Leiter (Ed.), *Costs and Benefits of Education.* Boston: Twayne, 1975.

McMahon, W. W., and Melton, C. "Measuring Cost of Living Variation." *Industrial Relations,* October 1978, pp. 324-332.

Maynard, J. *Some Microeconomics of Higher Education.* Lincoln: University of Nebraska Press, 1971.

Meeth, L. R. *Quality Education for Less Money: A Sourcebook for Improving Cost Effectiveness.* San Francisco: Jossey-Bass, 1974.

Meisinger, R. J., Jr. *State Budgeting for Higher Education: The Use of Formulas.* Berkeley: Center for Research and Development in Higher Education, University of California, 1976.

Mezvinsky, E. "Higher Education Strangling in Red Tape." *Congressional Record,* September 9, 1976, pp. H9662-9663.

Michigan Council of State College Presidents. "Unit Cost Study, Instruction and Departmental Research, 1966-67, A Study for the Public Colleges and Universities of Michigan." Mimeograph. Michigan Council of State College Presidents, 1968.

Millett, J. D. *Financing Higher Education in the United States.* New York: Columbia University Press, 1952.

Minter, W. J., and Bowen, H. R. *Independent Higher Education: Annual Report on Financial and Educational Trends in the Independent Sector* of American Higher Education. Washington, D.C.: National Association of Independent Colleges and Universities, 1978, 1980.

Mushkin, S. J., and McLoone, E. P. "Student Higher Education: Expenditures, Sources of Income." Mimeograph. Washington, D.C.: National Planning Association, 1960.

National Association of College and University Business Officers. *Fundamental Considerations for Determining Cost Information in Higher Education.* Washington, D.C.: National Association of College and University Business Officers, 1975.

National Association of College and University Business Officers. *Indirect Costs in Universities.* Washington, D.C.: NACUBO, 1976.

National Association of College and University Business Officers. *Cost Behavior Analysis for Planning in Higher Education.* Washington, D.C.: National Association of College and University Business Officers, 1977.

National Center for Education Statistics, U.S. Department of Health, Education, and Welfare. *Digest of Education Statistics.* Washington, D.C.: U.S. Government Printing Office, annual reports.

National Center for Education Statistics, U.S. Department of Health, Education, and Welfare. *Higher Education: Salaries and Fringe Benefits, 1971–72 and 1972–73.* Washington, D.C.: U.S. Government Printing Office, 1975.

National Center for Education Statistics, U.S. Department of Health, Education, and Welfare. *Higher Education: Salaries and Tenure of Instructional Faculty in Institutions of Higher Education, 1974–75.* Washington, D.C.: U.S. Government Printing Office, 1976a.

National Center for Education Statistics, U.S. Department of Health, Education, and Welfare. *Financial Statistics of Institutions of Higher Education, Current Fund Revenues and Expenditures.* Washington, D.C.: U.S. Government Printing Office, 1976b.

National Center for Education Statistics, U.S. Department of Health, Education, and Welfare. *Numbers of Employees in Institutions of Higher Education.* Washington, D.C.: U.S. Government Printing Office, 1976c.

National Center for Education Statistics, U.S. Department of Health, Education, and Welfare. *Projections of Education Statistics.* Washington, D.C.: U.S. Government Printing Office, annual reports.

National Center for Education Statistics, U.S. Department of Health, Education, and Welfare. *Salaries, Tenure, and Fringe Benefits of Full-Time Instructional Faculty in Institutions of Higher Education, 1975–76.* Washington, D.C.: U.S. Government Printing Office, 1977.

National Education Association. *Salary Schedule Provisions.* Washington, D.C.: NEA, 1953a.

National Education Association. *Salaries Paid in Degree-Granting Institutions.* Washington, D.C.: NEA, 1953b.

National Education Association. *Salaries Paid and Salary Practices in Universities, Colleges, and Junior Colleges.* Washington, D.C.: NEA, 1956–1964 (biennial).

National Education Association. *Salaries in Higher Education.* Also issued as *Salaries Paid and Salary-Related Practices in Higher Education.* Washington, D.C.: NEA, 1966–1972 (biennial).

National Federation of College and University Business Officers Association. *The Sixty College Study—A Second Look 1957–58.* Washington, D.C.: 1960.

National Science Foundation. *Characteristics of Doctoral Scientists and Engineers in the United States, 1975.* Washington, D.C.: U.S. Government Printing Office, 1977.

Oaks, D. H. "A University President Looks at Government Regulation." Address to the Association of Governing Boards of Universities and Colleges, St. Louis, Mo., October 18, 1976. (Excerpted in *AGB Report,* January–February 1977, pp. 41–46.)

Olscamp, P. J. "Quality, Quantity, and Accountability." *Educational Record,* Summer 1976, pp. 196, 201.

O'Neil, R. M. *The Courts, Government, and Higher Education.* New York: Committee for Economic Development, 1972.

O'Neill, J. *Resource Use in Higher Education.* Berkeley: Carnegie Commission on Higher Education, 1971.

Organization for Economic Cooperation and Development. *Public Expenditure on Education.* Paris: Organization for Economic Cooperation and Development, 1976.

Orr, K. B. "Higher Education and the Great Depression." *Review of Higher Education,* Spring 1979, pp. 1–10.

Pace, C. R. *Education and Evangelism.* New York: McGraw-Hill, 1972.

Pace, C. R. *The Demise of Diversity: A Comparative Profile of Eight Types of Institutions.* Berkeley: Carnegie Commission on Higher Education, 1974.

Pace, C. R. *Measuring Outcomes of College: Fifty Years of Findings and Recommendations for Future Assessment.* San Francisco: Jossey-Bass, 1979.

Palola, E. G., and others. "Program Effectiveness and Related Costs (PERC): An Overview." Saratoga Springs, N.Y.: Empire State College, 1975.

Radner, R., and Miller, L. S. *Demand and Supply in U.S. Higher Education.* New York: McGraw-Hill, 1975.

Riesman, D. *On Higher Education.* San Francisco: Jossey-Bass, in press.

Rock, D. A., Centra, J. A., and Linn, R. L. *The Identification and Evaluation of College Effects on Student Achievement.* Princeton, N.J.: Educational Testing Service, 1969.

Ruml, B., and Tickton, S. G. *Teaching Salaries Then and Now.* New York: Fund for the Advancement of Education, Ford Foundation, 1955.

Saunders, C. B., Jr. "Association View of Federal Impact on Education." *Educational Record,* Spring 1975, pp. 89–95.

Saunders, C. B., Jr. "Easing the Burden of Federal Regulation: The Next Move is Ours." *Educational Record,* Fall 1976, pp. 217–224.

Saunders, L. S. "The Productivity of Academic Departments." Unpublished doctoral dissertation, University of California, Berkeley, 1975.

Schumacher, E. F. *Small Is Beautiful: Economics as if People Mattered.* New York: Harper & Row, 1973.

Scientific Manpower Commission. *Salaries of Scientists, Engineers, and*

Technicians. Washington, D.C.: American Association for the Advancement of Science, 1964, 1971, 1977, 1979.

Scott, R. A. "The Hidden Costs of Government Regulations." *Change,* April 1978, pp. 16–23.

Seabury, P. (Ed.). *Bureaucrats and Brainpower: Government Regulation of Universities.* San Francisco: Institute for Contemporary Studies, 1979.

Silver, M. "Can Increased Spending Improve Our Schools? Dogma vs. Causal Analysis." In R. D. Leiter (Ed.), *Costs and Benefits of Education.* Boston: Twayne, 1975.

Sloan Study Consortium. *Paying for College: Financing Education at Nine Private Institutions.* Hanover, N.H.: University Press of New England, 1974.

Solmon, L. C. "The Definition of College Quality and Its Impact on Earnings." *Explorations in Economic Research,* Fall 1975, pp. 537–587.

Solmon, L. C. "Categorizing Costs and Benefits of Schooling and Implications for Subsidization." Los Angeles: Higher Education Research Institute, 1980.

Solmon, L. C., and Tierney, M. L. "Determinants of Job Satisfaction Among College Administrators." *Journal of Higher Education,* July–August 1977, pp. 412–431.

Southern Association of Colleges and Schools, Commission on Colleges. *Educational and General Expenditures of Member Colleges.* Atlanta: Southern Association of Schools and Colleges, 1975.

Southern Association of Colleges and Schools, Commission on Colleges. Colleges and Universities Speak Out on Cost of Federal Compliance in Higher Education. Atlanta: Southern Association of Schools and Colleges, 1976.

Spriestersbach, D. C., and Farrell, W. J. "Impact of Federal Regulations at a University." *Science,* October 1977, pp. 27–30.

State University System of Florida, The Board of Control. *Current Operating Expenditures by Function, 1958–59 and 1959–60.* Tallahassee: Florida State University, 1961.

Stigler, G. J. *Employment and Compensation in Education.* New York: National Bureau of Economic Research, 1950.

Stigler, G. J. *Trends in Employment in the Service Industries.* Princeton, N.J.: Princeton University Press, 1956.

Strein, C. T., and McMahon, W. W. "The University as a Non-Profit Discretionary Firm." Urbana: Department of Economics, University of Illinois, 1979.

Survey of Current Business, monthly issues, 1977–79.

Swords, P. deL., and Walwer, F. K. *The Costs and Resources of Legal Education.* New York: Council on Legal Education for Professional Responsibility, 1974.

Tennessee Higher Education Commission. *An Instructional Analysis of Tennessee Public Higher Education, Fall 1969.* Nashville: Tennessee Higher Education Commission, 1971.

Thurow, L. C. *Generating Inequality.* New York: Basic Books, 1975.

Tickton, S. G. *Teaching Salaries Then and Now—A Second Look.* New York: Fund for the Advancement of Education, Ford Foundation, 1961.

Triplett, J. E. "The Measurement of Inflation: A Survey of Research on the Accuracy of Price Indexes." In P. H. Earl, *Analysis of Inflation*. Lexington, Mass.: Heath, 1975.

Trivett, D. A. "Compensation in Higher Education." *Research Currents* (ERIC and American Association for Higher Education), February–March 1978.

Tuckman, H. P. *Publication, Teaching, and the Academic Reward Structure*. Lexington, Mass.: Heath, 1976.

U.S. Bureau of the Census. *Occupational Characteristics*. Special Report PE 1B, U.S. Census of Population, 1950. Washington, D.C.: U.S. Government Printing Office, 1953.

U.S. Bureau of the Census. *Earnings by Occupation and Education*. Special Report PC(2)-8 B, U.S. Census of Population, 1970. Washington, D.C.: U.S. Government Printing Office, 1973.

U.S. Bureau of the Census. *Historical Statistics of the United States*. Washington, D.C.: U.S. Government Printing Office, 1975.

U.S. Bureau of the Census. *Social Indicators 1976*. Washington, D.C.: U.S. Government Printing Office, 1977.

U.S. Bureau of the Census. *Statistical Abstract of the United States*. Washington, D.C.: U.S. Government Printing Office, annual reports.

U.S. Bureau of Labor Statistics. *National Survey of Professional, Administrative, Technical and Clerical Pay*. Washington, D.C.: U.S. Government Printing Office, 1960 and annual reports.

U.S. Bureau of Labor Statistics. *Salary Trends: Federal Classified Employees, 1939–1964*. Bulletin No. 1444. Washington, D.C.: U.S. Government Printing Office, 1965.

U.S. Bureau of Labor Statistics. *Salary Trends: City Public School Teachers, 1925–1965*. Bulletin No. 1504. Washington, D.C.: U.S. Government Printing Office, 1966a.

U.S. Bureau of Labor Statistics. *Wage Indexes: Long-Term Trend Data for Selected Occupations and Metropolitan Areas, 1907–1966*. Bulletin No. 1505. Washington, D.C.: U.S. Government Printing Office, 1966b.

U.S. Office of Civil Rights, Department of Health, Education, and Welfare. *Higher Education Guidelines, Executive Order 11246*. Washington, D.C.: U.S. Department of Health, Education, and Welfare, 1972.

U.S. Office of Education. *Higher Education Salaries*. Washington, D.C.: U.S. Government Printing Office, 1957–58 through 1970–71.

U.S. Office of Education. *Higher Education Planning and Management Data*. Washington, D.C.: U.S. Government Printing Office, 1958–1961 (yearly).

University of Iowa. *Recommendations from the University of Iowa to the State Board of Regents Concerning Legislative Requests for Operating Funds, Building Needs, and Related Improvements, 1969–1971*. Iowa City: University of Iowa Press, 1968.

University of Iowa. "Impact of Federal Regulations on the University of Iowa: A Compilation of Campus-Wide Responses." Mimeograph. Iowa City: Office of the Vice President for Educational Development and Research, University of Iowa, 1976.

University of Nevada System. *Cost of Instruction, 1968–69*. (n.p.; n.d.)

University of Toronto, Systems Research Group. *Cost and Benefit Study of Post-Secondary Education in the Province of Ontario: School Year 1968– 69, Phase I.* Toronto: University of Toronto, 1970.

University of Wisconsin. "Report on Questionable Federal Regulatory Activities." Mimeograph, n.d.

Van Alstyne, C., and Coldren, S. L. *The Costs of Implementing Federally Mandated Social Programs at Colleges and Universities.* Washington, D.C.: American Council on Education, 1976.

Verry, D., and Davies, B. *University Costs and Outputs.* Amsterdam: Elsevier, 1976.

Washington [State] Council for Postsecondary Education. *1974–75 Unit Expenditures Study.* Report No. 77–20. Olympia: Washington Council for Postsecondary Education, 1977.

Wasser, H. (Ed.) *Institutional Costs in American Higher Education. Proceedings of Conference on Economics of Higher Education: A Comparative Perspective of Policy and Dilemma.* New York: City University of New York, 1978.

Weathersby, G. B., and Jacobs, F. *Institutional Goals and Student Costs.* Washington, D.C.: The American Association for Higher Education, 1977.

Weisbrod, B. A. *The Voluntary Nonprofit Sector: An Economic Analysis.* Lexington, Mass.: Heath, 1977.

Wile, H. P. "What's So Special About Higher Education?" In *Studies in Management*, Vol. 3, No. 8. Washington, D.C.: National Association of College and University Business Officers, 1974.

Williams, G., Blackstone, T., and Metcalf, D. *The Academic Labour Market.* New York: Elsevier, 1974.

Wing, P., and Williams, R. "An Empirical Study of Factors Related to Expenditures and Revenues in Public Doctoral-Granting Universities." *Research in Higher Education*, 1977, 7, 207–228.

Withey, S. B. *A Degree and What Else? Correlates and Consequences of a College Education.* New York: McGraw-Hill, 1971.

Wolf, C., Jr. "A Theory of Non-Market Failures." *The Public Interest*, Spring 1979, pp. 114–133.

Wynn, G. R. *At the Crossroads: A Report on the Financial Condition of the Forty-Eight Liberal Arts Colleges Previously Studied in The Golden Years and The Turning Point.* Ann Arbor: Center for the Study of Higher Education, University of Michigan, 1974.

Index